George Brinton McClellan

Regulations and Instructions for the Field Service of the U.S. Cavalry

in Time of War

George Brinton McClellan

Regulations and Instructions for the Field Service of the U.S. Cavalry in Time of War

ISBN/EAN: 9783337814342

Printed in Europe, USA, Canada, Australia, Japan

Cover: Foto ©ninafisch / pixelio.de

More available books at **www.hansebooks.com**

Regulations and Instructions

FOR THE

FIELD SERVICE OF THE U. S. CAVALRY IN TIME OF WAR.

BY

GEO. B. M^cCLELLAN,

MAJOR-GENERAL U. S. ARMY.

TO WHICH IS ADDED,

THE BASIS OF INSTRUCTION FOR THE U. S. CAVALRY, FROM THE AUTHORIZED TACTICS;

INCLUDING THE FORMATION OF REGIMENTS AND SQUADRONS, THE DUTIES AND POSTS OF OFFICERS, LESSONS IN THE TRAINING AND USE OF THE HORSE;

Illustrated by Numerous Diagrams, with the Signals and Calls now in Use.

ALSO,

INSTRUCTIONS FOR OFFICERS AND NON-COMMISSIONED OFFICERS ON OUTPOST AND PATROL DUTY.

WITH

A DRILL FOR THE USE OF CAVALRY AS SKIRMISHERS,
Mounted and Dismounted.

FULLY ILLUSTRATED.

PHILADELPHIA:
J. B. LIPPINCOTT & CO.
1861.

Entered according to Act of Congress, in the year 1861, by
J. B. LIPPINCOTT & CO.
In the Clerk's Office of the District Court of the United States, in and for the Eastern District of Pennsylvania.

PUBLISHERS' PREFACE.

THIS volume contains a complete set of regulations for the field service of the United States cavalry in time of war. It is the result, after careful observation and comparison of the principal cavalry systems of the European armies, of the use and adaptation of all that was excellent and appropriate in them to our own cavalry. It forms a part of McClellan's extended report of his European commission.

Prepared when the author was a captain of cavalry, and a military commissioner—selected from that arm—from the United States Government to Europe, it is written with the intelligent and eclectic power of an adept in the art of war, and with a faculty of observation and combination unsurpassed in works of this character.

Published in this separate form, it is designed as a manual for cavalry officers in all the war-duties of their station; giving minute directions concerning the horses, their equipments, marches, advanced and rear guards, the posting of grand guards, pickets, vedettes:—in a word, presenting to an intelligent mind the proper mode of action under almost every variety of circumstances. It displays an acquaintance with the military character of general surfaces of country which would be astonishing, did we not regard it as the herald of his military powers displayed within a recent period.

Cavalry, long undervalued in our army, because our brief war-experiences had not demonstrated its importance, is more than restored to its true position. A very large force is being organized. Our horses and our men have no superiors in the world; and we may confidently expect to have a splendid cavalry force in the field. We only need time for organization and instruction, and proper methods of drill and duty. General McClellan's work, in this view, will be of the greatest assistance to officers, especially as they will be learning and practising what—however excellent in itself—has immediate additional value from being the recorded precepts of their distinguished commander.

To render the directions still more simple, there have been added: the Basis of Instruction from the authorized cavalry tactics; a set of Instructions for officers and non-commissioned officers on outposts and patrol-duty; and a Drill for cavalry acting as skirmishers, mounted and dismounted.

PHILADELPHIA, Oct. 3, 1861.

CONTENTS.

UNITED STATES CAVALRY.   PAGE
Introduction... 9
Tactics... 11
Cavalry School and Depot.. 14
Purchase of Horses... 15
Uniform... 15

REGULATIONS FOR FIELD SERVICE IN TIME OF WAR.

PART I.

Movements of Troops in the Vicinity of the Enemy..................... 18
Introduction.. 18

CHAP. I.—Arrangements for the March.. 18
  Art. 1. General Arrangements, and Remarks as to Marches...... 18
       2. Precautions to be observed on the March against Sudden Attacks... 19
       3. Arrangements during a Flank March.......................... 24
       4. Arrangement and Movement of the Trains................. 26
       5. The Defence of Trains... 30
       6. Of Short Halts during the March, Halts for the Night, and Halts for an Entire Day.. 33

CHAP. II.—Duties of the Commanders of the various Parts of the Troops during Military Marches.................................. 36
  Art. 1. Duties of the Commander-in-Chief................................ 36
       2. Duties of the Commander of the Advanced Guard......... 40
       3. Duties of the Commander of the Rear Guard............... 43
       4. Duties of the Commanders of the Advanced, Flank, and Rear Detachments... 44

CHAP. III.—Duties of Patrols during the March............................. 45

CHAP. IV.—In reference to Regulating Marches according to the Locality... 50

PART II.

Precautions to be observed in Camps for Security against the Enemy 57

CHAP. I.—Duties of all Parts of the Outposts................................ 57
  Art. 1. Of the Outposts in general.. 57
       2. Duties of the Vedettes of the Advanced Chain............. 59
       3. Duties of the Commanders of the Pickets..................... 63
       4. Duties of the Commander of the Main Guard............... 68

CONTENTS.

REGULATIONS FOR FIELD SERVICE, etc.—*Continued.*   PAGE

    ART. 5. The Reserves of the Outposts.................................... 71
         6. Independent Pickets.. 72
         7. The General Duties of all Parts of the Outposts........... 73
         8. Of the Duties of the Outposts in covering any March or Change of Position of the Troops under their Guard... 77
    CHAP. II.—The Arrangements of the Outposts at a Distance from the Enemy.. 79
    CHAP. III.—Of Visiting the Outposts..................................... 80
    CHAP. IV.—Of Patrols... 82
    CHAP. V.—Of the Command of the Outposts........................... 86
    CHAP. VI.—Of the Duties of Hunters, Friendly Indians, etc., at the Outposts.. 88
    CHAP. VII.—Of the Arrangement of the Outposts according to the Nature of the Ground.. 90
    CHAP. VIII.—Precautions to be observed in the Camp of the Main Body.. 100
    CHAP. IX.—Precautions to be observed for the Security of Cantonments 102
    ART. 1. Of Advanced Detachments... 102
         2. Precautions to be observed by the Main Body in Cantonments 104

PART III.

Of the Principal Operations of Special Detachments..................... 106
CHAP. I.—Of Sudden Attacks upon the Enemy 106
CHAP. II.—Of Reconnoissances.. 109
CHAP. III.—Of Convoys... 112
    ART. 1. The Defence of Convoys.. 112
         2. The Attack of Convoys... 114
CHAP. IV.—Of Foraging, and Attacks upon Foragers.................... 115
    ART. 1. Of Foraging... 115
         2. Of Attacks upon Foragers... 119

BASIS OF INSTRUCTION, CAVALRY TACTICS.

    ART. I.—Formation of a Regiment of five Squadrons in Order of Battle (or in Line)... 123
    Posts of the Officers and Non-commissioned Officers of the Field and Staff of a Regiment in Order of Battle............. 123
    Posts of the Officers and Non-commissioned Officers of a Squadron in Line... 124
    Posts of Officers and Non-commissioned Officers of a Company acting singly.. 125
    Assembly of a Regiment mounted... 126
    Assembly of a Regiment dismounted....................................... 126
    Formation of the Escort of the Standard.................................. 126
    Reception of the Standard... 127
    Salute with the Standard... 128
    Salute with the Sabre... 128

CONTENTS.

BASIS OF INSTRUCTION, etc.—*Continued.*   PAGE

ART. II.—Formation of a Regiment of five Squadrons in Column 128
    Order in Column by Twos or Fours 128
    Order in Column of Platoons.. 130
    Order in Column of Divisions.. 131
    Order in Close Column 131
    Compliments by Cavalry under Review......................... 132
    Form and Course of Inspection..................................... 134
ART. III.—Duties of Instructors.. 136
ART. IV.—Division, Order, and Progression of Instruction.............. 137
ART. V.—Gradation of Instruction... 138
    Recruits.. 138
    Recapitulation of the Time necessary to Instruct a Trooper to the School of the Platoon mounted, inclusive 139
    Corporals... 140
    Sergeants... 140
    Officers.. 141
ART. VI.—Instruction to Mount without Saddle, to Pack up, to Saddle, and to Unsaddle.. 141
    Manner of Vaulting.. 141
    Manner of Packing up the Effects................................. 142
    Manner of Rolling the Cloak.. 142
    Manner of Adjusting a Saddle..................................... 143
    Manner of Saddling.. 144
    Manner of Packing the Effects on the Horse................ 145
    Manner of Bridling... 147
    Manner of Unbridling... 147
    Manner of Unpacking... 148
    Manner of Unsaddling 148
ART. VII.—Of the Bit... 149
ART. VIII.—Manner of Training Young Horses............................. 153
    1st Lesson... 153
    2d Lesson... 155
    3d Lesson... 157
    4th Lesson 158
    Manner of Accustoming the Horses to Leap the Ditch and the Bar.. 158
    Assembly of the Young Horses in a Platoon................... 159
    Manner of Accustoming Young Horses to Firing and Military Noises... 160
    Horses that are Difficult to Train.................................. 161
    Lesson of the Longe... 162
ART. IX.—Definitions and General Principles.............................. 164
ART. X.—Signals 170

INSTRUCTIONS FOR OFFICERS ON OUTPOST OR PATROL DUTY.

ART. I.—On the Duties of an Officer or Non-commissioned Officer on Grand Guard.. 173
    SECT. 1. Parading the Grand Guard............................... 173
    2. Marching for his Destination..................................... 174
    3. If no Grand Guard was on the Spot before................ 174
    4. Relieving another Grand Guard................................ 175
    5. During his Tour of Grand Guard............................... 176
    Patrols... 177
    6. Placing the Vedettes 178
    7. Instructions for the Vedettes, and what the Officer commanding the Grand Guard has to do on their making Signals.. 179

CONTENTS.

INSTRUCTIONS FOR OFFICERS, etc.—*Continued.* PAGE
  SECT. 8. On the Arrival of a Flag of Truce.................................. 180
       9. Deserters coming from the Enemy............................... 181
     10. When the Grand Guard is attacked 182
          Grand Guards on the Flanks....................................... 182
          Reports 184
          Non-commissioned Officers.. 184
  ART. II.—Advance Guard of a Column in March 185
  ART. III.—Rear Guard.. 187
  ART. IV.—Patrols... 188
    SECT. 1. Side Patrols or Flankers.. 188
       2. Patrolling a Wood... 189
       3. Patrols of Discovery.. 189
       4. Secret Patrols.. 192
Conclusion... 193

SKIRMISH DRILL FOR MOUNTED TROOPS.
  ART. I.—Composition of Company and Posts, etc......................... 197
          To Mount... 199
          To Dismount and to Link.. 200
          Form and Course of Inspection..................................... 201
  ART. II.—Skirmish Drill.—Preliminary Remarks............................ 202
          To Take Open Order and Return to Close Order (in Line)... 204
          Open Order in Line.—To Break into Fours, Twos, and Files 204
          In Column of File to Form Twos, Open Order................ 205
          In Column of File to Form Fours, Open Order............... 205
          In Column of Twos, Open Order, to Form Fours, Open Order 206
          In Column of Fours to Form Twos, Open or Close Order...... 206
          In Column of Twos to Form Files, Open or Close Order...... 207
          To Deploy as Skirmishers from Line................................ 207
  ART. III.—In Open Order Column of Fours.—Action Front and Left.... 208
          In Open Order Column of Fours.—Action Rear and Left..... 208
          In Open Order Column of Fours.—Action Right................ 209
          In Open Order Column of Fours.—Action Left.................. 209
          In Open Order Column of Twos.—Action Front and Left.... 209
          In Open Order Column of Twos.—Action Rear and Left..... 210
          In Open Order Column of Twos.—Action Right................. 210
          In Open Order Column of Twos.—Action Left................... 211
  ART. IV.—To Deploy as Skirmishers when Dismounted..................... 211
          To Deploy as Skirmishers from Column of Fours............... 212
          After Deploying as Skirmishers, to Commence Action......... 212
          Column of Fours, Open Order, to Return to Close Order..... 213
          Column of Twos, Open Order, to Return to Close Order...... 213
          Column of File to form Fours in Close Order..................... 214
  ART. V.—To Sling and to Unsling Rifles.. 214
          Concluding Remarks.. 215

UNITED STATES CAVALRY.

INTRODUCTION.

THE nature of cavalry service in the United States being quite different from that performed by any in Europe, we ought not to follow blindly any one system, but should endeavor to select the good features, and engraft them upon a system of our own.

The proper organization of our cavalry must depend upon the consideration of three things: 1st, the nature of its service against the Indians; 2d, its employment against a civilized enemy invading our territory; 3d, its service in an offensive war, carried on against our neighbors.

The Indians, against whom our cavalry are brought to bear, are generally irregular light horsemen, sometimes living and acting altogether on the plains, in other localities falling back into the broken country when pursued: the difficulty, always, is to catch them; to do so, we must be as light and quick as they are, and then superiority of weapons and discipline must uniformly give us the advantage.

Any army invading our territory must necessarily be deficient in cavalry; in addition, the nature of the parts of our frontiers most liable to attack is not suited to the action of large bodies of cavalry, while in partial operations, light cavalry, well handled, ought always to be superior to heavy cavalry.

Canada, Central Mexico, and the West Indies, are also unsuited to the operations of masses of cavalry, and in none of them are we likely to encounter heavy cavalry, or large numbers of light cavalry; infantry and artillery must generally do most of the work, while light cavalry will afford invaluable assistance, and in Northern Mexico play an important part.

It would, therefore, seem that heavy cavalry would be worse than useless for our purposes, and that we need only light cavalry, in the true and strictest sense of the term.

I would propose that the regiments serving in localities where they are liable to be called upon to dismount, to follow the Indians on foot, be armed with the sabre, of a light pattern, the revolver, and the pistol-carbine, or else a rifled weapon, longer and more effective than the present carbine; that those serving on the plains be armed only with the sabre and revolver, giving to about 10 men in each platoon the pistol-carbine, or a long rifled carbine, in addition.

The accoutrements should be so arranged that when the men dismount to fight on foot, they can hang the sabre to the saddle; the pistol should always be carried on the person; the carbine slung over the shoulder.

The horses should be purchased by cavalry officers, and be selected for activity, hardiness, and endurance.

The men ought to be light, active, and intelligent.

The tactical unit should be small, that it may be handled with the greatest possible ease and celerity, and that it may never be broken. The regiments, also, should be small, for the same reasons.

The FORMATION OUGHT TO BE IN ONE RANK, as covering the greatest extent of ground, admitting the most rapid movements, and bringing every man to bear to the greatest advantage; suitable reserves should always be held in hand.

I would propose, as the unit, for interior service, and tactical purposes, the company, composed as follows:

1 captain.
3 lieutenants.
1 orderly sergeant.
1 quartermaster sergeant.
1 veterinary sergeant.
4 duty sergeants.
8 corporals.
66 privates.
2 trumpeters.
1 farrier.
1 saddler.

Total, 4 officers, 85 non-commissioned officers and men.

Of this number, 6 privates and the saddler to be dismounted, leaving the effective force of combatants, 4 officers, 78 men, and 78 government horses.

It would be advantageous to create the grade of first-class privates, say 20 in each company, as a means of rewarding good and faithful old soldiers who are not fitted to become non-commissioned officers; they should receive somewhat more pay than the second-class privates. The company to be divided into two platoons, four sections, and sets of fours. The lieutenants and non-commissioned officers to be attached to the same platoon and section, for the purposes of drill and interior service.

The posts of the officers, &c., to be as follows:

The captain in the rank, between the platoons; when necessary, he can move to the front, his place being left vacant; the 1st lieutenant, commanding the 1st platoon, on the right of the company; the 2d lieutenant, commanding the 2d platoon, on the left of the company; the 3d lieutenant, as file-closer, 4 paces in rear of the centre; this officer not to be replaced if absent; the orderly sergeant, as file-closer, two paces behind the right file; the quartermaster sergeant, two paces in rear of the left file; the veterinary sergeant, half-way between the orderly sergeant and the 1st corporal; the 1st duty sergeant, on the right of the 1st platoon; the 2d, on the left of the 2d platoon; the 3d, on the left of the 1st platoon; the 4th, on the right of the 2d platoon; the 1st corporal, as file-closer, 2 paces in rear of the centre of the 1st section; the 2d, behind the 4th section; the 3d, behind the 2d section; the 4th, behind the 3d section; the 5th, to be the left file of the 1st section; the 6th, to be the right file of the 4th section; the 7th, to be the right file of the 2d section; the 8th, to be the left file of the 3d section; the buglers, 2 paces behind the 2d files from the inner flanks of the platoons; the farrier, half-way between the quartermaster sergeant and the 2d corporal; the saddler and the dismounted men to remain with the train.

It will be observed that the strength of the company is the same as now authorized; it requires another lieutenant, in place of the brevet 2d lieutenant, and the addition of 2 sergeants, 1 veterinary, 4 corporals, and 1 saddler, while the number of privates is diminished by 8.

Regiments composed of 6 companies would be preferable to the present organization; by the addition of 2 companies to the 40 now in service, 7 effective regiments would be formed.

If this cannot be done, it would be well to decrease the number of companies in a regiment to 8, and form a 5th regiment of the 8 superfluous companies.

If neither of these plans can be adopted, it is believed that the modification proposed in the organization of the company will of itself produce very beneficial results.

To the staff of each regiment there should be added a chief veterinary, with the rank of sergeant major, or even as a commissioned officer, and a chief saddler; to the standard-company there should be allowed an additional sergeant as standard-bearer, and a corporal as assistant, or these two non-commissioned officers might be attached to the staff.

If a band is considered necessary, the men ought to be considered as belonging to the staff, in addition to the usual strength of the regiment, and not to be subtracted from the strength of the companies; it should be supported by the government, and not by the officers and regimental fund.

It would be advisable that the hospital attendants be placed on the same footing; and that a proper number of teamsters be authorized for the staff and each company, to be enlisted or hired as such, and not detailed from the companies; those for the companies should be under the sole control of the captains.

The junior field officers should have a direct, specific, and well-defined authority over a certain number of companies, the colonel taking the general direction; in a new organization it would be well to have 1 field officer for every 2 companies.

It ought to be laid down that detachments shall always be composed of men of the same company, and never of details from different companies; in the same company platoons or sections with their own officers and non-commissioned officers should, as far as practicable, be detached as units.

If legislation is called for, and obtained in effecting a re-organization of our cavalry, I think that it would be advisable to call the unit a *squadron*, instead of company, in order to distinguish it from the infantry unit in reports, returns, &c., without the necessity of circumlocution. It is also of importance to obtain authority to enlist supernumerary recruits, who might be kept at the cavalry school, or the European system of depot squadrons might be adopted; in time of war this system will be found to be absolutely necessary to maintain the cavalry regiments in a state of efficiency, and the requisite laws should be obtained in time of peace, that there may be no delay in taking the proper measures at the right time.

A proper organization would authorize a moderate number of supernumerary officers of all grades, for detail upon detached duty, so that the full number required by the tactics might always be present with the regiments and companies.

The efficiency of the arm would be increased were there a general of cavalry, whose duty it would be to inspect the troops of the arm, watch over their interests, and secure uniformity in the service. This officer ought to have a number of aides-de-camp, all cavalry officers, who could make, under his orders, more frequent inspections than any one man could accomplish.

TACTICS.

The individual instruction of man and horse should be regarded as the most important point of the whole system, and should be as simple as possible; the man should be taught to manage his horse with ease and address over all kinds of ground and at all gaits, to swim rivers, to go through certain gymnastic exercises,—such as vaulting,—to fence, to fire very frequently at a mark, and to handle his weapon with accuracy and effect at all gaits and in all situations.

Some of the preliminary instruction prescribed in the Russian and Austrian tactics might be introduced advantageously.

Every thing in reference to heavy cavalry, lancers, hussars, &c., should be omitted.

I would adopt the Russian sabre exercise as the basis of our own; insist upon the sabre being kept sharp in the field, provide the men with means of doing so, and lay it down as a rule that the strength of cavalry is in the "spurs and sabre."

The instruction on foot should be carried no further than its true object requires; that is, to bring the men under discipline, improve their carriage, and enable them to comprehend the movements they are to execute mounted.

The formation for review, parade, inspection, &c., to be: the companies deployed in one line, with intervals of 12 paces, or else in a line of columns of companies by platoons, according to the ground.

The Russian tactics will suggest excellent arrangements for the orders of battle of commands composed of regiments having ten, or fewer, companies, also for the movements of brigades, divisions, &c.

It should be laid down as a fixed rule that no cavalry force should ever charge without leaving a reserve behind it, and that against civilized antagonists the compact charge in line should be used, in preference to that as foragers.

Columns to be formed with wheeling distance, and closed in mass; when closed in mass, the file-closers close up to 1 pace from the rank, and the distance between the subdivisions to be just enough to permit each company to wheel by fours.

Marching columns to be by file, twos, fours, or platoons; by fours and platoons in preference when the ground permits.

Columns of manœuvre to be by fours, platoons, companies, or in double column; the latter always a regimental column, and to be formed on the two central companies, or platoons, without closing the interval between them.

Deployments to be made habitually at a gallop, and the individual oblique to be used as much as possible.

The instruction in two lines to be provided for.

The Russian tactics give a good basis for the system of skirmishers, and charging as foragers.

For the use of the mounted rifles, and cavalry acting as such, there should be a thorough system for dismounting rapidly, and fighting on foot.

CAVALRY SCHOOL AND DEPOT.

1st. To afford the young officers of mounted regiments, before joining their regiments, thorough instruction in the tactics, regulations for interior service, the general principles of field service, all necessary knowledge in regard to the horse, the use of weapons, &c.

2d. To perfect the instruction of lieutenants now serving with the regiments in the same branches.

3d. The instruction of non-commissioned officers sent from the regiments: it would be advisable to detail picked corporals, and insure, to a certain number of the best, promotion as sergeants immediately upon leaving the school.

4th. To instruct the recruits, that they may be well drilled and thoroughly instructed before joining their regiments.

5th. To break the remount horses, so that each recruit may take a well-broken horse with him when he joins his regiment, and that other remount horses may also be broken before being sent to the regiments.

6th. A veterinary school should be attached to the establishment, for the instruction of officers and veterinaries.

7th. A school for farriers.

8th. A school for trumpeters.

The systems of instruction and the organization of the French veterinary schools, and of the cavalry school at Saumur, afford, perhaps, the most accessible models for the basis of our own. The text-books there in use can readily be adapted to our own purposes, until experience enables us to have others of our own.

As a first step, we should have detailed special regulations for the use of mounted troops in garrison and the field.

To establish the veterinary school, I would propose the following, as probably the best and easiest plan:

Select an army surgeon who has served in the field with cavalry, is a good judge of horses, has turned his attention somewhat to the subject, and would be willing to assume the proposed duty; place him at the head of the veterinary school, and let him prepare the necessary course of instruction and text-books. In the first instance, at least, his assistants should also be of the medical staff.

It is very certain that no officer of the line possesses the technical and anatomical knowledge necessary to initiate an establishment of this kind.

Even if the school proposed cannot be established, there ought to be a work prepared by some of the medical corps on the veterinary science, for the use of cavalry officers. A small work on farriery would also be very serviceable.

The pupils for the veterinary school might be selected from among the best recruits; indeed, it is not improbable that the advantages of such an institution would induce excellent men to enlist, for the purpose of availing themselves of its benefits. Should such be found to be the result, it would then be well to require them to enlist for longer than the usual time, as a compensation for the time spent at the school. The pupils at the farrier school should be recruits who are blacksmiths by trade.

All the advantages of extra-duty pay ought to be secured both to the veterinaries and farriers.

PURCHASE OF HORSES.

It would be advantageous to detail officers of cavalry on this duty, just as they now are for the recruiting service. In cases when cavalry officers are recruiting in districts where horses abound, they could attend to both duties at the same time.

It might at present be proper to select the purchasing officers for their knowledge of horses; but it is believed that the effect of the education received at the proposed cavalry school would be such that, in a few years, all officers would be capable of purchasing. Animals bought in this way, as occasion offered, and not in large numbers at a time, would be obtained for a more moderate price, and more careful selections could be made.

They should all be sent to the cavalry school, when the commandant, and a certain number of the senior officers on duty there, would constitute a proper commission to inspect the animals and direct the service.

There should be regulations determining approximately the height, age, conformation, and qualities that the horses should possess; also a maximum, or rather an average, price, varying from time to time, according to the state of the market.

UNIFORM.

I would recommend that the epaulette be entirely dispensed with for regimental officers; it is useless, expensive, and inconvenient: the strap on the undress uniform is a sufficient distinction of rank.

For the men, I would replace the scales by a strap of cloth, of the same shape as that on the old fatigue uniform, but sewed fast to the jacket.

They should also have a police-cap, without visor, and of such a nature that it can be folded up, and carried in the pouch, or wherever may be most convenient; the Scotch bonnet, Turkish fez, a Greek cap of knit or woven wool, a flexible cap of the shape of the old forage-cap,—any of these would answer.

For service on the prairies, the men should have a loose flannel coat, leaving their uniform coat in garrison; the ordinary dark-blue sailor's shirt, cut open in front, and provided with a lining and pockets, is as good as any thing that can be devised.

The French fashion of giving the men a merino scarf in the field, instead of a stock, is worthy of consideration.

It would be well, on many accounts, to re-enforce the pants with thin leather.

The amount of clothing to be carried by each man should be limited; I do not see that they need more than 2 pairs of drawers, 1 shirt, 2 pairs of socks, a towel, soap, and hair-comb, in addition to what they wear; during very long expeditions, extra clothing should be carried in the train,—never on the horses.

The method of cold-shoeing, which is practised generally by the French cavalry, should be enforced, and the shoes carried by each man should have been previously fitted to the horse.

In "The Armies of Europe" will be found full information as to the cooking-utensils carried in the field by the European cavalry; it is very important that competent cavalry officers should fully consider this subject, and adopt a set suitable to the requirements of our own service; the proper principle would be to have small messes in the field, each mess consisting of the smallest number that are likely to be detached as a unit, so that they may always have their cooking-utensils with them; the utensils should be such that the men can habitually carry them on their own horses with convenience.

I would recommend that the shelter-tent be adopted as a part of our system.

The best model for a cavalry stable should be adopted, determining minutely the interior arrangements and the general plan as far as possible; and all stables built hereafter should be required to be in accordance with this plan; the drawings and descriptions furnished by the different members of the commission will afford the means of doing this understandingly.

The English system for the transportation of horses by sea, as followed in the Himalaya, is beyond doubt the most perfect that has been devised; sketches and a full description of this will be found in "European Cavalry," and it is recommended that it be inserted in our regulations, and adopted as our own system.

There are other suggestions as to the regulations and the service which I have already made in official and unofficial communications; I will here allude again only to the propriety of inscribing upon the colors of each regiment the names of the actions in which it has borne an honorable part, and of placing these same names on the army register, at the head of the list of the officers of the regiment; for few things are more important than those which tend to inspire and preserve a feeling of pride in the regiment, on the part of all its officers and men.

REGULATIONS AND INSTRUCTIONS FOR FIELD SERVICE IN TIME OF WAR.

PART I.

MOVEMENTS OF TROOPS IN THE VICINITY OF THE ENEMY.

INTRODUCTION.

§ 1. THE principal differences between marches near the enemy, and those during peace, are:

1st. That in the former case the troops are not so much divided, but move in larger bodies than in peace.

2d. That proper precautions are observed to guard against sudden attacks.

Remark.—In time of war, troops so far from the enemy as to be in no danger of attack observe only a part of the military precautions indicated below, increasing them as they approach the enemy.

CHAPTER I.

ARRANGEMENTS FOR THE MARCH.

ARTICLE 1.

General arrangements and remarks as to marches.

§ 2. Military marches may in general be: 1. Offensive; 2. In retreat; 3. To the flank.

§ 3. In each of these cases the troops may move in one or several columns.

§ 4. They move in several columns when in strong force, and having convenient roads, neither far apart, nor separated by impassable obstacles. But if it is necessary that a great number of troops follow the same road, the column should be divided into echelons, following each other at intervals, in order to avoid delay from crowding.

§ 5. It is impossible to determine with exactness the intervals between different columns, or between the echelons of the same column; these must depend upon the nature and relative positions of the roads, as well as upon the strength and degree of independence of each column. But it may be laid down as a general rule that these distances should be such that the commander can concentrate and form the whole, or at least the greater part, of his command before being seriously attacked.

§ 6. For the details of the distribution of the troops in the several columns and echelons, the rules laid down in the tactics for the formation of general columns must be taken as guides; observing that each fraction of the entire force must be so arranged that it can always form promptly to meet the enemy.

§ 7. On the march, cavalry may move by twos or by fours, but in preference by platoons when the road permits.

Artillery marches by piece or by section.

In a retreat, those parts of the rear guard nearest the enemy will always march by the rear rank.

§ 8. On the march, the distances permitted are: between companies, about 25 paces; between regiments, about 50 paces; between brigades, about 100 paces.

ARTICLE 2.

Precautions against sudden attack to be observed on the march.

§ 9. To secure troops, on the march, against sudden attacks, there are sent out from the main body: *an advanced guard; a rear guard;* and *flank detachments,* or *guards.*

§ 10. During offensive marches, the advanced guard consists of one-fourth, or one-fifth, of the whole force; it may be increased or diminished according to circumstances and the judgment of the commander. Its purpose is, to march at some distance in advance of the main body, in order:

1. To observe the enemy betimes, and give early information of his appearance, strength, and direction of march.

2. Having discovered the enemy, to follow, never losing sight of him, and endeavor to obtain all possible information concerning him.

3. Should the enemy approach and attack, to delay him long enough to enable the main body to form in order of battle.

4. To examine the country in advance, and remove all obstacles from the road.

5. During the arrangements of the main body for halting or encamping, to cover it on the side of the enemy.

§ 11. On the march, the advanced guard should be so far in front that, without incurring too great risk, it may delay the enemy long enough to enable the main body to prepare to receive him. Therefore, in proportion as the advanced guard is stronger and more independent, and as the time required for the formation of the main body is greater, the farther should the advanced guard be pushed forward, up to one-half a day's march, or farther. In small detachments, not requiring much time to assemble and form, the advanced guard does not move farther than from one and a half to three miles in front.

Remark.—When, under peculiar circumstances, the advanced guard is pushed forward a considerable distance, and therefore exposed to a separate defeat, or when the nature of the ground is such as to render its retreat difficult, there is sent out from the main body an "intermediate detachment," which holds itself in echelon between the two, to support the advanced guard if suddenly attacked. This detachment is under the orders of the commander of the advanced guard, who, upon meeting the enemy, either orders it up to assist him, or falls back upon it, according to circumstances.

§ 12. For the protection of its own march, an advanced guard should have an advanced guard of its own, consisting of one or more companies, or a platoon, according to the strength of the party; and on its flanks, flank guards, each of a platoon or section.

Remark.—The standard is always left with the main body of the regiment.

§ 13. The advanced and flank detachments keep themselves at from 500 to 1,000 paces from the head and flanks of the main advanced guard, according to their strength and the nature of the country.

§ 14. These detachments send out patrols in front and on the flanks, to examine the country and obtain early intelligence of the enemy. These patrols are usually at from 500 to 1,000 paces from their detachments, and ought to regulate their intervals so as never to lose sight of each other, and to form a continuous chain around the head and flanks of the main advanced guard.

§ 15. The general arrangement, without regard to the ground, of an advanced guard, composed of 10 companies of cavalry and 6 pieces of horse artillery, is shown in Fig. 1.

§ 16. An *advanced guard during a march in retreat* consists of a small number of troops, usually determined as in time of peace.

Its purpose is:

1. To open the way for the main body, and remove all obstacles from the road.

21

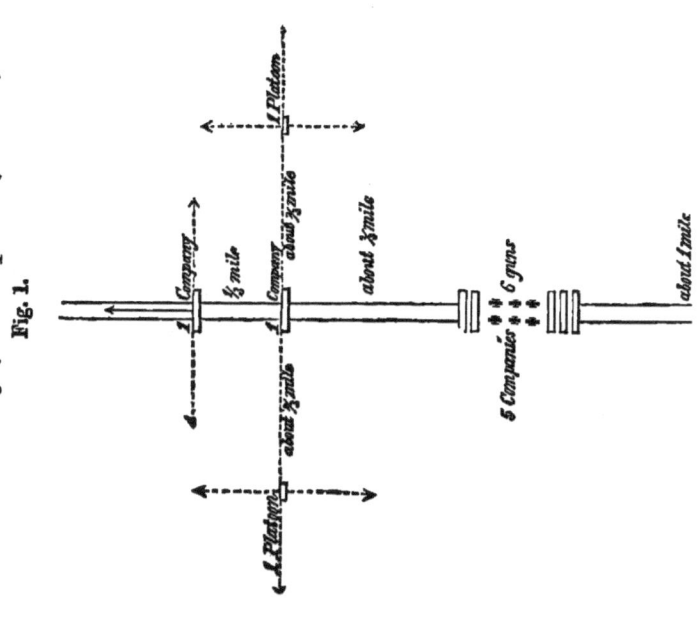

Advanced Guard, consisting of 10 companies of Cavalry and 6 guns.
Fig. 1.

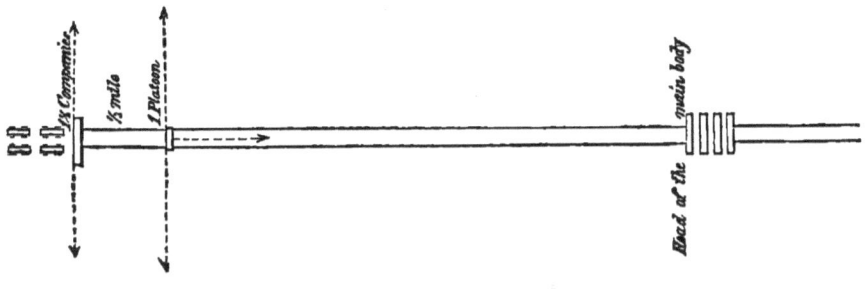

The arrows indicate the directions in which patrols are sent.

21

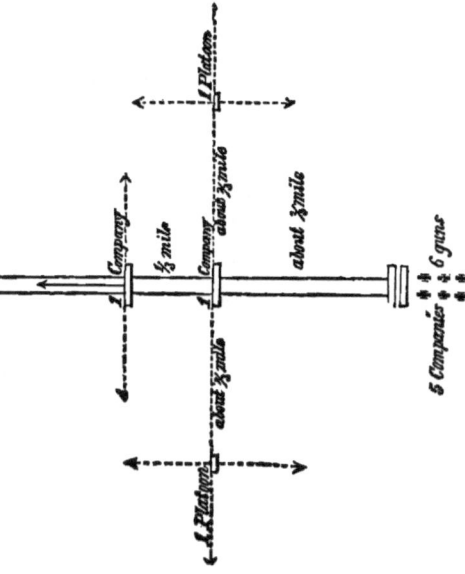

Advanced Guard, consisting of 10 companies of Cavalry and 6 guns.
Fig. 1.

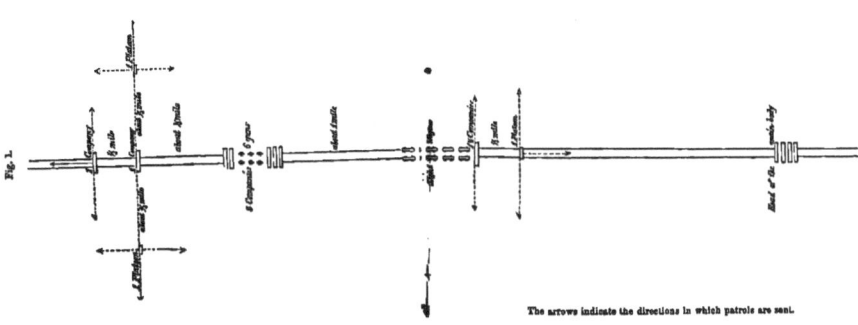

Fig. 1.

The arrows indicate the directions in which patrols are sent.

2. To serve as the escort of the train, which should move, at least, as far in advance of the main body as it does in rear of it during an offensive march.

§ 17. In this case, the advanced guard sends out front and flank detachments and patrols, which are arranged precisely as in offensive marches. Here the principal object to be kept in view is that all the detachments may be promptly united at any moment.

§ 18. During an *offensive march* the *rear guard* is formed according to the same principles as an advanced guard during a retreat. Its duty is as follows:

1. To watch over the preservation of order in the rear of the column.
2. To pick up stragglers.
3. To protect the rear of the column and the train against sudden attacks by parties of the enemy.

§ 19. In a *retreat*, it is the duty of the *rear guard* to cover the movements of the main body, as well as to repulse and delay the enemy in every possible manner. In this case, its duty becomes as difficult as that of the advanced guard in an offensive march, and sometimes more so, especially when the retreat is effected in sight of the enemy. The rear guard must, at every favorable point, use all means to check the enemy, and thus render it possible for the main body to retreat without precipitation. To effect this, it should always be much more independent than the advanced guard in offensive marches; for the latter can always retreat upon the main body, or be readily supported by it.

§ 20. With regard to the safety of the main body, the rear guard in a retreat observes the rules laid down in numbers 1, 2, and 5 of § 10.

§ 21. The strength of the rear guard depends upon several circumstances:

1. Upon our own and the enemy's designs.
2. Upon the proximity of the enemy.
3. Upon the nature of his operations.
4. Upon the distance from the main body, and the order of march of the latter.

If the enemy pursues vigorously, or if the main body ought to fall back a great distance behind the rear guard, then the latter should be strong enough to operate independently, and defend itself obstinately in all favorable positions. Such a rear guard should be one-fifth, or even one-third, of the whole force.

§ 22. The rear guard should cover its movements, both in the offensive and retreat, in the manner laid down for the advanced guard in §§ 12, 13, and 14.

§ 23. If the main body marches in several columns, all the rear guards should communicate with each other by means of patrols. They ought also to move in line,—that is to say, on the same general line perpendicular to the general direction of the march.

§ 24. To the advanced guard in all cases, and to the rear guard in retreat, mounted engineer troops are attached; in default of these, mounted working-parties with tools: in the first case, to remove obstacles in the road; in the second case, to retard the pursuit of the enemy, by destroying bridges, breaking up the road, &c.

§ 25. The distance of the rear guard from the main body depends upon its strength; generally, in a retreat, the rear guard is held at such a distance from the main body that the latter, even when the enemy attacks in force, may without precipitation or impediment select its own time and place for halting or encamping, without making a forced march. But if the rear guard is weak, and the enemy pursues vigorously, the main body should remain near by to support it. If the main body is obliged to pass defiles, or if its movements are in any way retarded, it must be at such a distance from the rear guard as to give it time to move off a sufficient distance, in spite of any unexpected delay.

§ 26. If the main advanced and rear guards move at the distance of some miles from the main body, each column of the latter detaches, in addition, small advanced and rear parties, (one or two companies, or a platoon,) which march at the distance of some few hundred paces from each column, and perform the duties of advanced and rear guards in time of peace.

§ 27. In cases where the nature of the ground, on the flanks of the roads, is such as to render the march of the columns insecure, small detachments are sent out as flankers; and from these patrols on the extreme flanks, as explained in §§ 12, 13, and 14.

ARTICLE 3.

Arrangements during a flank march.

§ 28. In a march to the flank, if it is in the power of the enemy to attack the flank of the columns in march, all the parts should be so arranged that they may promptly, and without a long movement, change from the order of march to that of battle, either by wheeling into line, or by changing the direction of the columns, and in such a manner as to be able to resist his attack: Therefore, in such cases, certain troops are designated who are to form the line of combatants in the order of battle, others to form the reserve, and others to guard the trains, on the road farthest from the enemy.

§ 29. During flank marches, flank detachments are sent out towards the enemy; they march parallel to the main column, watch the enemy, and, if necessary, oppose him long enough to enable the main body to form in order of battle.

§ 30. The duties of these flank detachments correspond to those of advanced guards in offensive marches, and rear guards in retreat; because the flank detachments protect the main body against a sudden attack, and enable them either to pass from one line of operations to another, or to gain a position on the flank of the enemy, or, finally, to turn him.

It should be observed, however, that flank marches should always be undertaken and executed with many precautions; for, when making them, it is easy to lose our own communications and line of retreat, if we have not time to gain the new line of operations. Therefore, that there may be no impediment during the intended flank march, every thing possible must be done to conceal it from the enemy, by taking advantage of the ground, and by the movements of the flank guard, which should be strong enough to offer an obstinate resistance, and keep the enemy away from the main body until the completion of the movement.

§ 31. The strength of the flank guard must be in proportion to the duties it has to perform; its strength must be determined upon the same principles as that of advanced and rear guards.

§ 32. The arrangements for the march, and the manner of operation of a flank guard, depend entirely upon the position of the enemy, the nature of the country, and the direction of the roads. To secure the march, the flank guard pushes out detachments and patrols on the exposed side, to cover the whole flank of the columns in march. The flank guard itself either marches opposite the main body, or remains in position, to occupy points where roads coming in from the side of the enemy would enable him to disturb the march of our own troops. In the last case, when the columns of the main body have passed beyond the point occupied by the flank guard, the latter either occupies another point, covering the march, by gradually sending troops there, or else places itself as a rear guard behind the marching column, while, in the mean time, any other points to be occupied have been held by other flank guards detached from the main body.

The first method is pursued when the ground permits the movement of the flank guard to be made without danger, as, for instance, along the banks of a stream over which there are few crossings; the latter in all cases where the march of the fractions of the flank guard would be exposed to danger from the attack of the enemy.

§ 33. The distance of the flank guard from the main body is regulated as in the case of an advanced guard in an offensive march.

§ 34. Fig. 2 gives an example, without reference to the ground, of the flank march of a division of cavalry, under the protection of a flank brigade and a battery of horse artillery.

§ 35. In addition to the main flank guard sent out in the direction of the enemy, each column of the main body detaches small advanced, flank, and rear guards.

When necessary, a special guard is detailed for the trains, which, in such cases, usually move in one body.

ARTICLE 4.

Arrangement and movement of the trains.

§ 36. To avoid confusion and delay in the march of troops, from the great number of wagons with them, the trains are divided into *three classes*.

§ 37. Trains of *the first class, which are needed during the march*, consist of the ambulances, provided with the means of dressing wounds, and accompanied by the surgeon of the day, an assistant surgeon, and a party of hospital attendants.

In the artillery, the spare carriages accompany the train of the 1st class; in the mounted engineer troops, the ponton-wagons, if there is any necessity for them. In addition to these, during marches near the enemy, the ammunition-wagons accompany the trains of the 1st class, that the troops may never be in want of cartridges.

§ 38. Trains of the 1st class follow immediately after their regiments, batteries, or other integral parts.

§ 39. Trains of the 2d class, which are needed by the troops only when in camp, consist of: the wagons for ammunition, money, papers and records, tools, baggage, medicines, field-forges, artillery-wagons, staff baggage-wagons, pack-animals of the field and company officers, wagons of the office of the commander-in-chief, wagons carrying provisions and forage for immediate distribution, and, finally, the sutlers' wagons. Ammunition-wagons are separated from the others, and compose in each column a separate section, marching near the troops: *i.e.* in an offensive march, they move at the head of the trains of the 2d

27

Flank march of a Division of Cavalry, with its batteries, under the protection of a flank brigade and 6 guns.

Fig. 2

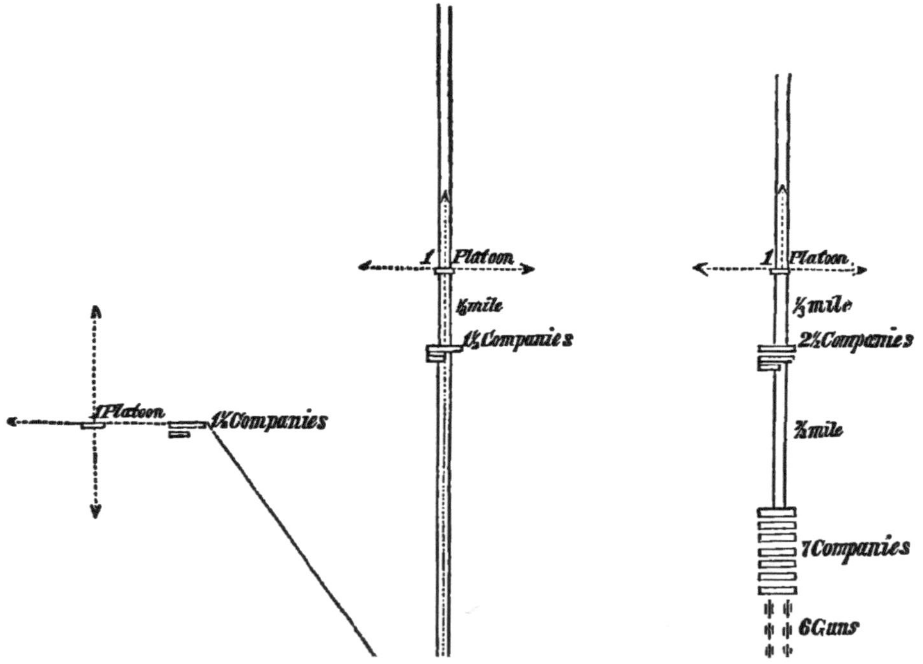

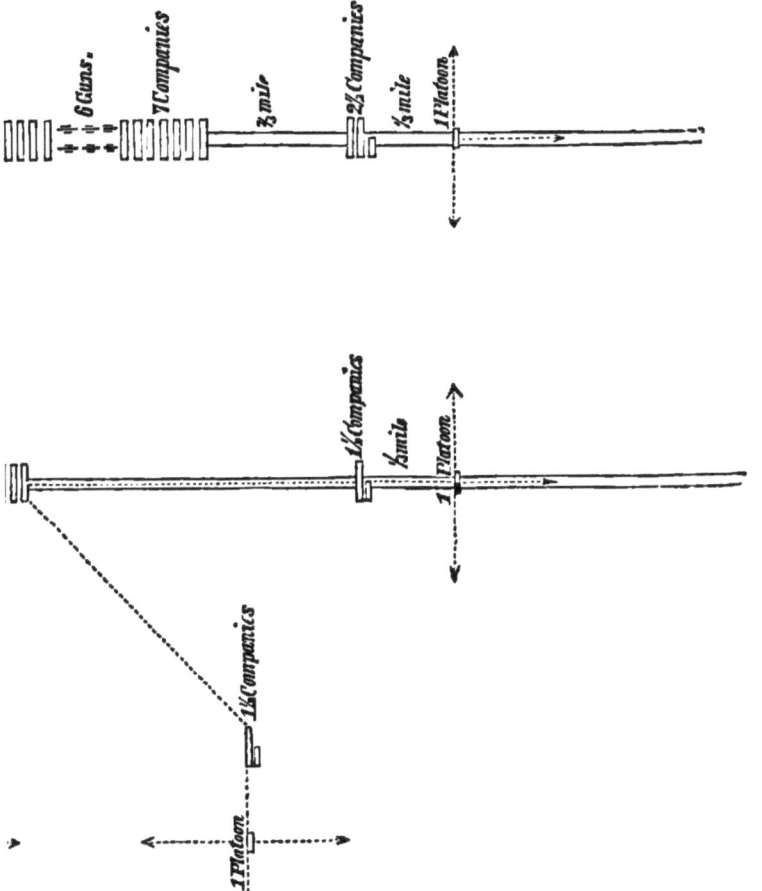

The arrows indicate the direction in which patrols are sent out.

Flank march of a Division of Cavalry, with its batteries, under the protection of a flank brigade and 6 guns.

Fig. 2

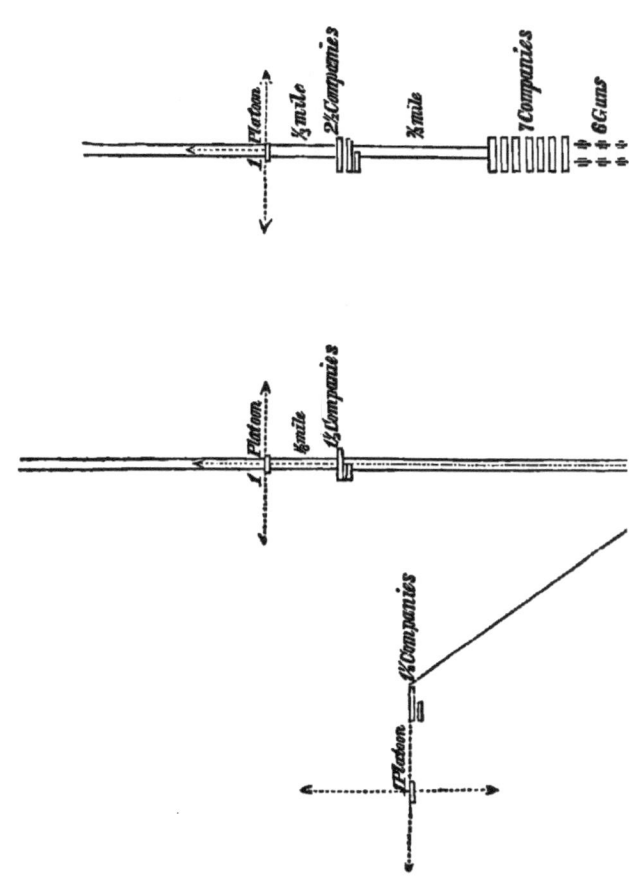

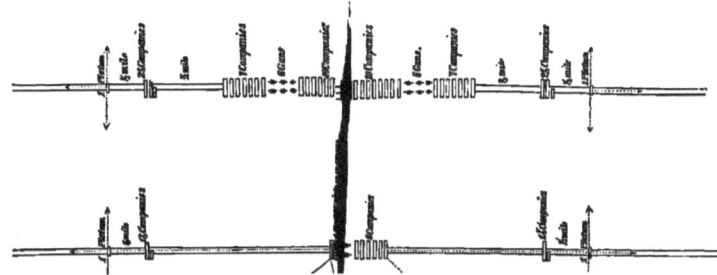

class, and in retreat, behind them. The other wagons of the 2d class move by kinds, and in the order named above.

§ 40. Trains of the 2d class march behind the troops, in the interval between the main body and the rear guard.

If there is no probability of meeting the enemy, or if the advanced guard is at a great distance (*e.g.* one-half a day's march) from the main body, then the wagons of the 2d class, belonging to the advanced guard, may march immediately after it; in like manner, if the general column moves by echelon, with intervals of half a day's march, then the wagons of the 2d class, belonging to each echelon, may march immediately behind it.

But when an affair with the enemy is anticipated, all the trains of the 2d class, except the ammunition-wagons, follow the main body, at a distance of not less than one-half a day's march; so that in the event of a retreat the wagons may not delay the movement. But in such cases the ammunition-wagons follow immediately after the troops to whom they belong. In a general retreat, the trains of the 2d class should be placed at least one-half a day's march in front of the troops, *i.e.* at such a distance that in no event can they impede or delay the movements of the active troops.

§ 41. *Trains of the third class* consist of *those for which the troops have no immediate or pressing necessity.* They are composed of provision and forage wagons, wagons loaded with hospital stores and equipments, ambulances for the sick who are in the general hospital, &c., &c.

§ 42. Trains of the 3d class always march in a distinct train, separate from the troops, on the principal road, and under the protection of a special escort; the strength of which depends upon the extent of the train and the position of the enemy.

§ 43. The number of wagons allowed in the 2d and 3d classes depends upon circumstances, and special orders issued during the campaign. Commanders of separate detachments may be allowed to vary the number of wagons in each class according to circumstances.

§ 44. In the march of a large number of wagons, any obstacle to a section, or a single wagon, delays all that follow, and thus extends to the whole train. To avoid this difficulty, large trains are divided into sections of about 100 wagons each, which march about one-third of a mile apart.

§ 45. If, in addition to the ammunition-wagons, there are some loaded with loose powder, they are formed in separate sections and placed in the part of the train least exposed to the enemy. No foreign matter is to be placed on these wagons.

§ 46. The head of each section must occasionally halt for a moment, that the rear may keep closed up.

§ 47. Detailed arrangements for the formation and march of trains should be made.

Article 5.
The defence of trains.

§ 48. The duties of troops detailed as the escort of a train are: 1st. To enforce the preservation of order. 2d. To assist their rapid and uninterrupted march. 3d. To defend them if attacked.

§ 49. A portion of the escort, detailed to watch over the order of march, distributes itself as a chain along the whole length of the train. If the escort is small, a certain number of privates, under the charge of a non-commissioned officer, are placed in charge of a section, or certain number of wagons, and are responsible for their order of march.

§ 50. When the roads are very bad, some of the escort are dismounted, in order to be in readiness to assist any wagons that may mire, break down, or meet with any impediment.

§ 51. A working-party marches at the head of the escort to repair the road. The strength of this party will depend upon the number of wagons, the state of the road, &c.

§ 52. The strength and composition of the escort of a train must depend upon the probability of attack, the extent of the train, and, finally, on the nature of the country through which the train is to pass.

§ 53. If the escort is of infantry, a small party of cavalry must be added to look out for the enemy, patrol, &c.

§ 54. In all cases, the commander of the escort has absolute control over all persons on duty with or accompanying the train.

§ 55. The commander of the escort should possess accurate information concerning the country through which the train is to pass, that he may make the proper arrangements for its security.

§ 56. A part of the escort always marches as an advanced guard, and another portion as a rear guard. The main body is concentrated at points determined by the danger; if necessary, it detaches flank guards, which send out patrols. In an open country, and when there is no reason to expect the enemy at any particular point, the main body of the escort marches alongside of the centre of the train. Under other circumstances, they are concentrated at the head or in rear of the train, according to the direction in which the enemy is expected.

§ 57. The advanced guard is thrown forward a sufficient distance to remove all obstacles that would delay the train. By

31

Arrangement of a Convoy, escorted by 10 companies of Cavalry, 2 pieces of Horse Artillery, and 2 regiments of Infantry.

Fig. 3.

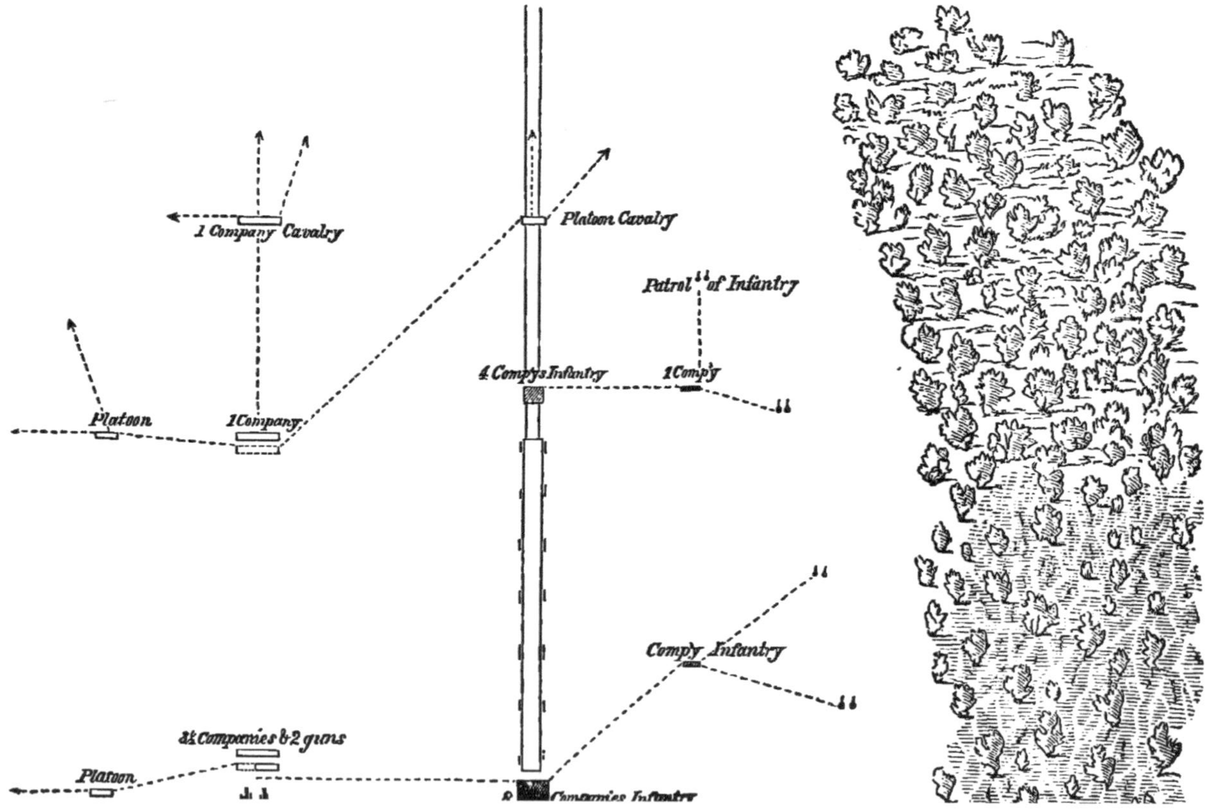

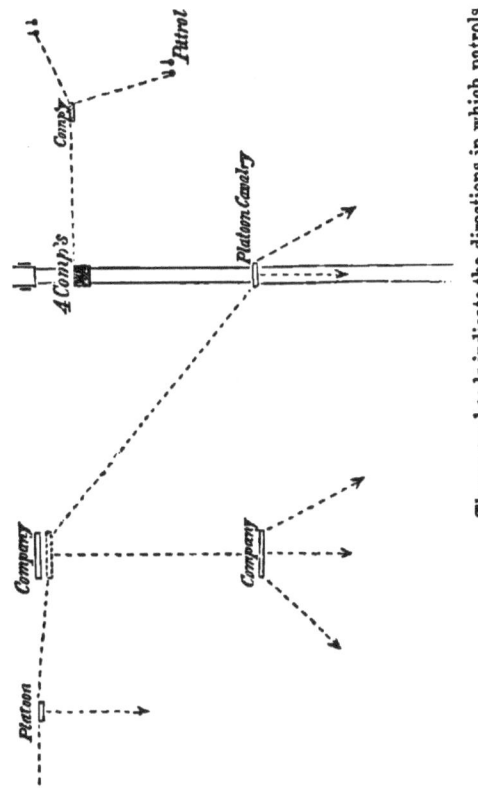

The arrow-heads indicate the directions in which patrols

·········· Cavalry.

━━━━━ Infantry.

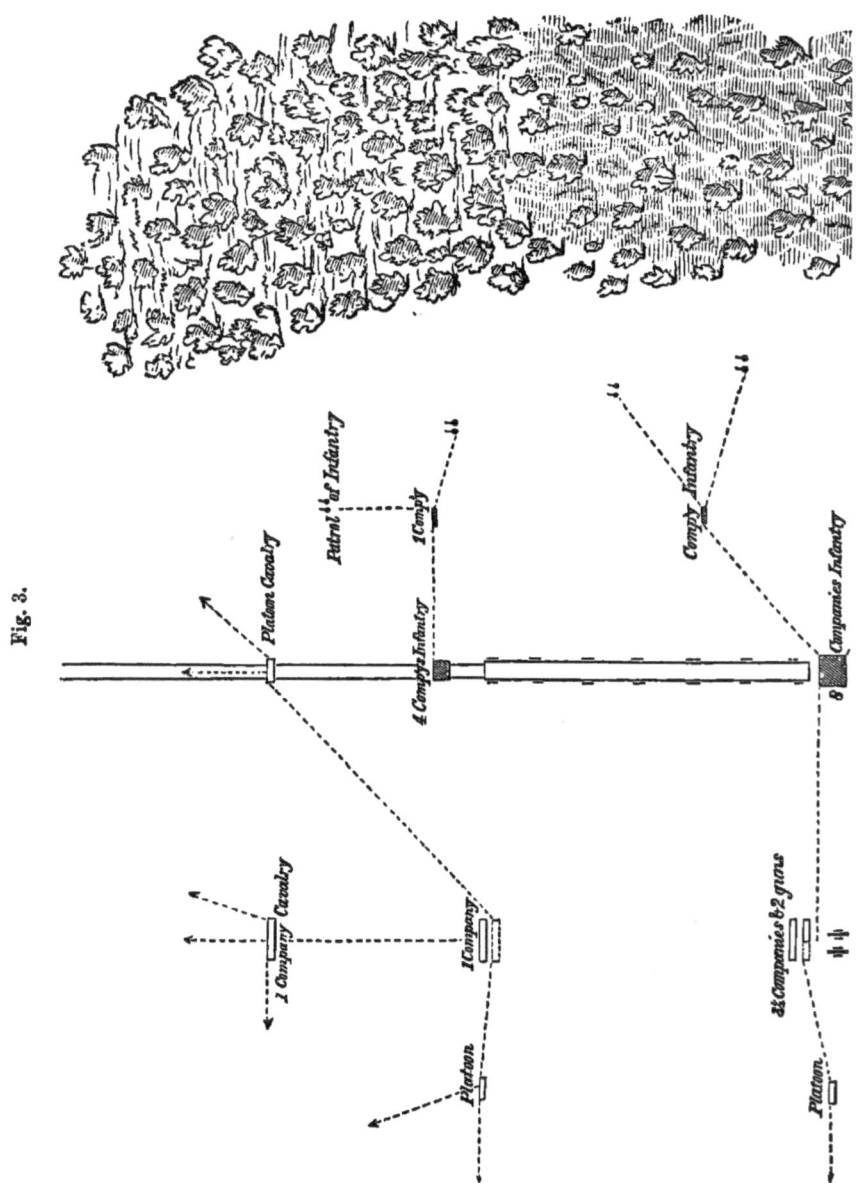

Fig. 3.

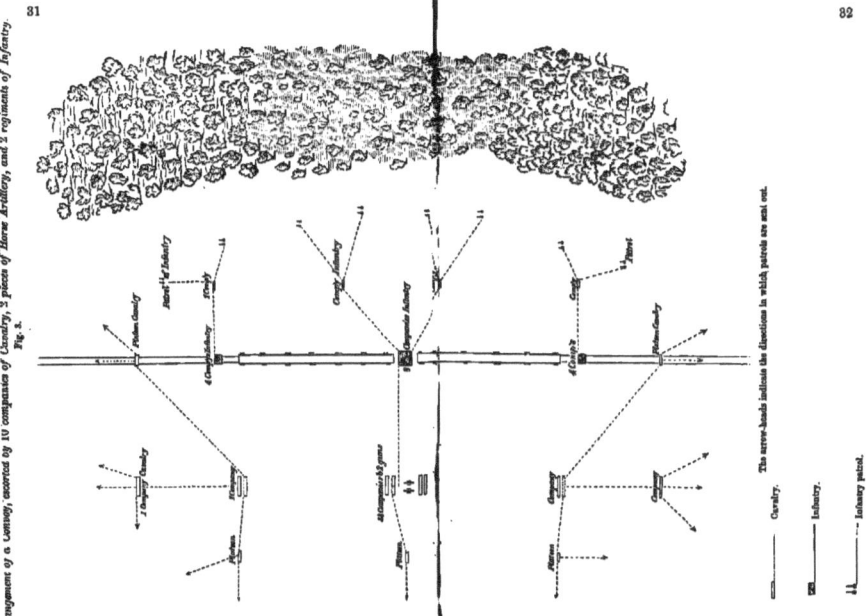

means of its patrols it examines the woods, villages, and defiles; keeps up its communication with the main body, and reports to the commander of the escort every thing observed.

§ 58. The advanced guard selects suitable positions for halting-places, camps, and for parking the train.

§ 59. The advanced guard occupies all defiles and positions which would enable the enemy to attack with advantage; it does not abandon them before the arrival of the main body of the escort, which last holds them until the train arrives. If necessary, the escort is relieved by a small flank detachment, or may itself remain in position until the whole train has passed by and is out of danger.

§ 60. If the enemy is expected from the rear, the suitable measures are taken; the rear guard destroying the bridges, dikes, &c., behind it, and throwing all possible obstacles in the path of the enemy. The rear guard should constantly keep up its communication with the main body by means of patrols.

§ 61. If the enemy threatens the flanks, and the ground is too much broken for the action of cavalry, the defence of the train becomes difficult for that arm. In such cases, small parties of cavalry are with the advanced and rear guards; but the main escort is composed of infantry, who occupy positions favorable for protecting the train before its head arrives opposite to them, and do not abandon those positions until the rear of the train has passed by.

§ 62. Fig. 3 gives an example of the march of a train escorted by 10 companies of cavalry, 2 pieces of horse artillery, and 2 regiments of infantry.

ARTICLE 6.

Of short halts during the march, halts for the night, and halts for an entire day.

§ 63. The length of a march near the enemy depends upon circumstances, and cannot be determined absolutely.

Under ordinary circumstances, the length of march may be about 17 miles; but in case of necessity it may be extended to 30 miles. Small detachments move with much greater rapidity than entire corps, or armies. As a general rule, troops should not be exhausted by forced marches.

Small detachments of cavalry may make marches of 40, 50, or even 70 miles; but this refers only to exceptional cases, when the success of the enterprise in hand depends upon the suddenness of their appearance.

The ordinary rate of march should be about 3 miles per hour.

When the roads are good, it is advisable to move at a moderate trot, walking for some distance before each halt, and before reaching camp; for it is proper to give the horses as much time as possible to feed and rest in camp.

Generals and other officers, furnished with an escort of cavalry, should regulate the rate of their march in accordance with what is laid down above, and are not permitted, except in cases of absolute necessity, to urge the escort to an immoderate speed for the sake of their own convenience.

§ 64. Short halts are made from time to time, as prescribed for marches in time of peace; that is, a halt for 10 or 15 minutes every hour, and in long marches, one or two long halts of about an hour each.

§ 65. When near the enemy, it is necessary to arrange the distances between the camps, or bivouacs, so that the columns of the main body can easily be assembled at the general point of rendezvous; then the reserves are to be placed near the roads by which the enemy is expected, in positions convenient to wood and water.

§ 66. The various parts of the army are so arranged that, if the enemy attacks, they can readily move out upon the roads, or quickly form in order of battle in a position chosen beforehand, either in front or in the rear of encampment or bivouac.

§ 67. The main body should always be secure from a sudden attack: therefore, (notwithstanding there is an advanced guard in front and a rear guard behind,) patrols are sent out from it, and a party is detailed, which does not unsaddle, and always remains ready for action; sometimes, to prevent being turned, separate posts are sent out on the flanks, and sometimes the troops are protected in their camp by advanced posts, arranged according to the rules laid down in Part II.

§ 68. The advanced and rear guards take measures not only for their own safety, but also for that of the main body, placing themselves for this purpose in positions suitable for action, and watching all the roads leading from the enemy.

§ 69. When it is perfectly certain that none of the enemy are in the vicinity, each column may pass the night by itself, on the road by which it marches.

§ 70. In flank marches of several days' duration, the camps for the night should be placed in such positions that the main body may be secure from attack, and in case of the appearance of the enemy in superior force be able to retreat, *i.e.* either to preserve the old road of march and communication, or in some manner to gain a new one. The arrangements for halts and camps for the night are the same as in offensive marches.

§ 71. In regard to the short halts of trains the following rules are prescribed: As in the case of cavalry, the head of the train occasionally makes short halts to enable the rear to close up, and if the train is divided into several sections, the head of each section does the same thing.

During these halts the wagons remain in the road, not turning to one side, or changing the arrangement of the wagons and escort from what it was during the march.

§ 72. Long halts, during which the animals are fed, are made only when the march is very long, or the roads very bad, and the animals fatigued. When the object is not to overtake the troops when at a halt, it is better to leave the train longer in camp, and then make the whole march without a halt; in this manner the animals are not kept so long in harness, and can therefore rest and feed better.

§ 73. During long halts, and camps for the night, the train is placed more compactly than usual; for which purpose a proper place is selected for placing all the wagons together, in order that, being less scattered, a better watch may be kept upon them, and better order be preserved. When danger is apprehended from the enemy, it is best to park the train in column, because this formation is changed more quickly than any other, and from it it is easier to take the road at the end of the halt, or when leaving camp.

Remark.—In this formation the average interval of 8 yards in width is allowed each wagon. The harness is either piled up behind the wagon, or hung on the wheels, and the animals are attached to the pole. The distance between each row of wagons in the column may be fixed at about 20 paces.

Light wagons of the 2d class, although they move in separate trains, are not brought together in camp, but bivouac in rear of the corps to which they belong. If there are wagons loaded with powder, cartridges, or other combustibles, precautions must be taken to guard them from fire, and it is, therefore, best to park them in a separate place, apart from the rest of the train. The escort bivouacs at the head, or on the flanks, of the train, as may be most convenient; guards and sentinels are posted to preserve order; if the teamsters are not to be trusted, and desertions are apprehended, the whole train is surrounded by a chain of sentinels.

§ 74. When an attack is expected, the train should be corralled, or else parked in a square with the hind-wheels outside, and the animals in the centre.

In this case, the escort places itself in a suitable position, keeping in view the defence of the position occupied by the park, and takes all the military measures of precaution necessary to secure itself and the train against a sudden attack.

CHAPTER II.

DUTIES OF THE COMMANDERS OF THE VARIOUS PARTS OF THE TROOPS DURING MILITARY MARCHES.

ARTICLE 1.

Duties of the commander-in-chief.

§ 75. The commander-in-chief must cause the roads by which he intends to march, as well as the country on each side, to be examined by officers of the general staff, or by patrols; but if, from the proximity of the enemy, or other causes, this is impossible, it is necessary, at least, to obtain information concerning their nature and practicability by inquiries of the inhabitants, &c.

§ 76. He must take steps to procure a sufficient number of reliable guides, so that each separate detachment may have its own; this is especially important in thinly-inhabited districts, and in movements by cross-roads.

§ 77. In relation to seeking and employing guides, the following rules are laid down: 1. To be watchful, lest the guides, for their own purposes, prejudice us in any manner; 2. To select guides from among hunters, woodsmen, stage or wagon drivers, and herdsmen, as well as peddlers and travelling beggars, because the country is well known to these classes of people; 3. To change the guides as seldom as possible, especially in localities where parties of the enemy may be met with; 4. To treat the guides kindly and mildly, and to reward them well; but to watch them closely and prevent them from passing over to the enemy, and to send them back by the road over which they came.

§ 78. He regulates the distribution of the troops, the order of march, and the precautionary measures; he arranges the disposition of the troops for the movement, by means of the maps of the country, and the information obtained concerning it and the enemy.

§ 79. The orders should be brief, clear, and positive. All minute details, which might, in unforeseen cases, trammel the subordinate commanders in the execution of their orders, should be avoided.

§ 80. The orders for the march should specify:

1. The number of columns; under whose command each column is to be; precisely where, and by what roads, the march is to be made.

2. The strength of each column, echelon, advanced, rear, and flank guard.

3. At what hour each column or party is to move.

4. Where and when the train is to assemble and move, and under the escort of what detachment. The road by which the train is to move should be carefully considered, in order that in the event of a sudden retreat the troops may find the most important roads clear.

5. The principal measures of precaution to be observed.

6. Where the commander-in-chief will be found during the march, so that the subordinate commanders may know whither to send their reports.

7. Finally, every thing rendered necessary by the circumstances is mentioned in the orders, and sometimes the general arrangements in case of meeting the enemy.

§ 81. In the distribution of the troops into several columns, for the march, the commander-in-chief will observe the following rules:—

1. The number of columns must depend upon the whole number of troops, and upon the number, nature, and degree of separation of the roads.

2. The movement of a large body of troops, as, for instance, an army corps, by one road, besides the difficulty of supplying them, renders the march difficult and slow; and, in addition, a long column requires much time to take up its order of battle. On the other hand, if the number of columns is very great, it may be difficult to keep up the proper connection; besides, when there are many roads near and parallel to each other, they are seldom of a nature favorable to the movements of large bodies of troops.

3. The intervals between the columns should always be such that they can give reciprocal support upon the appearance of the enemy, and not be in danger of being turned or separated. This interval will depend upon the nature of the country: the more broken it is, the nearer should the columns be to each other, for in this case more time is required to concentrate the troops, the transmission of orders and information is slower, and it is more difficult to watch the enemy. In addition to these considerations, the intervals between the columns should be regulated by the proximity of the enemy; the nearer he is, the less should these intervals be.

4. The principal masses of the troops move upon the roads

on which it is expected to meet the main body of the enemy, or by which the principal attack is to be made upon him.

5. Each kind of troops is moved towards the locality best suited for its operations.

6. If one flank is particularly threatened by the enemy, the columns on that side are reinforced, and the reserves drawn near them.

§ 82. To secure harmony of movement and the facility of mutual support, the commander-in-chief should—

1. Watch that the main columns are all equally advanced: therefore, he equalizes the rate of march on different roads, slackens the gait of certain columns, or increases the number and duration of the halts; regulating these things not only upon the length of march of each column, but upon all the circumstances that may influence the velocity of the movement, such as the nature of the road, the number of troops in the several columns, and the obstacles that may be encountered.

2. Take care that the columns do not cross each other.

3. Maintain a constant communication between the columns by means of patrols, which at the same time examine the intermediate country.

4. Take all precautions to enable the columns to unite at any moment: he therefore avoids separating the troops by insurmountable obstacles.

§ 83. That he may, under all circumstances, have it in his power to place the troops in position, the commander-in-chief should know not only where the troops ought to be at any given time, but also where they actually are. For this purpose, he requires every commander of an advanced guard, or chief of a separate column, to report not only the appearance of the enemy, as well as particular events and delays, but also his distance from known points on the road, and his arrival at halting-places and camps. These reports should be made the more frequently in proportion to the proximity of the enemy.

§ 84. To watch over the order of march, the commanders of the main and detached columns should occasionally halt and allow their commands to pass by them, so as to see that the column is not too much lengthened out, particularly in the march of large bodies on one road.

§ 85. The commander-in-chief and the subordinate commanders see that all persons belonging to the combatants, and for duty, march in the proper places. The non-combatants, dismounted men, led horses of the officers and men, march with the trains of the second class.

§ 86. In parties near the enemy, *i.e.* advanced guards, front and flank detachments, rear guards in retreat, patrols, &c., the firearms should be loaded. In the main body, the arms are loaded only when an affair is anticipated.

§ 87. When passing through towns or villages, by farms, inns, wells, and such places, the commander-in-chief and the subordinate commanders turn their attention to preventing disorder, by closely watching that no one leaves the ranks.

§ 88. In passing defiles and crossing rivers the commander-in-chief watches—

1. That the troops do not crowd together at the entrance, or stretch out in passing through, but that they preserve their proper distances.

2. That, in crossing rivers in boats or ferries, each party knows when and after what other party it is to cross.

3. That, as soon as any troops have crossed, they form in conformity with the orders they have received.

4. That the drivers of the artillery and train do not dismount without orders.

5. That, in crossing fords, the men follow each other at the prescribed distance; that the wagons do not drive in one after another, but that each waits until the one in front has gained a certain distance, or even reached the opposite shore. In case of necessity, some officers are left to superintend the crossing. At difficult crossings a detachment may be left to assist the artillery and train.

§ 89. During secret or night marches, trumpet signals are not used; orders are given in a low tone of voice. In secret night marches, smoking and striking fire are forbidden.

§ 90. The commander-in-chief watches that, during halts, as well as on the march, the troops are protected by advanced and rear guards, flank detachments, and patrols; also, when in camp, as explained hereafter in Part II.

§ 91. Upon approaching the place where the troops are to halt, bivouac, or encamp, the commander-in-chief sends forward betimes officers of the staff, with non-commissioned officers from every party, to mark the place to be occupied by each.

§ 92. Since the advanced and rear guards are more fatigued than the other troops, on account of their continual state of vigilance and preparation, the commander-in-chief should relieve them by fresh troops from time to time.

Article 2.
Duties of the commander of the advanced guard.

§ 93. Upon commencing the march, he sends out front and flank detachments, as explained in §§ 12, 13, and 14.

§ 94. He places an officer, or non-commissioned officer, in charge of every party detached, and explains to them what patrols they are to send out, and exactly in what direction, and gives them special instructions as to what they are to do in different cases.

§ 95. During the march he watches that the detachments and patrols maintain their communication with each other and himself, and that they perform their duties strictly. Not blindly trusting to the advanced and flank detachments for security, he should see that his command marches in the best order, and in the habitual formation, according to the nature of the ground.

§ 96. When in pursuit of the enemy, he should never lose sight of him, follow all his movements promptly and continually, and ascertain his strength, direction, and designs, as well as possible.

§ 97. He should exert himself to obtain reliable and detailed information concerning the enemy and the country in advance, by means of patrols, spies, inquiries from prisoners and the inhabitants.

§ 98. He interrogates deserters and prisoners as to—

1. The names and strength of their regiments, and the detachment to which they belong.

2. What brigade, division, and army corps they belonged to; the names of their commanders.

3. Where their corps are quartered.

4. What are the dispositions of their regiments, brigades, and divisions. If the corps is in position, the strength of its advanced posts, and whether it is carefully guarded.

5. What corps or divisions are near their own; where they are, and at what intervals.

6. When and where they left their regiments; whether detachments were sent out from the corps, in what force, and whether they expected support.

7. Whether there were any orders or rumors in regard to intended movements, and exactly what they were.

8. Whether provisions and supplies were abundant, and the situation of the magazines.

9. Whether there was much sickness, or any epidemics, and the situations of the main and temporary hospitals.

In few words, endeavor to obtain information about every

thing which relates to the arrangements of the enemy, his strength, designs, and means of all kinds.

§ 99. It is impossible to place much reliance upon the testimony of prisoners and deserters: on the one hand, they may be too ignorant to give a definite answer; on the other, they may, from fear, reply according to the wishes of the questioner, or they may deliberately falsify. It is therefore necessary frequently to repeat the same questions unexpectedly, so as to compare the different answers, and also to compare the statements of different individuals.

§ 100. The commander of the advanced guard will, without delay, report to the commander-in-chief every thing observed with regard to the enemy, every considerable detention, his arrival at remarkable points on the road, (such as towns, rivers, &c.,) and his arrival at halting-places and camps.

§ 101. Upon occupying any town, the commander of the advanced guard should take every means to obtain information as to military movements; for this purpose, he should at once seize the archives and papers of the authorities of the place, and also the letters and papers in the post-office.

§ 102. Upon receiving from the advanced parties or patrols any intelligence, especially if it concerns the movements of the enemy, he should endeavor to verify it in person, or by means of reliable officers, and then make his own report positively and distinctly, so that no unfounded or exaggerated report may unnecessarily alarm the main body and arrest its march. The nearer he is to the enemy, the more frequently should he send reports to the commander-in-chief.

§ 103. These reports are made either verbally through aides, or in pencil. The time and place whence the report is sent should be noted on the paper. The greatest attention should always be paid to giving the correct names of towns, villages, streams, &c.

§ 104. Reports should be written with the greatest care and attention, for upon the comparison of reports the movements of the main body must depend. The most important qualities of the reports are clearness, perspicuity, precision, and reliability. They should contain only what the sender has seen himself, or properly inquired into. Every thing which he could not examine himself ought to be stated separately, with the degree of confidence to be reposed in the source whence it was derived.

§ 105. When sending a verbal report, the commander of the advanced guard must satisfy himself not only that the bearer can repeat it word for word, but that he comprehends its precise meaning. If possible, it is best to send with all such despatches some of those who were ocular witnesses of the subject of the report. If the report is important, and there is danger of the bearer being captured, it is best to send a duplicate after the lapse of a short interval. It is useful to number all reports, for should one be captured or arrive before another sent previously, the series of numbers enables this to be detected. These remarks apply not only to the reports sent by the commander of the advanced guard, but, in general, to all reports sent in time of war. The adoption of a simple cipher will often be of advantage.

§ 106. The commander of the advanced guard attends to the repairs of the road, bridges, causeways, &c. If the repairs are heavy, and exceed the means at his disposal, he promptly informs the commander-in-chief.

§ 107. When the commander of the advanced guard is informed of the appearance of the enemy, he at once takes the measures rendered proper by the object of the march and the orders he has received : *i.e.*

1. He takes up a position in order to keep the enemy in check until the arrival of the main body; or,

2. Marches to meet and attack the enemy; or, finally,

3. Falls back upon the main body, endeavoring to delay the enemy as long as possible, so as to give the main body time to form and change from the order of march to that of battle.

§ 108. For camps, the commander of the advanced guard selects places advantageous for defence and secure against sudden attack. Entire detachments should not be placed in woods, defiles, towns, or villages, but they should be occupied only by a part of the command, the rest remaining near by. If there are defiles in advance, through which it is intended to march, their debouches should be occupied in force, in order to secure them for our ulterior movements.

§ 109. The commander of the advanced guard secures his camp by outposts.

Remark.—All the duties prescribed for the commander of the advanced guard in offensive marches apply equally to the commander of the flank guard during a march to the flank.

§ 110. In a retreat, the commander of the advanced guard follows the same rules as in the offensive, and takes great pains to remove all obstacles that might impede the march of the train and the main body. To repair the road, he detaches mounted engineer troops or working-parties, with the requisite tools, and pursues his march with the remainder of his command.

ARTICLE 3.

Duties of the commander of the rear guard.

§ 111. His principal duties, during a pursuit by the enemy, consist—

1. In indefatigable vigilance.
2. In the preservation of the best order and most severe discipline.
3. In sustaining the courage and spirits of his troops.

§ 112. He should use every exertion to ascertain the movements and designs of the enemy, that he may be able to take in time the measures necessary to thwart and oppose him.

§ 113. He secures and guards his march as the advanced guard does on the offensive. By a turning movement, the enemy may force the rear guard to accelerate its march, and thus throw it into disorder; for this reason, the commander should pay especial attention to his flanks and to the cross-roads, by which the enemy might turn and attack him; if necessary, he may send out, instead of the usual small detachments, large and independent parties which can resist the attack.

§ 114. The rear guard should always be in a condition to form in order of battle; therefore, those portions near the enemy retreat by the rear rank, so that they have only to face about.

§ 115. That he may be able to preserve order in the rear guard when retreating in sight of the enemy, especially during the rigor of his pursuit, the commander ought not to conduct the retreat with all the troops at once, but with one portion fighting to protect the other, which latter in the mean time retreats, occupies an advantageous position in rear, and then receives the shock of the enemy in turn, thus allowing the first portion to pass by to the rear.

§ 116. The portion of the rear guard covering such a retreat ought to avoid engaging in a decisive combat, and merely check the enemy long enough to enable the portion in retreat to gain its newly-chosen position.

§ 117. The commander of a rear guard, in a retreat, should resort to all means of retarding the pursuit of the enemy; for this purpose, he orders the roads to be broken up, bridges to be destroyed, defiles to be blocked up, &c.

§ 118. During an offensive march, if there is no danger of an attack upon the rear of the column, the duties of the commander of the rear guard are as in peace: he superintends the preservation of order in the train, and picks up stragglers, &c.

§ 119. In all cases, the commanders of rear guards ought to

report to the commander of the main body every thing that occurs to their party.

ARTICLE 4.

Duties of the commanders of advanced, flank, and rear detachments.

§ 120. They send out patrols, as laid down in § 14, to examine the greatest possible amount of ground on all sides, and to obtain information of the enemy; the number of the patrols must depend upon circumstances and the nature of the country.

In open country they are small, and at great intervals apart. In a rough, broken country, in foggy or very rainy weather, in night marches, the number of patrols is increased, and they remain near their detachments. Patrols are not sent out in very dark nights, unless it is absolutely necessary.

§ 121. The commanders of detachments upon sending out patrols should instruct them in what direction to march, what intervals to preserve, and to what objects and places their attention should chiefly be directed.

§ 122. If there are defiles, woods, villages, &c., in front, the advanced and flank detachments should examine them by patrols before entering them, lest they should be suddenly attacked and cut off.

§ 123. On approaching a village, the commander of a detachment orders his patrols to seize, in some way or other, some of the inhabitants for interrogation, as to whether the enemy is concealed in the village, or its vicinity; whether he has passed through it; if he has passed, in what force, with what kind of troops, when, and in what direction. The inhabitants seized should not be dismissed until the whole detachment has left the village.

§ 124. Commanders of advanced, flank, and rear detachments, upon receiving reports from their patrols, should endeavor to verify them in person, particularly in important cases, and ought not to make their own reports until fully satisfied of the truth of those of the patrols.

§ 125. Commanders of detachments should endeavor to maintain a constant communication with the parties on their flanks by means of patrols. Flank detachments should not be long separated from their corps by impassable places, such as woods, marshes, lakes, &c.; but if these obstacles are not very extensive, the detachment and its patrols march on the outer side of them, in order to examine the country more fully.

§ 126. If the enemy appears, or attacks in force, the commanders of the advanced, flank, and rear detachments call in their patrols, and, without accepting combat, retreat upon their column under cover of skirmishers, merely endeavoring to delay the enemy as long as possible. If, however, an opportunity offers to capture one of the enemy's patrols, without delaying its own march, the detachment should undoubtedly avail itself of the chance.

CHAPTER III.

DUTIES OF PATROLS DURING THE MARCH.

§ 127. Patrols are parties of various strength detached either from troops on the march to examine the country, or from troops in position to obtain news of the enemy.

In this chapter, patrols of the first kind are alone treated of; the duties of patrols sent out by troops in position will be given in Part II., Chapter IV.

§ 128. The principal duty of patrols is to discover the enemy betimes, and thus secure the detachment to which they belong, as well as the rest of the army, against sudden attacks.

§ 129. Patrols should not consist of less than 12 or 15 men; for they ought to be able to attack the enemy's patrols by surprise, without too much risk.

§ 130. The men composing a patrol should not keep too close together, but stretch out as much as the ground and the force of the patrol will permit; never forgetting that it is very important that they should not all be captured at once.

§ 131. Patrols on the march move at a fixed distance from their detachment, keep up their communications, never lose sight of each other if they can avoid it, and form a continuous protective chain around the army.

§ 132. In a patrol of 15 men, the commander arranges them as follows: two or three of the most intelligent and best mounted men are sent in advance; if one is sent back with a report, the others remain in advance, and keep sight of the object reported The rest of the patrol march according to the arrangement indicated in fig. 4, at 150 or 200 paces behind these advanced men, having their rear guard about 100 paces behind.

§ 133. Fig. 5 shows the arrangement of a patrol of 30 men.

Remarks.—1st. With every 10 men a non-commissioned officer is sent; 30 men and over are commanded by an officer.

2d. The men in front, on the flanks, and in rear of a patrol, are called *patrollers*.

§ 134. The flank patrollers regulate themselves on the position

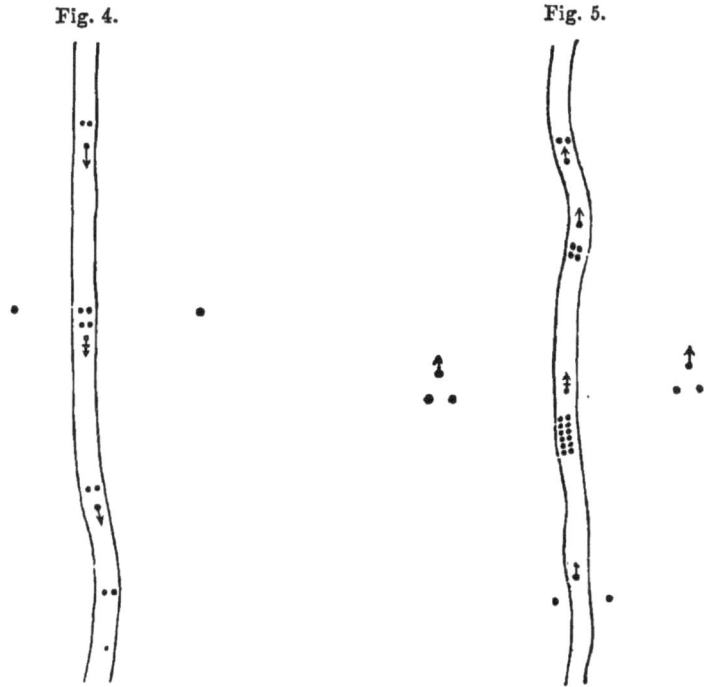

Fig. 4.   Fig. 5.

of the patrol, which is on the road, and endeavor not to lose sight of it. They take care not to be separated from it by impassable obstacles; for this reason, when they meet with such places, they join the advanced patrollers, or the main patrol itself, until the obstacle is passed.

§ 135. During the night the patrols draw near to their detachment, and endeavor to connect with each other by a chain of men, that the enemy may not slip through the intervals under cover of the darkness.

§ 136. It is impossible to regulate with exactness the space to be covered by patrols, but the following remarks will serve as guides:

Patrols should cover and protect the march, but ought not to scatter so much as to be unable to assemble quickly if they meet the enemy. In a level country, where they can see a great distance in advance, there is less danger in stretching out than in a broken, wooded, or mountainous region. The main consideration is, that the patrol should be able to survey at a glance the whole of the space confided to it; the extent of this space will, therefore, depend upon the nature of the ground, as well as upon the weather, and whether the march is at night or in the daytime.

§ 137. A detachment destined to attack the enemy by surprise should not send out its patrols so far as one intended merely to reconnoitre; because the enemy, being warned by the appearance of the patrols, would be on the alert.

§ 138. Patrollers should look around carefully on all sides, and often halt to listen. If they hear the slightest suspicious noise, however indefinite in its nature, particularly at night or in an obstructed country, or if they observe dust, smoke, the glitter of arms, or any signs whatever of the enemy, such as the sound of footsteps, rumbling of wheels, noise of horses, &c., they at once inform the nearest non-commissioned officer, who reports to the commander of the detachment. The whole party then halts, the flank patrols face outwards, the rear guard faces to the rear, and the march is arrested until the cause of the noise is ascertained, or the object which attracted attention examined.

Remark.—Reports should be made in a clear, calm tone of voice.

§ 139. The flank patrols ascend every eminence on the side of their route, and remain there, facing outwards, until the detachment passes by or sends another patrol to relieve them.

Remark.—In ascending a hill to reconnoitre, one man should precede the others, riding very slowly; when near the top, he takes off his cap and moves up just far enough to see over, covering himself by trees, bushes, &c., as well as possible; in this manner he may see the enemy without being discovered by them.

§ 140. Patrols turn their attention to every thing which may disclose the movements of troops passing by, notice the direction of their march, &c.

§ 141. Patrols should examine carefully every thing which may conceal the enemy, such as houses, woods, coppices, ravines, &c. In passing by such places, the patrols endeavor to ascertain whether they are occupied by the enemy, and then either occupy them themselves, or pass by with the utmost precaution. Defiles, bridges, ravines, hollow ways, dikes, and rivers, should be carefully examined; having passed them, the front patrollers should at once place themselves on the highest bank to observe the environs.

§ 142. A special **patrol** of 2 or 3 men is sent to examine any remarkable object which is too far off to be visited by the flank patrollers; the rest halt, and await their return: such patrols should move at a moderate gait.

§ 143. If it is necessary to pass through a village, the operation is conducted as follows. One of the front patrollers approaches it. If it is in the day, he rides through several streets and asks for the chief person of the place; in the mean time the other front patrollers ride along the skirts of the village. Having found the chief person of the place, the front patroller conducts him to the commander of the advanced guard, which now approaches the village; the patroller then rides through the village with his comrades, and halts on the farther side in some elevated position. There they await the arrival of the advanced guard.

§ 144. If a village is to be passed at night, the front patrollers go quietly to the first house, call out its master, take him away, and obtain the necessary information from him; afterwards they go for the chief person of the place.

§ 145. Before entering a woods, the front patrollers must ascertain that the enemy does not occupy the skirts, and one or two men should ride around the whole woods, if it is not too extensive; all the cross-roads should be examined to the distance of several hundred paces by flank patrols, who afterwards overtake the patrol. Before entering open fields in a forest, patrollers should ride all around the edges.

§ 146. The patrols detain all persons met on the road, and send them to the commander of the detachment for examination. The commander retains, under guard, all who are suspicious characters, as well as those who have witnessed important movements, or whose testimony is of such importance as to need verification.

§ 147. Upon the appearance of hostile patrols and patrollers, flags of truce, or deserters, our own patrollers, even if in considerable force, at once inform the commander of the patrol, who, satisfying himself of the true state of the case, at once takes the necessary measures.

If he sees a weak patrol of the enemy, or single soldiers straggling off for pillage, he quietly endeavors to seize and disarm them; he stops the flag of truce, blindfolds, and places him under the charge of a trustworthy soldier, who, not allowing him to turn back, conducts him to the commander of the detachment.

§ 148. Whenever the commander of a patrol perceives, from a distance, the approach of the enemy in strong force, he at once informs the commander of the detachment, and at the same time endeavors to get nearer the enemy to ascertain his strength, &c.;

finally, he retreats upon the detachment without exposing himself.

Remark.—In this, and all similar cases, the party falling back should move as slowly and in as good order as possible.

§ 149. A patrol only gives notice of the approach of the enemy by firing when it is suddenly driven in and has no time to send a report. Therefore, a patrol should be in no hurry to fire when it discovers the enemy; for it may happen that we see him before he discovers us, and then, if we are only engaged in watching him, we should endeavor to fall back on the detachment without being observed.

§ 150. Upon the first shot fired by the patrollers, the whole patrol forms, and the commander acts according to circumstances. If the enemy is the stronger, he falls back upon the detachment, covering himself by skirmishers; but, if it is possible, he endeavors to capture the enemy's patrollers, and sends back those taken to the commander of the detachment.

If attacked by surprise, the patrol should defend itself to the utmost, and fire a few shots, even if in the air, to warn the detachment of its danger. In such cases, it is not always advisable to retreat by the direct road.

Remark.—The commanders of parties must bear in mind that there are few circumstances which can justify the surrender of cavalry; proper precautions on the march render a surprise next to impossible; and when a party of cavalry is attacked, no matter how suddenly, or by what superiority of force, a determined and instantaneous charge will always enable the greater part to escape in safety. Officers and men should therefore always have their wits about them, and their weapons in constant readiness for use.

§ 151. During the march, patrols are not permitted to wander out of the way, nor to halt to rest at their discretion.

§ 152. To be certain that their orders are executed, the commanders of patrols should be alternately at the head and on the flanks; in a word, everywhere, that they may see and superintend every thing for themselves.

§ 153. Should it happen that two patrols or patrollers meet on the march, even if they belong to the same regiment, they should challenge each other, as directed in § 337.

§ 154. During halts, the patrols continue to secure the troops against a sudden attack. Choosing positions from which it is easy to examine the country around, they halt in the same order as that in which they marched, and face outward.

CHAPTER IV.

IN REFERENCE TO REGULATING MARCHES ACCORDING TO THE LOCALITY.

Of advanced guards.

§ 155. It is but seldom that any one arm is exclusively employed when near the enemy; on the contrary, it is usual to operate with a combined force of cavalry, infantry, and artillery, so that it may be always possible to employ one or the other arm, according to circumstances and the locality.

§ 156. If the main body is composed of the different arms, then the advanced guard is similarly constituted, that it may be able to act in all localities.

§ 157. The composition of such an advanced guard depends—

1st. Upon the object and nature of its intended operations. During marches in pursuit it is reinforced by cavalry; but if it is to make an obstinate resistance, it is strengthened with much infantry and artillery. In general, light cavalry are the best for advanced guards, wherever the nature of the ground permits them to operate; but infantry are necessary to support them. Mounted rifles and mounted engineer troops are of great service in advanced guards.

2d. The composition of the advanced guard depends also upon the locality: if the ground is broken, much infantry is required; if it is open, much cavalry, and, in general, light troops.

§ 158. The order of march of an advanced guard depends, principally, upon its composition, the order of march of the main body, the locality, &c. The main rule is, that it should never be too much divided, so that there may always be a considerable force in hand to seek the enemy more boldly and detain him longer. Therefore, even when the main body moves in several columns, the principal part of the advanced guard marches on the main road, sending only small parties on the others to watch the enemy and detach patrols as far as possible in all directions. In an open, level country, the cavalry marches at the head; in a broken country, there is only a small detachment of cavalry at the head, to furnish advanced detachments and patrols. An advanced detachment of cavalry, which sends out patrols in front and on its flanks, moves at the distance of a few miles in front of the advanced guard. Small detachments of cavalry move in a line with it on the other roads; also others on the

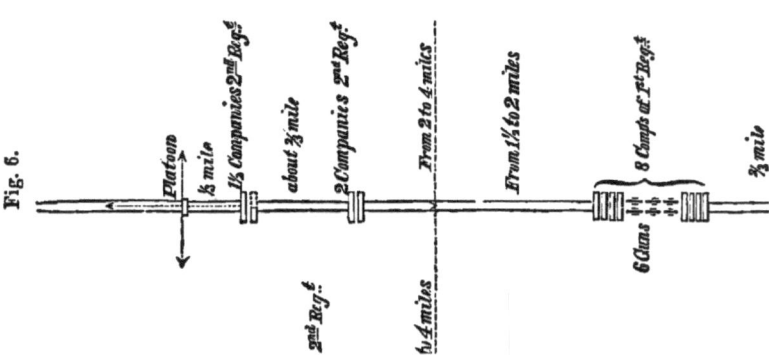

Fig. 6.

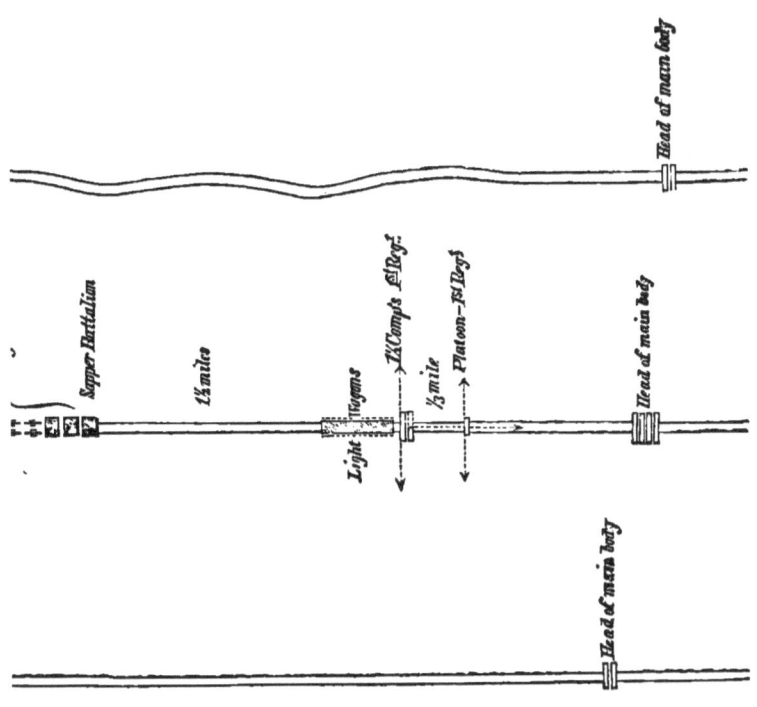

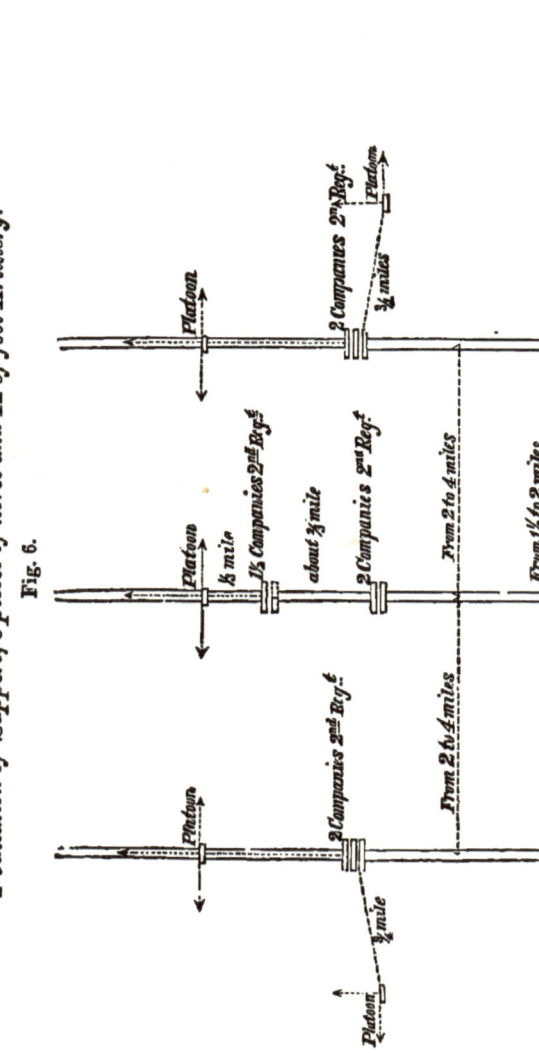

March of an Advanced Guard composed of 1 brigade of Cavalry, (20 companies,) 2 divisions of Infantry, (8 battalions,) 1 battalion of Sappers, 6 pieces of horse and 12 of foot Artillery.

Fig. 6.

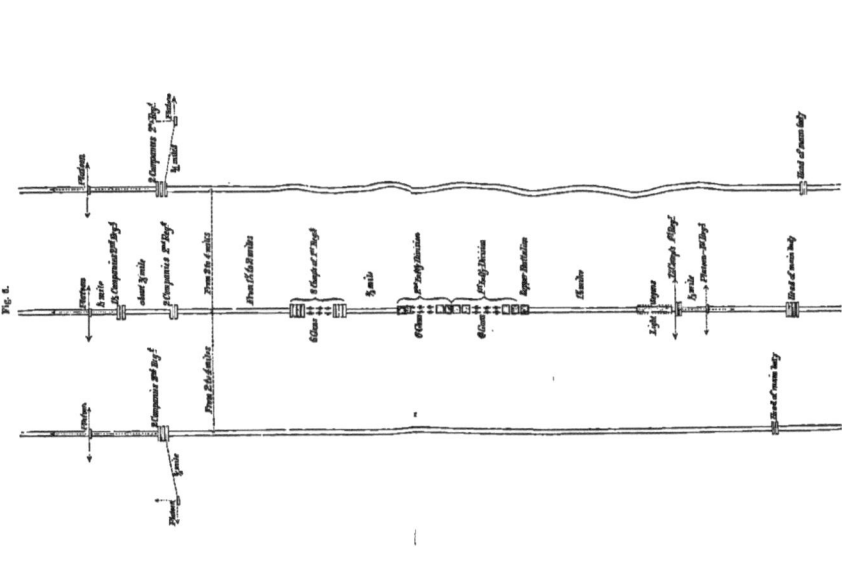

March of an Advanced Guard composed of 1 brigade of Cavalry, (20 companies,) 2 divisions of Infantry, (8 battalions,) 1 battalion of Sappers, 6 pieces of horse and 12 of foot Artillery.

Fig. 8.

flanks of the main advanced guard, to secure it against being turned. All the front and flank detachments maintain a constant mutual communication by means of patrols, and thus keep in sight the whole space in front of the main body over a great extent. But if the flank columns of the main body march at a great distance from the main road followed by the advanced guard, then, in addition to this last, each flank column detaches a small advanced guard for its own security.

§ 159. If the advanced guard is composed of different arms, its distance from the main body depends not only upon its strength, but also on the following circumstances: 1. On its composition. Cavalry may advance much farther than infantry. 2. Upon the locality. The more fully the nature of the country secures the advanced guard against being turned, the farther may it move from the main body. 3. Upon the object in view. Prior to defensive combats in position, it is advantageous to have the advanced guard as far from the main body as possible, in order to secure time for making the necessary arrangements; but if the main body is already concentrated for a decisive attack upon the enemy, it is sometimes well to be entirely without an advanced guard; during a pursuit, the main body should follow the advanced guard as closely as possible. 4. Upon the order of march of the main body. The longer the time needed by the main body to form in order of battle, on account of the intervals between the columns, the nature of the ground between them, the length of the columns, &c., so much farther forward should the advanced guard be pushed. In general, the distance of the advanced guard from the head of the main body should be a little greater than the interval between the outside columns of the main body.

§ 160. Fig. 6 gives an example of the arrangement of an advanced guard composed of one brigade of light cavalry, 8 battalions of infantry, one battalion of sappers, 6 pieces of horse artillery, and 12 pieces of foot artillery; the main body following in 3 columns. Disregarding minute details, this is established as the basis of the arrangement of an advanced guard, without regard to the ground.

Whatever slight changes may be made necessary by the nature of the country can easily be made with the aid of a map and the special information obtained in other ways.

§ 161. If the country is partially broken and obstructed, it is advantageous to have four or five companies of infantry just behind the leading detachment of cavalry, to examine places that are difficult or dangerous for the latter.

§ 162. Upon the plains the patrols are of cavalry; in a

mountainous region, of infantry. In the latter case, not only the advanced detachments and patrols are of infantry, but also the head and rear of every column; the cavalry and artillery march in the middle, under the protection of the infantry.

§ 163. In passing through a village, the infantry enter it first, if there are any with the advanced guard; the cavalry either ride rapidly around it, or, according to circumstances, halt a little before reaching the village, and wait until the infantry have passed through.

§ 164. The passage of important bridges, ravines, and defiles, should be effected in the same manner, the infantry examining them. As soon as the infantry have crossed and formed on the other side, the cavalry send out patrols to a great distance to examine the ground in front, before the main body of the advanced guard begins to cross.

The advanced guard, having crossed rapidly, forms in front of the passage to cover the debouche of the main body. The distance of such a position from the passage should be such that, in the event of being attacked, the advanced guard may not be too quickly forced back upon the main body while debouching, and that the latter may have ample time to form without disorder.

§ 165. Since attacks should be most expected when passing through defiles, or when issuing from them, they should be traversed rapidly, and with the most extended front possible, to prevent the column from stretching out. In passing long defiles, the troops should occasionally halt for a moment, to close up and re-establish order.

§ 166. As for the rest, an advanced guard, possessing a certain degree of independence, without neglecting any of the precautions here laid down, should not be too apprehensive, and, in examining the country, ought not to detain itself with objects which, from their nature, cannot conceal the enemy in sufficient force to make him dangerous to the advanced guard.

§ 167. In very mountainous regions it is necessary to rely upon the infantry alone; the cavalry and train remaining in rear, and not entering the defiles until they have been occupied. Here the infantry patrols are sent out as far as possible, and occupy the heights from which the direction of the columns may be seen, until relieved by the patrols of the rear guard, which is also of infantry. In this manner the cavalry, which the enemy would attack in such places in preference, is protected. Not a gorge or defile should be left unexamined; for in the mountains an attack may be expected at any moment.

§ 168. In a wooded country the commander of the advanced guard takes nearly the same precaution as in the mountains.

If the forest is deep, but not broad, detachments of cavalry ride along the skirts, which are occupied by infantry skirmishers as supports; if the forest is dense, but not deep, the infantry lead. The infantry place themselves along the skirts of the wood on both sides of the road; the cavalry then passes through at a fast trot, forms on the plain beyond, and there awaits the rest of the column.

§ 169. When the road passes through a country but little obstructed by defiles, villages, or other obstacles to the movements of cavalry, and there is no infantry with the advanced guard, mounted rifles are very useful; finally, the enemy, in retreating through such a country, leaves infantry at these obstacles to arrest the pursuit of the cavalry, and delay until the arrival of the infantry; in such cases mounted rifles or dismounted dragoons will produce sure results by acting against the enemy's infantry.

OF THE MAIN BODY.

§ 170. It remains to be said, in reference to this, that the nature of the country must determine its order of march, whether cavalry or infantry are to lead. If the country is broken, particularly if it is wooded, there is great danger in placing the cavalry at the head; for it may not only be unable to act, but, if forced to retreat, may carry disorder into the infantry following.

The artillery should march in the midst of the other troops; but a few pieces may move with the head of the column, to protect it in case of meeting the enemy suddenly.

§ 171. If there are infantry, then in traversing extensive forests, in which parties of the enemy may easily conceal themselves, the flank detachments and patrols of cavalry are replaced by infantry.

OF THE REAR GUARD.

§ 172. In § 19 the duties of a rear guard in a retreat are described as being important, and sometimes even more important than those of the advanced guard in the offensive. Therefore, not only the force but the composition of the rear guard should correspond to the importance of its duties; if the main body consists of troops of the different arms, the rear guard should be composed in like manner.

§ 173. Its order of march must depend not only upon the locality, the number, direction, and separation of the roads, and the degree of security of the flanks, but also upon the order of march of the main body, and the manner in which the pursuing enemy operates. Frequently the march of the rear guard becomes a fighting retreat. If the enemy does not follow directly on its heels, its arrangements will generally be nearly the same as those of an advanced guard in the offensive; but in this case it is necessary to turn the closest attention to the roads on the flanks, because the pursuing enemy usually endeavors to turn the retreating rear guard with a part of his force, in order to keep it constantly in retreat and prevent it from holding the positions it has selected. For this reason, there should be on the flank roads not only patrols from the rear guard, but parties strong enough to hold the enemy in check.

§ 174. In districts where there are extensive plains, the rear of the rear guard is reinforced by all its cavalry, so that the infantry may move forward to occupy any hills, woods, or other favorable positions.

§ 175. As in a mountainous, wooded, or broken country, the cavalry of the advanced guard marches in rear of the other troops, so, in a rear guard retreating through a similar country, the cavalry forms the head of the column, marching under the protection of the infantry, with which latter there is only a small party of cavalry for sending rapid information of the approach of the enemy.

§ 176. It is stated in § 115 that, to preserve the requisite good order, the retreat of the rear guard should not be by all the troops at once, but by alternate portions, so that one part may fight to protect the retreat of the other. According to this, upon approaching a defile or bridge, around which the cavalry cannot pass, the greatest part of it should be sent on early to pass through.

A few guns are placed in front of such obstacles, under the protection of a party of infantry, to keep the enemy at a distance, while the rest of the infantry and artillery pass the defile, availing themselves of all the heights on both sides to protect those in retreat against the attack of the enemy, and to cover the flanks. Therefore, the ground should be examined early, that it may be occupied betimes for defence by infantry and artillery. After having passed the defile, the cavalry forms in order of battle, out of cannon range.

If the enemy endeavors to pursue the rear guard beyond the defile, the cavalry should, if the ground permits, stop or delay his pursuit by an attack upon the front and flanks of the head of his column, so as to give the infantry and artillery time to gain the necessary ground. In such cases, there is an advantage in having passed the defile, so as to attack with a superior front the head of the enemy's column as he debouches.

§ 177. If a village is to be traversed, it is first occupied by a sufficient force of infantry, and the cavalry then either passes around it, or, which is quicker, rides rapidly through it, if this can be done without masking the fire of the infantry. Having passed beyond the village, the cavalry and horse artillery come into position to cover the retreat of the infantry.

§ 178. In a retreat, dismounted rifles or dragoons, availing themselves of the obstacles of the ground, may arrest the pursuit of the enemy, without fearing, as in the case of infantry, to remain behind the main body of the rear guard.

§ 179. Finally, if the enemy acts imprudently, the rear guard may form ambuscades for him, or force him to slacken the pursuit by resuming the offensive for a time.

§ 180. The commander of the rear guard should always regulate himself upon the movements of the main body, always holding every position as obstinately as possible, lest a premature retreat on his part should bring the enemy suddenly upon the main body.

PART II.

PRECAUTIONS TO BE OBSERVED IN CAMPS* FOR SECURITY AGAINST THE ENEMY.

CHAPTER I.

DUTIES OF ALL PARTS OF THE OUTPOSTS.

ARTICLE 1.

Of the outposts in general.

§ 181. The outposts are detachments upon whom is imposed the duty of securing the other troops against sudden attacks.

§ 182. They are independent of, and in addition to, the camp and quarter guards, whose duty it is to watch over the interior order and police of the camp.

§ 183. Light cavalry are employed on outpost duty wherever

(*) The term *camp* is here used in its most general sense, including all the arrangements of the troops when halted, whether in tents, huts, bivouac, or villages, provided they are not in cantonments or winter quarters. The term *encampment* refers particularly to a camp of tents or huts.

the ground permits them to act; in cases of absolute necessity, the outposts consist of infantry.

§ 184. The outposts consist of:
1. A chain of double vedettes.
2. Pickets, which are the immediate supports of the vedettes.
3. Main guards, placed as supports in rear of the pickets.

§ 185. If the outposts are pushed very far to the front, or if the nature of the ground is such as to render their retreat difficult, parties, called *reserves of the outposts*, are placed between the outposts and the troops guarded, to serve as a reserve and support for the former.

§ 186. The outposts should enclose all the places and observe all the roads by which the enemy can approach the camp guarded.

§ 187. The chain of outposts is placed in front of the general position of the troops, so as to intersect all the roads leading towards the enemy. It forms a curved line, falling back on the flanks.

§ 188. The outposts should be pushed so far to the front that, while in no danger of being cut off, they may give timely notice of the enemy's approach, and keep him long enough in check to enable the troops guarded to prepare to receive him.

For this purpose the chain of mounted vedettes is usually placed at not more than three miles in front of the camp; the pickets not more than three-fourths of a mile in rear of the vedettes; the main guards at about the same distance behind the pickets.

§ 189. The interval between the pairs of vedettes composing the chain should be such that in the daytime they can see each other, and in the night hear every thing that happens between them.

§ 190. The object of the pickets and main guards being merely to receive the chain, they are composed of small numbers of men. Therefore, a picket consists of about a platoon, and a main guard of about a company.

§ 191. The commander-in-chief determines approximately the general direction and extent of the chain; in conformity therewith, there are detailed the number of men necessary to guard the space designated. The subordinate commanders carry out the details as follows:

§ 192. A field officer, or captain, commanding two companies, conducts them to the place where the main guard is to be posted; leaving one company there, he takes the other to form the pickets and vedettes, and accompanies one of the platoons himself, to superintend the proper posting of the vedettes. Separating gradually,—one moving to the right, the other to the left,—the two platoons continue to move on until the interval between them is about three-fourths of a mile, and their distance from the main guard about the same; they then halt. The commander of each platoon, having cut off 6 men for patrols and carrying reports, divides the rest of his platoon into 3 reliefs.

He then conducts the first relief to the chain. The non-commissioned officer designated to post the vedettes accompanies the relief; if there is but one officer with the platoon, the senior non-commissioned officer takes command of the picket until the return of the officer.

The commander of the picket having conducted the first relief to one flank of the line he is to occupy, posts the vedettes so that they may be in full communication with the vedettes of the neighboring pickets. The captain of the company which furnishes the pickets will command the more important of the two pickets.

§ 193. Supposing each platoon to consist of 30 men, the main guard will consist of 60, and each picket, deducting the six men for patrols, of 24 men; each picket will thus furnish 4 pairs of vedettes, the two together 8 pairs; supposing the intervals between the pairs of vedettes to be from 300 to 500 paces, the line occupied will be from 2,400 to 4,000 paces. In this manner two companies, each 60 strong, will furnish a main guard and two pickets, which may watch a space of about 2 miles. (See fig. 7.)

Article 2.

Duties of the vedettes of the advanced chain.

§ 194. In each pair of vedettes, one is designated as the chief vedette. Both remain mounted; the one in front has his carbine advanced, or pistol drawn; the vedette in rear is permitted to sling his carbine.

§ 195. For the purpose of challenging all who approach the chain, the vedettes are furnished with the countersign; they are to remember it and keep it secret.

§ 196. They must be always vigilant and cautious; therefore, every thing which may in the least distract their attention is strictly forbidden, such as talking, smoking, whistling, singing, &c.; even horses that are much in the habit of neighing are not placed in the chain.

§ 197. They must keep in view all the space between them, so that individuals may not cross clandestinely.

Therefore, one man in each pair should, in turn, look and listen carefully, lest any thing occur in the direction of the

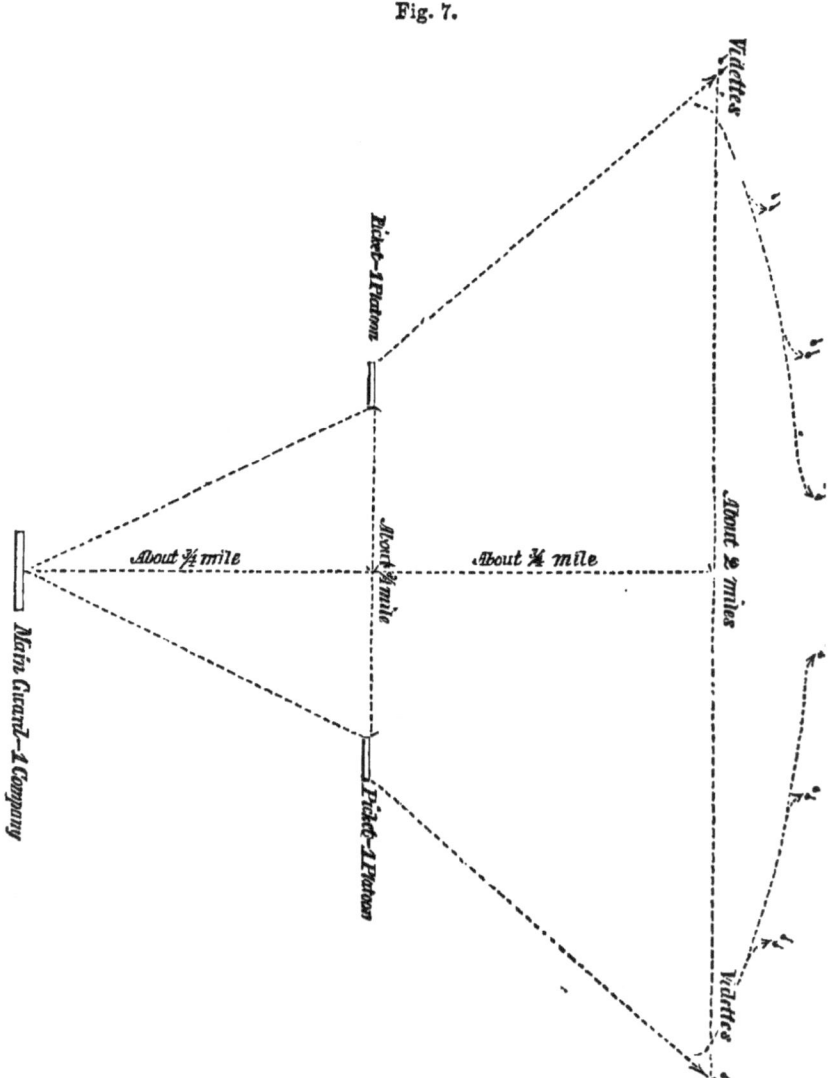

Arrangement of the chain of vedettes, pickets, and main guard furnished by two companies.

enemy or of the next pairs; the other man places himself some paces behind the first, to relieve the tension of sight and hearing.

During the day, in open aountry, they merely look towards the neighboring pairs; in a rough, obstructed country, at night, or in a fog, when it is impossible to see the next pairs, one man, in his turn, carrying his weapons as prescribed for the front vedette in § 194, must constantly ride along the chain to the next pair, or until meeting one of its members. When they are posted in sight of the enemy, or very near him, they may give each other preconcerted signals, (such as tapping the carbine, or some such noise,) being careful, however, that the signals employed are of such a nature as not to attract the attention of the enemy.

§ 198. Upon observing any thing whatever in the direction of the enemy, as, for example, extraordinary movements, dust, noise, kindling or extinguishing fires, changes in his outposts, drawing them in or reinforcing them, &c., the chief vedette sends in the other to inform the commander of the picket, remaining himself on the spot to continue watching what attracted his attention.

In the daytime, when in full view of the picket, instead of one of the vedettes riding in to report, they may, in certain cases, act as follows: If any thing suspicious is observed in the direction of the enemy, such as dust, glittering of arms, &c., one of the vedettes will move his horse in a circle at a walk; upon this, the commander of the picket will take 3 or 4 men and at once ride to the vedette to examine the matter for himself. If the vedettes discover a party of the enemy advancing towards them, but at a great distance, one of them will move his horse in a circle at a trot, on which the officer will act as just prescribed. If the vedettes discover a party of the enemy coming towards them, and not more than a mile off, one of them will at once move his horse in a circle at a gallop, on which the officer will act according to circumstances.

By both the vedettes riding in a circle at the same time, in the same and opposite directions, and at the different gaits, the number of signals may be much increased.

§ 199. Unless they have special orders to the contrary, the vedettes permit no one to cross the chain towards the enemy, except officers' detachments and patrols personally known to them. If they observe any one attempting to steal over, they detain him until the arrival of the relief or patrol, and then send him to the commander of the picket.

§ 200. If the commander of the picket approaches in the daytime, they do not challenge him, but both vedettes advance carbine or draw pistol, and the chief vedette alone reports whether any thing worthy of the slightest attention has been observed.

§ 201. If any person, not personally known to the vedettes, approaches along the chain, the front vedette halts him at 50 paces from the post, by crying, in a low tone, *"Halt! Who comes there?"* If the reply is satisfactory, and the orders are to pass persons with the countersign, he then cries, *"Advance, and give the countersign!"* or, if it is a party that has approached, he directs one person to advance and give the countersign, not allowing him to approach nearer than ten paces for the purpose. If the party challenged does not reply, and persists in attempting to pass the chain, the front vedette cocks his piece, goes to meet him, aiming at him, halts close to him, and twice repeats the challenge, *"Halt! Who comes there?"* If the person does not reply to the third challenge, the vedette shoots him.

Remark.—It is to be understood that vedettes fire only upon persons who are armed, or resist; with regard to others who approach the chain without the countersign, they are merely stopped, and treated as directed in the following section.

§ 202. If the person approaching has the countersign, then, in the daytime, the vedette allows him to pass, but not nearer than 10 paces to the post; if he has not the countersign, the vedette directs him to halt at 50 paces from the post, and turn his back to it, (if he is on horseback, he is made to dismount,) and awaits the arrival of the relief or patrol, to whom he turns him over as a prisoner, to be taken to the commander of the picket.

§ 203. In the night, when it is impossible to recognize the faces of those approaching, the vedettes act in the following manner: If the reply to the challenge, *"Halt! Who comes there?"* is, a *general, an officer, patrol, relief,* or *rounds,* the countersign is demanded, as already explained, and if it is properly given, the party is allowed to pass. If the party does not know the countersign, one of the sentinels at once rides to the commander of the picket and receives his orders. But other military employés, and enlisted men, even if they have the countersign, are not permitted to cross the chain at night, but are treated as is directed in the preceding section for people who do not know the countersign in the day.

§ 204. Whilst the chief vedette interrogates the person who has approached the chain, the other cocks his piece, and watches in all directions with redoubled attention.

§ 205. If a flag of truce, or, in general, any one whose business is of such a nature as not to permit him to await the arrival of a relief or patrol, approaches the chain, the chief vedette sends in the other to report to the commander of the picket.

Flags of truce are not received at night, except under very peculiar circumstances.

§ 206. If any one whatsoever approaches the post from the direction of the enemy, even if of their own command, the vedettes halt them, and do not allow them to approach within 50 paces; the junior vedette then rides in to report to the commander of the picket.

The only exception to this rule is the case of a returning patrol, if it consists of men of the same regiment as the vedettes, and if the latter recognize the persons of the officer and men composing it.

§ 207. If deserters from the enemy approach, the vedette halts them also at 50 paces, orders them to lay down their arms, to dismount, if mounted, and to retire a little beyond the 50 paces.

Then the junior vedette rides in to report to the commander of the picket, while the other, cocking his piece, watches the new arrivals.

§ 208. If the vedettes discover the approach of the enemy, they at once inform the commander of the picket; but if he appears suddenly in front of the chain, they give the alarm by firing. They should fire only when he approaches resolutely: to fire without necessity, and without being satisfied that it is really the enemy, would be merely to create useless alarm.

§ 209. Upon hearing a shot, the other vedettes redouble their vigilance and attention, exerting themselves to discover what is going on where the shot was fired, but not leaving their posts without receiving a signal or special orders to do so, unless driven in, when they will rally on the picket.

ARTICLE 3.

Duties of the commanders of the pickets.

§ 210. With every picket there must be an officer and a trumpeter.

§ 211. The officer detailed for duty with a picket should have the *parole, watchword,* and *countersign* for the day.

Upon reaching his post, he communicates the *countersign* to all the men; he gives the *watchword* only to the non-commissioned officers who are to be sent out with patrols and reliefs.

§ 212. Having conducted his platoon to the position it is to occupy, he acts as directed in § 192, and posts the 1st relief in person. The non-commissioned officer who is to post the next relief rides with him; if there is no other officer present, the senior non-commissioned officer remaining with the picket sees that all the men remain mounted and fully ready to move, until the return of the commander.

§ 213. The first relief is posted as in time of peace.

§ 214. When posting each vedette, the commander of the picket gives them their instructions where to stand, and to what their attention should be chiefly directed; he points out the direction in which they are to retreat in case of necessity, and designates the number of each post. He designates the most reliable and experienced man of each pair of vedettes as chief vedette.

§ 215. In arranging the intervals between the pairs of vedettes, he should endeavor to post them in positions whence they can see as far as possible in all directions and at the same time be as little conspicuous to the enemy as practicable; for this purpose it is best to place them on the heights during the day, and behind the hill, at its foot, during the night.

§ 216. The intervals between the pairs should be such that they can see all the ground between them; no precise rules can be laid down in respect to this, as in some cases the chain will be close, and in others scattered; as in an open country there is no advantage in an unnecessarily close chain, so in an obstructed country it is improper to place the vedettes far apart. In some localities it may be necessary to post them not more than 100 paces apart, while in others the intervals may be 500 paces.

§ 217. If the chain, or a portion of it, is placed in advance of a stream, ravine, wide ditch, or other obstacle, the commander of the picket must see that the passages across are in good condition, so that in case of attack the vedettes can easily rally on the picket, and the latter have free communication with its vedettes.

§ 218. It is also absolutely necessary that the commander of the picket should see that no pair of vedettes is entirely composed of men ignorant of the duty, but that as far as possible one of them should be an experienced and reliable soldier, to be designated as chief vedette; he should also watch that no nearsighted person is placed on the chain during the day, nor any one dull of hearing in the night.

§ 219. Upon posting the chain of vedettes, it becomes evident whether the picket can furnish a sufficient number of men to keep one-third on duty; if there is a deficiency in the chain, the requisite number of men are taken from the picket, which is reinforced from the main guard. If there are more men than necessary, the commander of the picket disposes of the supernumeraries in accordance with the orders of the commander of the main guard.

§ 220. Having posted the 1st relief of vedettes, the commander returns to his picket, and places it in the best position; that is to say, one convenient for receiving and supporting the vedettes, not visible from the side of the enemy, and which the latter cannot pass around; it is selected in preference on a road leading towards the enemy, and especially at cross-roads.

§ 221. At the picket a sentinel is posted, mounted or dismounted according to the locality, and so placed that he can see the whole or the greater part of the chain, and observe what occurs there. If this sentinel is mounted, he carries his weapons as directed for the front vedette in § 194.

§ 222. After this, the commander orders the men to dismount; during the day, one-half of the men at a time may be allowed to unbit and feed their horses. In the night, all the horses ought to be bitted, and one-half the men in perfect readiness to mount. One-half of the men may be allowed to sleep in the daytime. Under certain circumstances it may be necessary to keep the whole or a part of the picket mounted during the night.

§ 223. Having arranged the vedettes and picket, the commander reports his dispositions, as well as every thing he has observed, to the commander of the main guard, unless the latter was present at the time.

§ 224. All reports concerning the outposts are made either verbally, through a non-commissioned officer, or in pencil, with the most concise expressions, and not observing the ordinary forms. Here the main point is, that the report is well founded and clearly expressed. The report should be numbered, state what party it refers to, and the date and hour when sent.

§ 225. For patrols and orderlies, 6 men are detailed from the picket, independently of those who supply the vedettes; two of these, besides any already sent out, should always be in readiness to start in an instant; the others may rest, and in the day unbit their horses.

§ 226. The pickets should always be vigilant, careful, quiet, and ready to move. The arms ought to be loaded, the men fully accoutred, all the horses saddled, and the whole picket in an effective condition; the horses are sent to water in parties of two or three at a time, under charge of a non-commissioned officer, and take every thing with them. The horses should not be hobbled or picketed. The use of fire is forbidden, without special permission. The men change their dress, from the uniform to the overcoat, and the reverse, one at a time. Under peculiar circumstances, in the night, one-half the men (by turns) may be allowed to take off their shakos and sleep, but the rest must be on the alert, or stand to horse.

§ 227. When a relief is sent out, which habitually is done every two hours, but oftener in bad weather, severe cold, or after great fatigue, the whole picket mounts, and so remains until the return of the relief.

§ 228. It being easy for the enemy to approach the chain during the night, in order to make a sudden attack at daybreak, the whole picket should be mounted some time before dawn.

§ 229. If it appears to be necessary to draw in the vedettes upon the picket, or to close in the vedettes on each other for the night, then, by the special order of the commander of the outposts, the chain removes to its new position upon the approach of twilight. The decrease of the intervals between the pairs of vedettes is regulated by the darkness of the night and the weather; in a dark night, with heavy rain, a thick fog, or, most especially, with a wind blowing towards the enemy, this interval is made very small. The extra men needed in these cases are supplied by the main guards or the reserve of the outposts. At daybreak, the chain again advances to the position designated for it during the day.

§ 230. If the ground occupied by the vedettes during the day is so advantageous that it would be injurious to throw them back at night, and it is necessary to decrease their distance from the picket, then the chain is left where it stands, the intervals between the vedettes are diminished, and the picket moved up closer to the chain.

§ 231. Besides the original posting of the chain, the commander of the picket should also superintend its removal to the night position; and if the vedettes were originally posted at night, he should be present when they take up their new position for the day, also when his picket is relieved by other troops. The other reliefs of the vedettes not only may, but ought to be made by non-commissioned officers, so as not to take the commander from his picket, where his presence may be very necessary.

§ 232. All the men of a relief, while marching, carry their weapons as prescribed for the front vedette in § 194, and the act of relieving is performed as in time of peace; the instructions are given quietly, and all orders in a low tone.

§ 233. The returning relief is received at the picket as in time of peace, with the difference that the whole picket is mounted.

§ 234. When the rounds arrive at a picket, they are received as directed below in Chapter III., *on visiting the outposts;* in this case, all orders are given in a low tone, and the necessary quietness is preserved.

§ 235. At the proper hours, the commander of the picket will send out patrols to verify the exactness of the vedettes, (see Chapter III.;) he should also despatch the reliefs punctually, and report to the commander of the main guard after every relief, although there may be nothing new.

§ 236. When a report comes in from the chain of the arrival of men without the countersign, or in the night of those who (see § 203) are not entitled to pass with it, the commander of the picket at once sends a non-commissioned officer and two men to bring them in. Upon their arrival, he demands the *parole*, *watchword*, and *countersign;* and if all their replies are correct, he permits them to pass freely; but if they do not know the parole, he sends them, under guard, to the commander of the main guard.

§ 237. If a flag of truce or deserters from the enemy arrive at the chain, the commander of the picket goes there himself, taking with him a non-commissioned officer and some privates. When near the flag of truce, he demands who he is, by whom and to whom sent; and then, having blindfolded him, directs the non-commissioned officer and two privates to conduct him to the commander of the main guard. If deserters have arrived, he directs his escort to take their arms, and bring them within the chain; he then calls up one of the deserters and questions him, and having ordered them all to be searched, lest they carry concealed weapons, he sends them to the commander of the main guard, with an escort in proportion to their number.

§ 238. If a report arrives from the chain of any thing important in the direction of the enemy, or of his appearance, the commander of the picket verifies it in person, at once sends a report to the commander of the main guard, and informs the neighboring pickets; in the mean time the picket mounts.

§ 239. If it appears that the enemy, in small force, merely alarms the outposts, the vedettes commence firing, the pickets advance, and either endeavor to overthrow the enemy's detachment or to keep him in check until the arrival of the main guard or the reserve of the outposts.

§ 240. If it appears that the enemy is not in superior force, then the pickets should attack and drive him off; afterwards they resume their original positions.

§ 241. If it is ascertained that the enemy attacks vigorously in force, and has already approached so near the chain that the vedettes are in danger of being cut off, the commander of the picket gives them the signal to retreat, and, using them as a chain of skirmishers, he begins, if it is necessary, his retreat upon the main guard, again reporting the state of affairs to the commander of the latter, and the nearest pickets.

§ 242. While retreating, he should endeavor to delay the enemy as long as possible, also to observe, as well as he can, his force, kind of troops, and direction, taking care, however, not to be cut off.

§ 243. In the night the enemy does not see the strength of the picket, and moves over ground with which he is unacquainted, while the picket knows the ground. Therefore, it is sometimes advantageous for cavalry pickets, in the night, to commence their retreat by attacking: if the attack fails, nothing is lost, and the picket falls back upon the main guard; if it succeeds, even if it is impossible to drive the enemy off, his pursuit is at least delayed, and his force more closely examined.

§ 244. Upon hearing firing at the chain, the commander of the picket at once sends to learn the cause, and causes the picket to mount: if the enemy really attacks, the commander acts as directed above; but if the firing was only upon individuals, he at once sends word to the main guard and neighboring pickets, to prevent unnecessary alarm.

§ 245. The other pickets mount at once upon hearing firing at any part of the chain; and if the picket attacked retreats, they regulate their movements on it, so as to keep up the communication and not be cut off, and at once inform the next picket on the opposite side.

§ 246. After every skirmish the commanders of the pickets make an inspection to ascertain whether any of their men are captured or missing; if there are any such cases, they at once inform the commander of the main guard. Until the countersign is changed, the commanders of the pickets forbid the vedettes to allow any one to cross the chain, even with the old countersign; this they do in all cases when a man is missing from the vedettes or pickets, even if there has been no skirmish.

ARTICLE 4.

Duties of the commander of the main guard.

§ 247. The main guard is commanded by a field officer or captain; there must always be a trumpeter with him.

§ 248. He communicates to the commanders of the pickets the *parole, watchword*, and *countersign*.

§ 249. Having reached the position designated for the main guard, its commander details and sends forward the platoons that are to supply the pickets and vedettes. Having turned over the command of the main guard to the next in rank of those remaining with it, he goes himself to the advanced chain, to superintend the posting of the pickets and vedettes; he gives all the parties their instructions, how they are to act upon the appearance of the enemy, and how in case of retreat; he carefully examines the ground. The main guard remains mounted until the vedettes and pickets are posted.

§ 250. If it is impossible for the commander of the main guard to be present at the original posting of the pickets and vedettes, he should at least ride over all the ground committed to his charge.

§ 251. If in any of the pickets one relief is short of men, the commander of the main guard supplies the deficiency from it; if a picket has more men than enough, he either directs the superfluous men to join the main guard, or sends them to reinforce another picket which has not men enough, or, finally, directs the picket which has the most men to occupy a greater portion of the chain than its neighbors.

Remark.—In these cases, it is absolutely necessary to bear in mind that the parties sent to the outposts must be units, so that their interior organization may not be disturbed; especially that two companies of the same regiment must furnish a main guard and the corresponding pickets and vedettes. From this there will result greater unity in the conduct of the outposts, and each officer, being with his own men, can assign them to the particular duty best suited to the character and capacity of each.

§ 252. In the disposition of the vedettes and pickets, the commander of the main guard should look to the connection of the whole chain and all the pickets under his charge, and particularly to the facility of communication with the neighboring main guards.

§ 253. Having returned to the main guard, its commander arranges it as follows: the guard dismounts; during the day one-half, by turns, unbit and feed their horses, holding them by the reins; the rest of the men remain with their horses, in perfect readiness, some 20 to 50 paces in front of those who are feeding. During the night all the horses must be bitted, and one-half the men perfectly ready to mount.

§ 254. Having arranged the main guard, its commander reports to the commander of the outposts his arrangements, and every thing of importance that he has observed.

Remark.—Sketching the ground occupied by the outposts is a part of the duty of the staff officers; but if there are none present, the commander of the main guard should annex to his report a rough pencil sketch of the ground, for the better elucidation of his arrangements.

§ 255. A sentinel is placed at the main guard, as at the picket, (§ 221;) he challenges all who approach in the same manner as the vedettes. All other precautions are observed by the main guard as by the pickets. (§ 226.)

§ 256. If it is necessary to cook in a covered place, and the commander of the outposts has given permission to use a fire, the men do not leave their position to eat, but the food is brought to them, and they eat, a few at a time.

§ 257. The commander of the main guard receives the rounds in the same manner as the commander of a picket does. (§ 234.)

§ 258. If men without the countersign, flags of truce, or deserters from the enemy, are sent in from the pickets, the commander of the main guard interrogates them, and then sends them, under guard, to the reserve, if there is any, or direct to the commander of the outposts.

§ 259. Upon receiving from the pickets news of the approach of the enemy, or on hearing firing at the chain, the commander of the main guard at once sends an officer, or a sergeant, with two men, to ascertain what is taking place, and reports to the commander of the outposts. That part of the main guard whose horses are bitted mount and ride to the front to receive or support the retreating pickets in case of necessity; in the mean time the other portion prepare, and, if the firing continues, join the advanced party.

§ 260. If the commander of the main guard is satisfied that the enemy attacks really and decidedly, he reports again to the commander of the outposts, and acts according to the preceding instructions; that is, he either endeavors to resist the enemy and hold his ground, or keeps up the firing and retards his advance, or simply falls back upon the reserves.

§ 261. In the night, the main guard may, as in the case of a picket, (§ 243,) try an immediate attack; but this should be made by only a part of the main guard, holding the rest in reserve to support the attacking party.

§ 262. The commander of each main guard should constantly keep up his connection with his pickets and the nearest main guards by patrols; if the enemy advance, he must regulate his movements in conformity with those of the other main guards, so that, being as nearly as possible on the same line, they may be in a condition to render mutual assistance.

§ 263. The commander of a main guard should be very careful as to his reports; upon receiving any news about the enemy from the pickets, he should endeavor to verify it in person; if that is impracticable, it is best to send to the commander of the outposts the original report received from the picket.

§ 264. If the same two companies remain upon outpost duty for several days, the pickets are usually relieved every 24 hours. It is best to relieve them in the morning, that the new pickets may be able to see the country. If the two companies are detailed for 24 hours only, the pickets may be relieved during the day, especially if they have been alarmed and have not had time to unbit their horses. Such reliefs should be effected one or two hours before sunset, to give the new reliefs time enough to become acquainted with the ground.

ARTICLE 5.

The reserves of the outposts.

§ 265. These may be employed with two objects:
1. To facilitate the retreat of the outposts, if they are very distant from the camp; or,
2. To retard the advance of the enemy if the outposts are close in.

In the first case, the reserve need not be very strong; if the ground permits the action of cavalry, it is composed of that arm in preference; from two to four companies or more may be detailed for the service. In the second case, the composition of the reserve depends upon the ground and the length of time it is desired to detain the enemy; in localities at all favorable to infantry, the reserve is composed of that arm, and it is of cavalry only on perfectly open plains; in this last case, the deficiency in defensive strength is supplied by the addition of horse artillery.

§ 266. In general a reserve of the outposts is detailed only for the protection of a considerable body of troops, as, for instance, 3 or 4 divisions. For detachments consisting only of a division or so, there is no reserve of the outposts; the detachment itself constitutes the reserve.

§ 267. The bivouac of the reserve of the outposts is selected as near as possible to water, wood, straw, forage, &c.; but in no case should any military advantages be lost sight of, they being much more important in such a case than any considerations of mere convenience.

§ 268. An inlying picket, of from $\frac{1}{4}$ to $\frac{1}{3}$ of the entire reserve, is detailed, which should be perfectly ready to mount, to support the outposts if necessary. The inlying picket is placed a little in advance of the rest, and acts as the guard of the artillery, if there is any; its men should wear their accoutrements, and have their horses constantly saddled and bitted.

§ 269. The rest of the horses are not unsaddled, but stand at the picket-ropes, or are hobbled, except the horses of the guns, which are fed in harness, and are unhitched only to go to water, and that by turns; the caisson-horses may be unhitched.

§ 270. The reserve always bivouacs in order of battle,—that is, with the companies in line; the guns ought to be in position, in full readiness for action, a little in advance. If the reserve is partly composed of infantry, the cavalry is so placed that the party standing to horse may be covered by the infantry.

§ 271. The arms should be loaded. The men change their dress, and unsaddle to examine their horses' backs, a few at a time; in a company by section, in a regiment by companies. The men who are reposing may take off their shakos, but not their accoutrements.

§ 272. The use of fire is allowed, unless peculiar circumstances render it improper.

§ 273. The reserve secures itself by camp and quarter guards, posted as in time of peace. The duty in the reserve is performed as in ordinary bivouacs; guards and sentinels present arms as usual, but no signals by drum or trumpet are allowed.

§ 274. When the outposts take up their positions, if it becomes necessary to reinforce any of the main guards, or to establish new pickets, it is done from the reserve.

§ 275. The commander of the outposts is habitually with the reserve; therefore, all reports from the main guards and independent pickets are sent thither, that its movements may be regulated in conformity with the reports received.

§ 276. When the commander of the reserve receives a report of the approach of the enemy, he acts according to circumstances; that is, he either sends a reinforcement to the pickets, or advances to support them with the whole reserve, or joining them himself does every thing that is necessary or possible. It is the duty of the reserve to prevent the enemy from falling suddenly in force upon the main body, and to use every exertion to retard his advance, in order to afford the main body time to prepare to receive him, and take the measures necessary under the circumstances. The more vigorously the enemy attacks, the more stubbornly must the reserve resist him.

§ 277. The troops composing the reserve may relieve the main guards and independent pickets; this relief is effected once or twice in 24 hours. The reserve itself is relieved by the special order of the commander of the main body.

ARTICLE 6.
Independent pickets.

§ 278. If there is near the advanced chain any point the occupation of which is necessary or very advantageous,—for example, if it will strengthen a flank of the chain not sufficiently secured by the nature of the ground, if it commands an extensive view, or if the enemy must necessarily pass over it, and its distance is such that the chain cannot be extended to it without a considerable increase in the number of men,—then this point is occupied by a special detachment, called an *independent picket*.

§ 279. They are sent out from the nearest main guard, or from the reserve of the outposts, and are under the orders of the commander of the outposts. They are posted as the ordinary pickets, with the difference that their vedettes are solely for their own security, and are so placed as to prevent the enemy from attacking the picket unawares.

§ 280. Not having a direct connection with the other parties, they must maintain it by means of patrols, and should also send patrols in the direction of the enemy; therefore the strength of an independent picket will be determined by the indispensable number of vedettes and patrols to be furnished. For example, if it is necessary to post two pairs of vedettes and one sentinel at the picket, and to send out patrols on two roads leading towards the enemy, and on one towards the nearest picket, then, each patrol consisting of two men, there will be 11 men in each relief, or 33 privates in the whole picket.

§ 281. The greater the distance of an independent picket from the other parties of the outposts, the stronger should it be. In all cases it should have a secure retreat.

§ 282. It is the duty of independent, as of ordinary, pickets, to be always prudent, to watch the enemy, to obtain information of his nearest parties and distant movements; but as they are more exposed than the others to be attacked and cut off, they should redouble their vigilance and precautions.

ARTICLE 7.

The general duties of all parts of the outposts.

§ 283. Precaution and indefatigable vigilance are the first duties of all parts of the outposts. Independently of the security of the outposts themselves, this duty assumes a peculiar importance from the fact that upon its fulfilment depend the tranquillity, safety, and sometimes the existence of the troops guarded.

§ 284. If the positions of the outposts are not already occupied by our own troops, the parties detailed for outpost duty will march to their posts with all the usual military precautions;

that is, with advanced, flank, and rear patrols. Besides this, it is well, upon approaching the ground, to send out small patrols in all directions, to examine the country and ascertain whether the enemy is concealed in the vicinity. It is safer not to commence posting the chain until the return of the patrols; at all events, not until they have occupied points whence they can see for a long distance in all directions.

§ 285. At the outposts it is necessary to preserve quietness, and to avoid every thing which might discover them to the enemy. For this reason the use of trumpet signals is forbidden, except in case of a skirmish; directions, orders, and challenges are given in a low tone; the use of fire is prohibited, except at the reserve, and is permitted there only when there is no particular reason for forbidding it.

§ 286. Every commander despatching a party for outpost duty under his orders must give its chief detailed instructions; he must satisfy himself that the instructions are fully understood, and must exercise the greatest personal vigilance in watching over their execution by his subordinates.

§ 287. If it is impossible to carry out the instructions fully, the subordinate must at once report to his superior, explaining the cause of the impossibility.

§ 288. The gradation of subordination is as follows: the vedettes are immediately subordinate to the pickets from which they are detached; the pickets to their main guards, the main guards and independent pickets to the reserve of the outposts. The commander of the reserve is immediately subordinate to the commander of the outposts; the latter to the commander of the advanced guard.

§ 289. The commander of every post should at once report to his immediate superior, and, if necessary, to the commanders of the nearest parties, every thing he has observed in person, or learned through his subordinates, especially what refers to the movements of the enemy.

§ 290. The subordinate should always endeavor to verify the information in person, and then make his report; always remembering that an unfounded report may produce serious consequences to the whole army.

§ 291. If it is impossible for him to verify the information in person, he should forward to his superior the original report received.

§ 292. Reports should be written clearly and with precision, especially with regard to the force of the enemy, noting not only his numbers, but of what arms, and the direction in which he marches. In reports positive facts should be distinguished from probabilities,—noting the degree of confidence to be reposed in the latter.

§ 293. If it is unnecessary to forward the original report received, it is preserved until, by the progress of events, it has lost all importance and significance.

§ 294. All reports to the commanders of main guards are of especial importance, and those to the commander of the outposts still more so. Every exaggerated or ill-founded report renders it necessary to turn out and fatigue the troops uselessly; on the contrary, contempt for the enemy, and tardiness in reporting, may not only compromise the one making the report, but even endanger the security of the army and place it in a precarious situation.

§ 295. It is the duty of every party of the outposts to preserve its connection and communication with the nearest corresponding parties, with those subordinate to it, and with that to which it is immediately subordinate.

§ 296. The commander of every post should carefully examine, in person, the ground in his vicinity, not only in reference to his relations with the nearest posts, but in regard to his movements if attacked. He must also find suitable watering-places.

§ 297. In case of an attack it is the duty of every party not only to reinforce and support the parties immediately subordinate to it, but also to assist the neighboring parties whenever it is necessary and possible. If a retreat is ordered, or forced upon them, each party rallies on that to which it is subordinate.

§ 298. In conformity with what has been said before, if firing at the chain is heard, the portions of the pickets and main guards ordered to be in constant readiness at once move forward, even if they have received no reports as to the advance of the enemy. In such cases, the reserve, although fully ready to meet the enemy, makes no movement, without orders, until the pickets and main guards are driven in.

§ 299. Upon an attack by the enemy, the commander of every party should regulate his movements in accordance with those of the nearest parties, so that he may not expose them to be cut off by a premature retreat on his part, or expose himself either by too tardy a retreat, or by moving to the front with unnecessary rapidity.

§ 300. It is the duty of all parties of the outposts and of all vedettes to hold their positions as long as possible. In the event of an attack they do not retreat without orders or pressing necessity; because, although there may be no difficulty in the retreat, and although the ground abandoned may easily be reoccupied, yet the enemy gains something of which we cannot deprive him,

—that is, a knowledge of the ground, which may have been the only object of his attack.

§ 301. If any party is ordered to defend itself to the utmost, then, although the enemy is in superior force, they resist him on the spot, and, if necessary, unhesitatingly sacrifice themselves to the last man.

§ 302. The commanders of all the posts should see that their subordinates have betimes the *parole, watchword,* and *countersign.*

§ 303. The commanders of pickets allow all persons who know the *parole, watchword,* and *countersign* to cross the chain in any direction, both by day and night, without obstacle. Therefore, in time of war, the parole is not given to the men, but only to those persons whose duty renders it necessary for them to possess it, and they preserve it with the utmost secrecy.

§ 304. On this principle the parole is given only to the commanders of the main guards and pickets, and to those persons who are intrusted by the proper authorities with missions which render it necessary for them to cross the chain without detention.

The watchword is given only to the non-commissioned officers sent out with patrols and reliefs, and serves for mutual challenges.

The countersign is given to all on duty at the outposts, and serves to challenge all who approach the chain.

§ 305. Upon the arrival at any post of people who, by the regulations, or by special orders, are not to be allowed to pass, the commander of that post sends them to his immediate chief. Upon the arrival of flags of truce he watches that they do not enter into conversation with any but the authorized persons.

§ 306. At the outposts arms are not presented, nor the men mounted, for any of the commanders. Upon the approach of a superior officer, the party on duty at once stand to horse, the commander of the post orders the rest to do the same, and places himself in that position; if the superior stops at the post, its commander reports what he has observed.

§ 307. Upon the approach of the commander of the advanced guard, or of the main body, to the position of the outposts, he is met and accompanied only by the commander of the outposts; the commander of each post remains with it.

§ 308. When a post is relieved, the old commander will explain to the new one every thing which is, in his opinion, of importance, and every thing that he has observed in reference to the enemy and the locality.

§ 309. If the commander of a party, newly placed on duty at the outposts, finds any thing wrong in the original arrangement of the vedettes, pickets, or main guards, he must report it, through his immediate chief, to the commander of the outposts, and ask his permission to rectify the dispositions; until he receives this permission, he preserves the former arrangement.

§ 310. The commanders of all posts watch over the punctual despatch of the reliefs of vedettes and posts sent out from their commands. It is best to relieve all the parties of the outposts before dawn; for the enemy can advantageously avail himself of the darkness to approach the chain, in order to attack at daybreak, and the presence of the reliefs at this time doubles the force of the outposts.

§ 311. The commanders especially see that the required rounds and patrols are sent at the proper times, never sending them at known hours or regular intervals; for, as they are sent to verify the exactness of the posts, it is best that they should be constantly expected.

ARTICLE 8.

Of the duties of the outposts in covering any march or change of position of the troops under their guard.

§ 312. If the troops, covered by the outposts, are ordered to make any movement, then to avoid a change of troops the parties who have formed the outposts constitute, if there is no special reason to the contrary, the advanced guard, if the march is to the front; the rear guard, if it is in retreat; in the latter case, it is the duty of the vedettes and pickets to cover the retreat of the rear guard.

§ 313. If the movement is to be concealed from the enemy, particular precautions are required on the part of the outposts.

They must redouble their vigilance, and take measures to insure that no one from the side of the enemy, neither patrols nor reconnoissances, penetrates our position; and they must manage these measures of precaution in such a way that the enemy may not observe what is going on among us, or that any thing extraordinary is being undertaken.

§ 314. Besides keeping all the posts perfectly ready for action, the means of effecting this consist in *not* sending more patrols than usual *in front* of the chain, but in sending them *behind* it as secretly and frequently as possible, to prevent the enemy's patrols from crossing it.

In addition, if it is necessary to place a party of troops near the chain, under cover, they should be in ambuscade, that they may attack the enemy unexpectedly if he endeavors to break through the chain.

§ 315. In these cases, the outposts are ordered to resist the enemy as obstinately as possible, not only to prevent him from penetrating within our lines, but to hinder him from seeing any thing. Sometimes, in order to distract the attention of the enemy, attacks are made upon his outposts during the retreat of our own troops. Such attacks promise greater success in the night than in the day, because when, on the alarm, the supports of the enemy's outposts approach the chain, they may thence perceive things that were imperceptible, even to the strongest vision, from their usual posts.

§ 316. If a retreat is to be effected secretly, it is best not to relieve the outposts by fresh troops before their retreat, because the sight of the new troops may excite the attention of the enemy; while, on the contrary, the sight of old troops and posts may tend to diminish his vigilance.

§ 317. Secret retreats are usually made at night, during which time it is endeavored to keep up the bivouac-fires, that the enemy may not observe the absence of the troops.

§ 318. To facilitate the retreat of the outposts themselves, should they be attacked during the night, certain measures of precaution are adopted. The officers should thoroughly acquaint themselves with the roads of retreat, placing several posts on the roads, for greater security, and especially at crossings of streams, on cross-roads, and in places where the roads diverge.

§ 319. A little before dawn, all the main guards are assembled and gradually retreat in the required direction; after them follow the pickets, and finally, at dawn, the whole chain commences its retreat, joining the pickets at a trot or gallop.

§ 320. With a certain, although small, extension of the line of outposts, it is impossible for them all to retire by one road without serious delay. Therefore there should, if possible, be designated for their retreat several roads which unite with the main road, even if at a great distance; if this is impossible, it is best to concentrate them rapidly on one point, in order thus to form a detachment of sufficient strength to resist the attempts of the enemy.

§ 321. As a general rule, the moment when troops are breaking up their camp is the most favorable for the enemy to attack; it is, therefore, best to execute such things secretly, although there may be no other reason than this. If the means thus adopted are successful, the main body may sometimes accomplish the object of its movement before the enemy perceives its absence.

CHAPTER II.

THE ARRANGEMENTS OF THE OUTPOSTS AT A DISTANCE FROM THE ENEMY.

§ 322. If the enemy is so far from us that he cannot pass over the intervening space in a single march, and is, therefore, obliged to move by the roads, it will be sufficient to limit the operations of the outposts to watching the roads.

§ 323. In such cases it is only necessary to send out independent cavalry pickets on the roads leading towards the enemy; they communicate with each other by means of patrols.

§ 324. As far as regards obtaining information of the enemy, it is best to push out these pickets as far as possible, but, on the other hand, it is more dangerous for the pickets themselves; therefore they should not be pushed so far in advance as to be in great danger of being cut off.

§ 325. The distance to which they may be advanced will be increased in proportion to the number of roads occupied, the difficulty which the enemy must experience in moving secretly by each road, the distance to which patrols are sent out from each post, and the distance of the enemy from our position. It is necessary to be more cautious, and to draw in the pickets as the enemy approaches.

§ 326. The force of each independent picket must depend upon the number of vedettes and patrols it is to furnish, and upon the degree of strength it ought to possess.

§ 327. Every such picket is posted according to the rules laid down in §§ 220 and 221. The routine of duty and the measures of precaution are exactly as in ordinary pickets.

§ 328. As a general rule, they preserve their mutual communication by patrols; in addition, they send out patrols as far as possible towards the enemy, to obtain the earliest possible news of him.

§ 329. If they are far from the army, they must be supported by small detachments placed in reserve at points where several roads unite, or at places whence it is easiest to afford prompt assistance to those pickets which may be expected to be attacked first.

§ 330. Intelligent irregular cavalry, *inured to war*, may be employed advantageously as independent pickets and patrols; but the supports must always be of the regular cavalry.

§ 331. Sometimes, even when at a great distance from the

main body of the enemy, there may arise the necessity for the greatest precautions; for example, when the population is disposed to insurrection, or when the country is full of hostile partisans.

In such cases the precautions should be in proportion to the danger.

CHAPTER III.

OF VISITING THE OUTPOSTS.

§ 332. Small parties, consisting of a non-commissioned officer and two good men, are sent out by the pickets and main guards to ascertain whether the vedettes observe the proper vigilance and precaution. These parties are called *patrols*. Patrols also offer the advantage that they may happen to stumble upon the enemy stealing across the chain.

§ 333. The non-commissioned officer of the patrol must have the *watchword* and *countersign*.

§ 334. A patrol sent to visit the vedettes proceeds as follows: the non-commissioned officer has his sabre at a carry; the two men follow him with carbines advanced, or pistols drawn and cocked. They proceed to one flank of the chain belonging to their command; cross to the outside of the chain near the flank vedettes, and approach the chain silently from the outside to test the vigilance of the vedettes. When the vedette challenges, the non-commissioned officer replies, "*patrol*," and, at the command, "Advance, sergeant, with the countersign," advances to about 10 paces from the vedette, and gives the countersign in a low voice. The patrol then proceeds, in the same manner, to the first vedette of the next picket, or main guard, near which it recrosses to the interior of the chain, returns to its party, and reports whatever has been observed.

§ 335. If the non-commissioned officer finds the post of any pair of vedettes abandoned, he leaves one of his own men there, and sends in a man of the next pair to inform the commander of the picket.

§ 336. The patrol must carry back with it all persons found detained at the chain, and all met with without the countersign.

§ 337. If two patrols meet at night, and cannot recognize each other's faces, the one which first perceives the other cries, "*Halt! Who comes there?*" and, having received the reply, "*Patrol!*" cries, "*Advance, sergeant, with the countersign!*" the non-commissioned officer of the second patrol gives the countersign, and, in his turn, then demands the watchword; if the replies are all correct, both patrols then proceed on their march, each having informed the other of any thing extraordinary observed or suspected.

§ 338. Upon suddenly meeting the enemy, patrols act as prescribed for vedettes.

§ 339. The number of patrols sent to visit the vedettes must be increased in proportion to the difficulty of seeing the vedettes from the pickets, the darkness of the night, the obstructions of the ground, the thinness of the chain, and the fatigue of the men, whether arising from a long march or a combat.

Under these circumstances, patrols are sent out continually, that is, on the return of one, another is at once sent out.

In the daytime, in clear weather, and in open country, but few patrols are despatched, though the vedettes must be kept in constant expectation of them.

§ 340. To inspect the pickets and main guards, the commander of the outposts sends out "*rounds*," from time to time.

§ 341. *Rounds* consist of an officer with two privates; all the main guards and pickets should be informed betimes what officers are ordered to make the rounds.

§ 342. The officer making the rounds must know the *parole*, *watchword*, and *countersign*.

§ 343. In reply to the challenge of the sentinel at the main guard or picket, the officer making the rounds answers, "*Rounds!*"

To receive the rounds, that part of the main guard or picket which is ordered to be in constant readiness mounts, without drawing sabre; those reposing are not disturbed. In other regards the rounds are received as in time of peace.

§ 344. The commander of the party visited reports to the rounds the number of men under his command, the arrangements of all his posts, the number of men absent on duty, the number present, and every thing that has been observed.

§ 345. After this the officer making the rounds examines the command, satisfies himself that they are in the required state of preparation, and verifies the general number of men. Then, if he has been ordered to test whether the whole command can be promptly in the saddle, he notifies the commander of the post, who at once orders all the men to mount.

§ 346. Every thing prescribed here should be done quietly, and all orders be given in a low tone. After this the rounds proceed to the next post; but the officer may demand an escort from the party just inspected.

§ 347. The rounds are not limited to visiting the main guards and pickets, but may be required to visit the vedettes; in this case they act as prescribed for patrols sent for the same purpose.

§ 348. The rounds are not sent out at fixed hours; the hours of their visits depend upon the judgment of the commander of the outposts, and should be so regulated that the parties to be visited may not know when to expect them; they are sent out most frequently at night, and just before dawn.

§ 349. Upon the return of the rounds the officer reports to the commander of the outposts the condition in which he found affairs, and every thing he observed.

CHAPTER IV.

OF PATROLS.

§ 350. The duties of *patrols sent out by troops on the march* were described in Part I., Chapter II., Article 5.

In this chapter will be described the duties of *patrols sent out by troops in camp.*

§ 351. Besides the patrols sent out to visit the vedettes, (§§ 332 to 339,) patrols are sent out for other purposes, namely:

1. To keep up the communication between the different parties of the outposts.
2. To reconnoitre the enemy; and,
3. To examine the country.

§ 352. When a patrol is sent out to keep up the communication between different parties of the outposts, it rides to the post whither it is sent, reports to the commander whatever it was directed to communicate, and every thing observed on the way; having received his instructions, the patrol returns to its party.

§ 353. To insure the safety and tranquillity of the troops it is not sufficient for the outposts merely to watch the space visible from the chain, because the enemy may send out small parties to make partial attacks, in order to exhaust the troops by forcing them to assemble on continual alarms. To secure the outposts against such attacks, as well as to discover the enemy and examine the country, patrols are sent out in advance of the chain.

§ 354. Such patrols are divided into *near* and *distant patrols;* they are composed of light cavalry in preference.

§ 355. *Near patrols* consist of a non-commissioned officer with two or three prompt men, and are sent out by all parties of the outposts. They move on all the main roads leading towards the enemy, and do not go more than one or two miles from the vedettes, so that they may give prompt information of the approach of the enemy; they limit themselves to watching him. These patrols are sent out the more frequently in proportion as the enemy can approach more secretly; so that in an obstructed country, in thick fogs, dark nights, and close to the enemy, they are sent out continually,—that is, one immediately upon the return of another.

§ 356. *Distant patrols* are sent out to discover the enemy and examine the country at considerable distances, (from 2 to 10, and even more, miles,) and are composed of a greater number of men, (of 10, 20, 30, and more,) that they may sometimes be able to attack hostile patrols, and make prisoners. They are usually commanded by an officer, to whom are explained, in detail, the object of his mission, the means of accomplishing it, and the direction he is to take; he is also instructed whether to engage the enemy's patrols or to avoid a combat.

§ 357. Distant patrols sometimes consist of a company, or more, especially if they cannot return the same day. They are sent out by the advanced guard or main body, and take the name of *flying detachments*. As a general rule, all distant patrols are under the orders of the commander of the outposts.

§ 358. The moment a patrol passes beyond the chain, it should detach front, flank, and rear patrollers, to secure itself against sudden attack. In figs. 4 and 5 are given examples of the arrangements of patrols of 15 and 30 men; larger patrols are arranged according to the same principles. Smaller patrols are arranged according to their strength: for example, a patrol of five men sends out one in front, and one on each side; a patrol of three men places one in front, the others move at a little distance apart,—one watching to the right, the other to the left.

§ 359. It is a great advantage for a patrol to see the enemy before being discovered itself; this renders it possible to avoid a stronger force, and to apprize the outposts of its approach, or to attack, by surprise, an equal or inferior force.

§ 360. In order to secure themselves against a sudden attack, patrols should use all possible precautions, and observe the deepest silence; the *patrollers* carry their pieces cocked. In the night, and in thick weather, all precautions are redoubled. The patrol should occasionally halt and listen; the men in front and on the flanks, dismounting by turns, place the ear to the ground, &c.

§ 361. On their return march the patrols should be even more cautious; because the enemy, having perceived them, may select this very time for the attack, on the supposition that the outposts, being relieved from apprehension by the return of the patrols, may somewhat relax their vigilance.

§ 362. The commander of a patrol should concert certain signals with his *patrollers* by which they are to indicate their discoveries. If the necessary precautions are observed, it is impossible for the enemy to attack unawares; therefore the commander of a patrol is always held responsible for its loss.

§ 363. In Part I., Chapter II., Article 5, are explained the precautions to be observed by patrols sent out by troops on the march; these measures are equally applicable in the present case, and the following are prescribed in addition:

§ 364. If a patrol leaves in its rear defiles by which it is intended to return, a few men should be left to hold them,—in preference, the men having the worst horses. If these men are driven off by a superior force, they can, by means of preconcerted signals, (such as rockets, lighted straw on poles, &c.,) inform the patrol of the fact, so that it may seek another line of retreat.

§ 365. As these patrols are usually intended merely to discover the enemy and examine the country, they should generally avoid a combat unless success seems certain.

§ 366. That he may be able to avoid the enemy when still unperceived by him, the commander of a patrol pays special attention to the ground, so that in case of necessity he may avail himself of its accidents for concealment.

§ 367. Upon meeting the enemy in superior force, the patrol should at once commence its retreat if already discovered.

§ 368. If a patrol suddenly stumbles upon the enemy in the night, it is best to attack at once; in the night the advantage is always on the side of those who attack first, for to the habitual disorder following a sudden attack is added the uncertainty as to the strength of the attacking party. In such cases, decision and the advantage of the initiative insure success. When the enemy is beaten off and retreats, he ought not to be pursued far, lest we fall into an ambuscade; and it is best, not being allured by success, to avail ourselves of it, and retreat in good order.

§ 369. The guides of patrols ought to be chosen for their thorough knowledge of the country and fidelity; but their suggestions should not be blindly followed: to verify them, constant inquiries should be made of the inhabitants, and of all persons met on the road; for greater security, the guides should be detained until the patrol is in perfect safety.

§ 370. To rest and feed the horses, the patrol avails itself of some covered place off the road, as a forest, ravine, &c.

During the halt, the patrol secures itself by means of vedettes, small patrols, and the precautions described for independent pickets. In these cases the use of fire is rigorously forbidden, no matter how well concealed the place may be. If any inhabitants are found on the spot, they must be detained until the patrol departs. During the winter, halts are made at isolated houses, or small hamlets, taking care that none of the inhabitants pass beyond the chain of sentinels established by the patrol.

§ 371. Patrols being in small force, in order to avoid the danger of being cut off, should never remain long in any one place.

§ 372. All patrols, especially those intended to examine the country, should, if possible, return by a different route from that by which they advanced; besides thus increasing their own security, they examine a greater space, and bring back information concerning two roads instead of one.

§ 373. It is very desirable that the commander of a patrol sent to examine the country should make sketches of the ground passed over, or at least describe in great detail all the objects met with of any importance in a military point of view, such as roads, rivers, forests, and defiles. Whether the roads are practicable for all kinds of troops; the nature of the road-bed; whither the roads lead; and whether they are the shortest. The extent of the forests; whether they are dense or open, marshy or dry. The size of the villages; whether they are situated on heights or in hollows; whether they contain churches and mills; whether a stream runs through them in one channel, or in several branches, or around them; whether the inhabitants have many cattle and much provisions. With regard to rivers, he observes their depth, fords, and bridges; whether the bottom is boggy or hard; the declivity and height of the banks; which bank is the higher, and where it is easiest to cross. As to marshes, he notes their extent; whether they are passable; whether there are dikes across them, and of what kind. In reference to defiles, he notes their length and breadth; describes the adjacent country, and whether the defiles can be turned. Where the commanders of patrols cannot go in person, they interrogate the inhabitants concerning these things, and compare the various replies received.

§ 374. Since special acquirements are necessary for the successful accomplishment of the object of these patrols, an officer of the staff is sent with each of them, or is placed in command.

§ 375. Sometimes patrols are sent out to alarm the enemy's outposts. These attempts usually succeed when the latter are very much scattered; for then, to repulse the attack, he collects his posts; but the patrol, having gained its object, that is, having alarmed the enemy, in the mean while retreats in safety.

§ 376. Such attacks are made in preference in the night, or in dark and bad weather. The patrol, concealing its weakness, should silently steal up to the enemy; for on this depends its success.

Having approached the outposts, it should rapidly, noisily, and with warm firing fall on them as foragers, create an alarm, seize, if possible, some of the vedettes or pickets, and then retreat rapidly before the enemy recovers.

§ 377. As a conclusion to the rules laid down in this chapter, it may be stated that the principal duties of the commander of a patrol are the following:

1. To be always cautious.
2. Always to provide for the security of his retreat.
3. Never to allow himself to be surrounded and captured.
4. To examine the country carefully, and remember its features.
5. To obtain all possible information from the inhabitants.
6. To understand how to select guides and how to treat them; and,
7. To endeavor to examine every thing in person.

§ 378. As for the rest, it is impossible to give the commander of a patrol instructions in sufficient detail to cover all the exceptional cases that may arise; therefore the success of his mission must depend chiefly upon his discretion and presence of mind.

Rashness, equally with cowardice, both here and everywhere, fails to secure the desired advantages.

CHAPTER V.

OF THE COMMAND OF THE OUTPOSTS.

§ 379. In order to secure unity in the arrangements and operations of the outposts, a field or general officer is detailed as the commander of the outposts; all the parties are under his command.

There is usually detailed for duty with him an officer of the staff, whose particular duty it is to prepare an accurate and rapid description of the ground.

§ 380. The commander of the outposts may either be detailed

for a certain length of time, or be relieved at the same time with his troops; in the latter case, he is usually the senior officer of the troops detailed for outpost duty.

§ 381. Having received from the commander-in-chief, or the chief of staff, instructions as to their operations, the general direction and extent of the chain, information of the number of troops, and destination of the parties detailed for the service, he sees to the prompt occupation of the places designated for the positions of the outposts,—making, in general, such modifications of the arrangement as may appear necessary.

§ 382. He receives every day from the commander-in-chief, in writing, and under an envelope, the *parole, watchword,* and *countersign;* he communicates these to the commanders of the main guards for the use of their posts.

§ 383. He gives the necessary instructions to the commanders of the main guards, pickets, and other posts, and maintains a constant watch over their punctuality and vigilance in the execution of their duty, and sees that they keep up the necessary connection with each other.

§ 384. He should be informed of every thing that happens at the chain; nothing should escape his attention with respect to the posts, and guarding the ground around them; it is his duty not only to correct, but anticipate, negligence, and to give all necessary directions.

§ 385. He makes the distribution of patrols, determining from what parties, by what roads, and how far they are to move; he despatches distant patrols, and gives to their commanders detailed and precise orders.

§ 386. He arranges the despatching of rounds to visit the outposts, and also goes around in person. He informs betimes the commanders of the main guards and pickets as to who will be sent on the rounds. The hours of sending out the rounds depend upon his judgment; usually they go out during the night and before dawn.

§ 387. Upon the arrival of flags of truce, deserters, or strangers, he acts according to the instructions received from the commander-in-chief, or chief of staff, to whom he ought to refer in all doubtful cases.

§ 388. The post of the commander of the outposts is with the reserve, whither all reports are sent from the outposts; but if there is no reserve, he places himself with the main guard which is nearest the centre of the general position. In every case he notifies all the commanders where he will be, that they may know where to send their reports.

§ 389. But he so arranges matters that, if he is not found at the place designated, the report, no matter what it is, may be forwarded direct to the commander of the advanced guard, and also that this may in general be carried out in cases where the point from which the report originates is nearer to the commander of the advanced guard than to his own habitual position; but he takes care that he himself shall, in all cases, be promptly informed of every thing that occurs.

§ 390. The commander of the outposts, having received reliable reports from all his parties, regulates their operations in conformity with his instructions, and conducts their movements, either so as to repulse the attempts of the enemy, or to concentrate the parties, or to afford support to any of them, or, finally, to make a general retreat.

§ 391. He promptly reports to the commander-in-chief every thing deserving attention that has been observed, and also sends him early reports of his intentions.

§ 392. Upon the arrival of the commander-in-chief at the outposts, their commander accompanies him over the whole position.

CHAPTER VI.

OF THE DUTIES OF HUNTERS, FRIENDLY INDIANS, ETC., AT THE OUTPOSTS.*

§ 393. Outpost service is performed by these kinds of troops rather differently from the manner pursued in the regular cavalry. Adopting for them the rules herein contained, and which can be explained to them by their chiefs, they may be advantageously employed in advance of the regular cavalry.

§ 394. The main difference is, that the advanced chain does not consist of double vedettes, relieved every two hours, but of pickets of 3 or 4 men each, on duty for 24 hours, and relieving each other in the task of watching the enemy.

§ 395. These pickets are placed at such a distance apart that they can see each other, or at least that the enemy cannot slip through without being seen by one or other of the pickets.

§ 396. In each picket one man, mounted, or on foot, with his horse bridled by his side, constantly watches the whole space committed to the picket; another remains behind him in full readiness to mount; but the others repose, feed their horses, lead them to water, and even go in search of forage.

---

* This chapter is taken from one in the Russian regulations, relating to the duty of Cossacks at the outposts.

§ 397. If the pickets are pushed very far in advance of the regular cavalry, lines of supports are placed behind them. These supports are placed in preference near roads, or points of special importance, where they may serve as points of assembly for the chain of pickets.

§ 398. The supports usually consist of from 6 to 12 men each. One of them, usually standing to horse, places himself in sight of the chain of pickets, also turning his attention to the ground on each side. Of the rest of the men a part hold themselves in readiness, while the others rest, feed and water their horses, and, if necessary, go for forage.

§ 399. The remainder of the companies, or the regiment on duty, usually form a reserve, about a mile in rear of the lines of supports, on the principal road, or behind the centre of the chain. A part of this reserve is held in readiness to mount, but the greater part repose, and even hobble or picket their horses.

§ 400. The quick sight, activity, and vigilance of the men, referred to in this chapter, are such as to allow a greater interval between these pickets than between the pairs of ordinary vedettes. The supports, not being intended to relieve the chain, but merely to serve as rallying-points, may also be placed farther apart than the pickets of regular cavalry. Finally, instead of main guards, there is in this case but one main reserve. From these facts it would appear that reliable men, of the kind alluded to here, may guard a given space with a smaller number of men, and less fatigue, than regular cavalry. Reserves of light cavalry should be posted on a line with the main reserve of the irregulars. The Indian horses being peculiarly capable of enduring the fatigue of outpost duty, the friendly Indians, if there are any present, should compose the outposts in preference.

§ 401. During the night and in dark weather the intervals between the irregular pickets must be decreased, as prescribed for vedettes.

§ 402. Regular patrols and rounds need not be so much resorted to, but each particular chief should often ride around the whole circuit of his command.

§ 403. The irregular reserve will from time to time send out patrols of 5, 10, or 15 men to reconnoitre in all directions.

CHAPTER VII.

OF THE ARRANGEMENT OF THE OUTPOSTS ACCORDING TO THE NATURE OF THE GROUND.

§ 404. The art of arranging the outposts according to the nature of the ground is founded upon : 1. The proper general direction of the advanced chain; 2. The distribution of the supports; and, 3. The composition of the supports. The object to be gained is to discover the enemy at the greatest possible distance with the smallest possible number of men, without exposing any of the posts to be cut off.

§ 405. The general line of the outposts is generally determined by some natural objects, such as the banks of rivers, creeks, borders of ravines, marshes, skirts of woods, crests of heights, &c.

§ 406. The chain of vedettes should cross objects favoring the view of the surrounding country, and its flanks should rest on impracticable places. It should be neither too far advanced nor too close in: in the first case, it would be difficult for the vedettes to retreat; in the last case, the troops guarded would not have the necessary time given them.

§ 407. The chain should not be so placed as to have close in front of it covered places, villages, woods, and such objects; if it is not possible to throw the chain in advance of these places without too great an extension, it is best to draw it a great deal to the rear. If this last cannot be done, for want of space, it only remains to redouble vigilance and send out more frequent patrols.

§ 408. If the chain is placed behind an impassable object, such as a broad river or a very bad marsh, it may be made thinner than usual, or even be entirely dispensed with; in the latter case, patrols must be sent out, more or less frequently, in proportion to the degree of impracticability of the ground and the difficulty of examining it. In no case should any portion of the ground remain entirely unwatched, however impracticable it may appear to be.

§ 409. In mountainous regions, where the broken nature of the country embarrasses communications and facilitates the concealment of the enemy's movements on all sides, the outposts draw nearer together than the specified normal distances, and sometimes the camp is entirely surrounded by a chain of vedettes.

§ 410. In the general line of the outposts there may be places unfit for the operations of cavalry; such portions are necessarily occupied by infantry, all the rest by cavalry: in such cases, one part of the chain will consist of mounted vedettes, the rest of pairs of infantry sentinels. In this case, the outposts are formed of cavalry and infantry, each guarding the ground destined for it according to the rules laid down for that arm; but such a chain of outposts should form one general whole, and the different parts must maintain a constant union, unless separated by wholly impassable obstacles.

§ 411. The vedettes should be posted at the points commanding the most distant views; in the day they are placed on the summits of the hills, at night they fall back to the foot of the slope. They should also be concealed by some natural object, which, at the same time, permits them to see all around. Between the pairs of vedettes there should be no covered places which might conceal the approach of the enemy.

§ 412. In the distribution of the supports of the chain, that is, the pickets, main guards, and reserves, they are posted in preference at places around which the enemy cannot pass, or, at least, at places where he may most probably be expected; therefore, they are usually posted near the roads, especially at crossroads.

§ 413. Another condition in the distribution of the supports is that each should, if possible, see the parties directly subordinate to it, and to which it ought to give immediate support. This is particularly important for the pickets in relation to the vedettes, because on the approach of the enemy the latter form part of the former.

§ 414. A third condition for the proper distribution of the supports is that they should be concealed until the moment for action arrives.

§ 415. Finally, a fourth condition is that they should be placed in positions suitable for their operations; that is, cavalry should have an open unobstructed space in their front, but infantry, an obstructed country. This condition is of peculiar importance in regard to the reserve, which is expected to make a more obstinate resistance than the main guard and pickets.

§ 416. In order to preserve the general union between all parts of the outposts, and more especially between the outposts and the troops guarded by them, there should be no impassable obstacles between them; this is to avoid exposing any party to being cut off and defeated separately. If there is behind the chain of vedettes a place across which communication is difficult, it is best to place the main guards or pickets near it, that they may hold the crossings, and permit the fulfilment of the other conditions for a good arrangement.

§ 417. Pickets relieving vedettes should always be composed of the same kind of troops as their vedettes; the main guards and reserves are composed according to the nature of the ground between the pickets and the camp; in places suitable for cavalry they consist of that arm, in defensive positions they are of infantry.

§ 418. To secure their greater independence, the reserves of the outposts may sometimes be composed of all three arms; but in an open, unobstructed country they may be of cavalry and horse artillery alone.

§ 419. *Example of the arrangement of outposts composed of cavalry alone.* (Fig. 8.)

It is supposed that an advanced guard, consisting of a brigade of cavalry and a division of infantry, is in the village A, and that it is necessary to guard it against the enemy, expected by the roads B.

§ 420. To determine the line of observation to be occupied by the outposts, the whole ground between the position of the advanced guard and the points accessible by the enemy must first be carefully examined on the map; from the selection of the line of observation results the composition of the chain and its supports.

§ 421. In this example, according to the conditions already mentioned, the most advantageous line of observation is that proceeding from the village L, through the villages M and N, thence following the ridge O to the lake P. This line is favorable, because:

1. The right flank, resting on the marsh near the village L, cannot be turned, and requires no further extension.

2. The left flank, resting on the lake, allows us to observe from the ridge the distant movements of the enemy; the ridge also conceals our own movements from the enemy in that direction.

3. Without being too far off, the chain is at such a distance that every movement of the enemy can be discovered in season to enable the advanced guard to take all its measures for operating against him.

§ 422. Upon the nature of the ground over which the line of observation extends must depend the kind of troops who are to hold it.

In this example, from the appearance of the ground towards the enemy and towards the advanced guard, it seems that cavalry can act with advantage; therefore all the outposts are of that arm.

The extent of the line is a little more than 5 miles: therefore,

REGULATIONS FOR FIELD SERVICE. 93

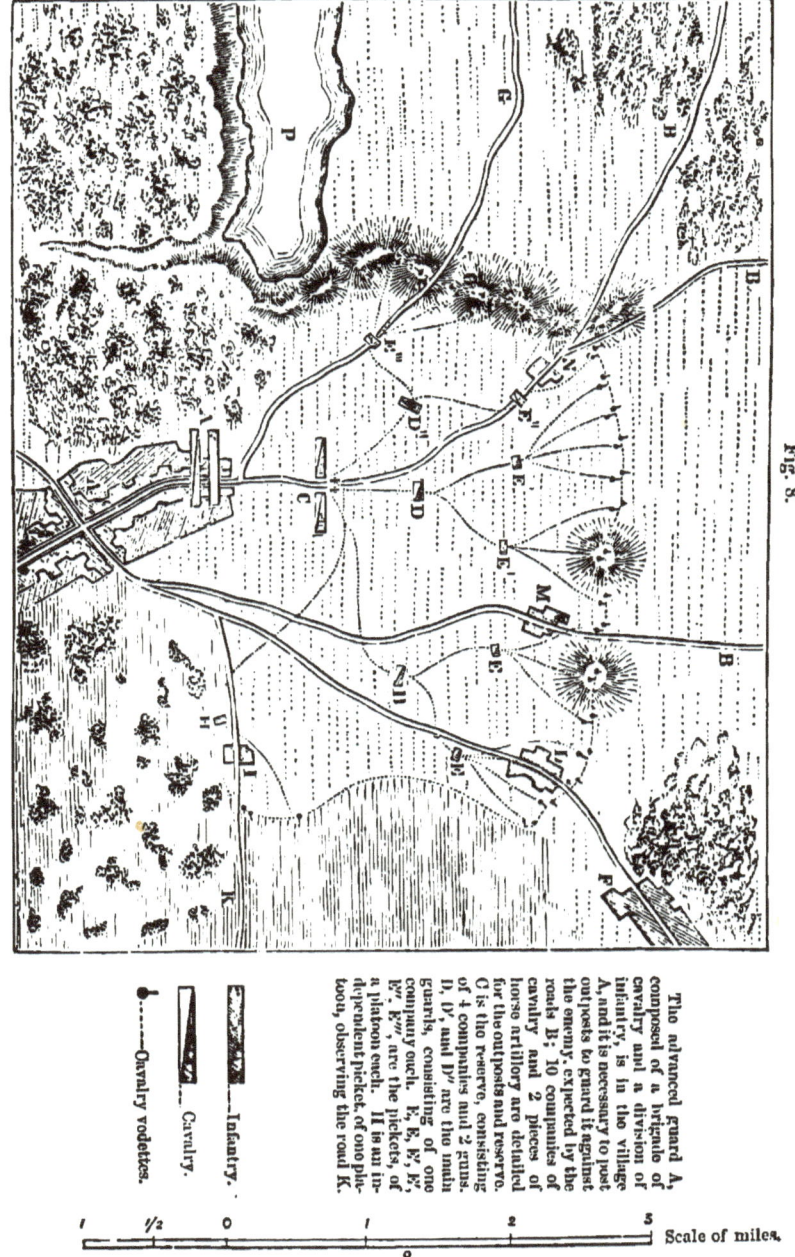

Fig. 8.

The advanced guard A, composed of a brigade of cavalry and a division of infantry, is in the village A, and it is necessary to post outposts to guard it against the enemy, expected by the roads B: 10 companies of cavalry and 2 pieces of horse artillery are detailed for the outposts and reserve. C is the reserve, consisting of 4 companies and 2 guns. D, D', and D" are the main guards, consisting of one company each. E, E', E', E", K''', are the pickets, of a platoon each. F is an independent picket, of one platoon, observing the road K.

●·········· Cavalry vedettes.
▭ Infantry.
▰ Cavalry.

Scale of miles.

according to the estimate in § 193, 6 companies will be required for the vedettes, pickets, and main guards. As the ground opposes no obstacles to the action of cavalry, the reserve should also be of that arm. This reserve, consisting of 4 companies of cavalry and 2 pieces of horse artillery, is posted at the central point C, whence it can easily move to all parts of the outposts.

§ 423. In accordance with the principles just explained, the commander of the advanced guard issues in this case instructions to the following purport:

1. The Nth regiment of cavalry and 2 pieces of the Nth battery of horse artillery are detailed for outpost duty. These troops will post a chain of vedettes from the village L, through the villages M and N, and along the ridge O to the lake P.

2. Patrols will be sent out: from the village L to F; from the picket E''', along the road G; and from the other posts, in the direction in which the enemy is expected.

3. If the enemy attacks in force, the outposts will fall back upon the advanced guard.

With these instructions as a basis, the commander of the outposts makes his assignments; each company is directed where to take position, and between what points to occupy the line of observation; all the parties are posted as explained above and shown in Fig. 8.

§ 424. If, in the example given in Fig. 8, the right flank of the advanced guard is not regarded as sufficiently protected by the marsh, then an independent picket, consisting of a platoon, is posted at H, to watch the road leading through the village I; this picket posts two pairs of vedettes.

§ 425. *Example of the arrangement of outposts composed of both cavalry and infantry.* (Fig. 9.)

It is supposed that the advanced guard A, consisting of a brigade of cavalry and a division of infantry, is placed behind the village B, and that outposts are to be posted to guard against an attack by the enemy arriving from the direction of the village C.

§ 426. With this arrangement of the advanced guard, it is best to place the outposts on the left side of the creek M, because if the line of posts were limited by the stream it would be difficult to obtain information of the movements of the enemy's advanced guard.

§ 427. The best line of observation is from the lake N to the corner of the village B, then along the edge of this village to the marsh Q. On account of its shortness and the nature of the objects on which its flanks rest, this line is very advantageous. From the lake N to the village B (about $1\frac{1}{3}$ mile) it may be held

REGULATIONS FOR FIELD SERVICE. 95

Fig. 2.

The advanced guard A, consisting of a brigade of cavalry and a division of infantry, is placed behind the village B, and outposts are to be posted to guard against an attack by the enemy arriving from the direction of the village C: 4 companies of cavalry, 2 regiments of infantry, and 2 pieces of foot artillery are detailed to furnish the outposts and reserve.

D is the reserve, consisting of 1½ companies of cavalry, 11 companies of infantry, and 2 pieces of foot artillery.

E is a main guard of 3 companies of infantry, which furnishes the two pickets F, each of which posts 5 pairs of sentinels.

E' is an infantry main guard of 2 companies, which supports the two cavalry pickets H, each of which consists of a platoon and posts 3 pairs of vedettes.

E'' is an infantry main guard of 2 companies, to support the cavalry picket H', which posts 4 vedettes, and H'', which posts 1 vedette. E''' is an infantry main guard of 2 companies, which holds the cemetery and supports the cavalry picket H''', posting 3 redettes.

▬▬ Infantry.
▬▬ Cavalry.

0 ½ 1 2 Scale of miles.

by cavalry; along the edge of the village, (about ¾ of a mile,) by infantry.

§ 428. To prevent the line from being turned, independent pickets must in this case be posted on the left flank, near the lake N and the height O, on the right flank on the road L; to support the pickets and defend the villages and crossings, it is best that all the main guards should be of infantry.

§ 429. Thus the line will consist of 2 cavalry and 2 infantry pickets, holding the main line of observation, of 3 independent cavalry pickets, and of 4 infantry main guards. To supply these, 5 platoons of cavalry and about 9 companies of infantry will be necessary; so that for the whole outpost service, including the reserve, there may be detailed 4 companies of cavalry, 2 battalions of infantry, and 2 pieces of foot artillery.

§ 430. On this basis the commander of the outposts receives the following instructions:

1. Four companies of the Nth regiment of cavalry, the Mth and Nth regiments of infantry, and 2 pieces of the Nth foot battery are detailed for the outposts.

2. The cavalry will occupy the line of the outposts from the lake N, along the ravine P, to the corner of the village B; the infantry, from this last point, along the edge of the village to the marsh Q.

One independent cavalry picket will be posted near the village R, another in front of the village I, a third on the road L.

3. The main guards will be of infantry, posted as follows: one, of 2 companies, in the cemetery near the end of the village B; another, of 3 companies, in that village; a third, of 2 companies, in the village G; a fourth, of 2 companies, in the village I.

4. The rest of the troops detailed will form the reserve of the outposts, and be posted at D, on the main road, behind the crossing over the stream M.

5. As long as the enemy does not show a strong force of infantry, every effort will be made to keep him beyond the villages.

Under the foregoing instructions the outposts may be arranged as shown in Fig. 9.

§ 431. Finally, among the examples of the disposition of outposts according to the ground may be considered the case of a locality which permits the enemy to approach only by a few passes. If he is separated from us by a river, a marsh, rough hills, &c., and can approach only by known fords, passages, or narrow defiles, then, if these points are occupied by independent pickets, there will be no necessity for a continuous chain of vedettes.

Remark.—Whenever the camp is behind a river, the outposts should convey to their own side all the boats and other means of crossing.

§ 432. In such cases, the independent pickets are posted at points which the enemy cannot turn.

§ 433. For their own safety, they post vedettes; if the ground permits, they communicate with each other by means of patrols.

§ 434. If it is necessary to support the independent pickets, reserves are placed as directed in § 412.

§ 435. *Example of the arrangement of the outposts in a locality where the enemy can approach only by a few passes.* (Fig. 10.)

It is supposed that a detachment, composed of a brigade of cavalry and a division of infantry, is placed at the village A to guard, in connection with another detachment at B, the troops following from the north, and that outposts are to be posted; and that it is known that the advanced troops of the enemy, approaching from the south, have not yet occupied the village N, and that they cannot turn the passages over the stream P.

§ 436. It is evident that it is unnecessary, in this case, to post a continuous chain of vedettes, and that it will be sufficient to place independent pickets on the main roads, at proper distances from the advanced detachment to be supported by it, and keep up the communication with the detachment at B.

§ 437. Upon examining the ground in front of A and B, it is evident that the stream P is the most advantageous line of observation, and that the main detachment will be perfectly secure if the crossings of the stream are occupied by independent pickets.

§ 438. The crossings are at the points Q, R, S, T, U, and V. Supposing the crossing at Q to be occupied by a picket from the detachment at B, and that each picket consists of a platoon, the detachment at A must furnish 5 platoons, or 6 if the flank picket at K consists of a company.

§ 439. Main guards, consisting of a company each, are posted near the villages F and I; and there may be a reserve of 4 or 5 companies and a few guns at the village D.

§ 440. The pickets posted near R, S, and T, should send out patrols to the village N, and the pickets near U and V send patrols to the village W; a small detachment should be sent through the village N, to keep on until it finds the enemy; this should be composed of a company.

§ 441. On these principles the commander of the outposts receives the following instructions:

1. The Nth regiment of cavalry and 2 pieces of the Nth horse battery are detailed for the outposts.

Fig. 10.

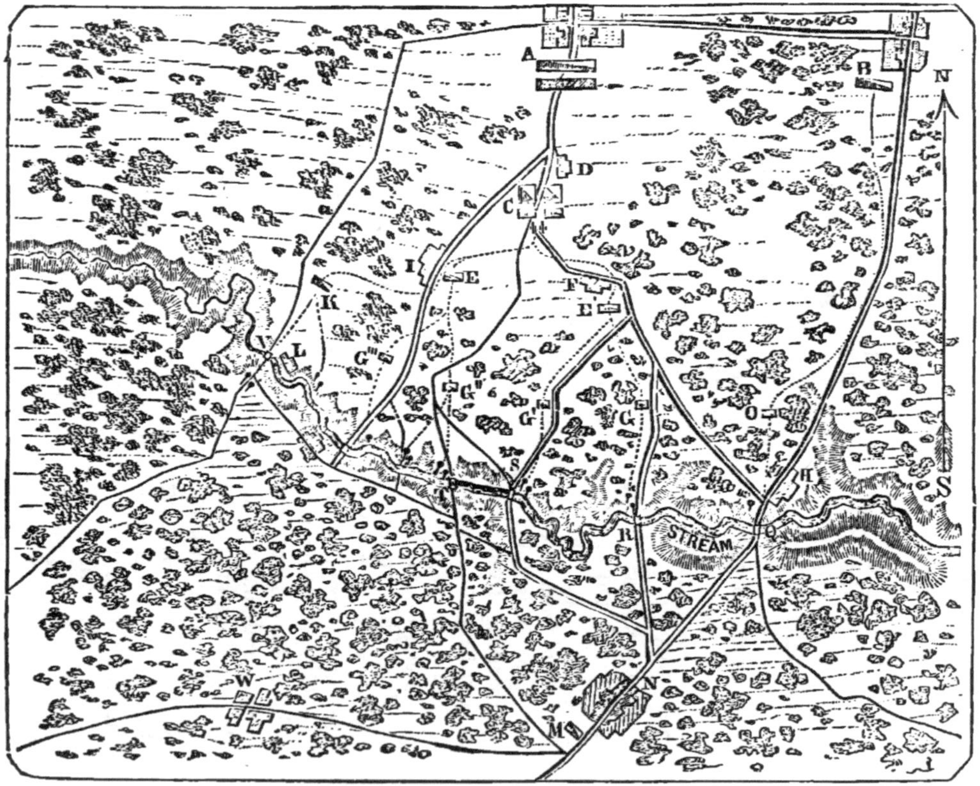

The enemy is beyond the village N; our own detachments occupy A and B; the force at A consists of a brigade of cavalry and a division of infantry; 10 companies of cavalry and two pieces of horse artillery are detailed from A to furnish the outposts and reserve. C is the reserve, consisting of 5 companies and 2 guns. K is a main guard of 1 company, supporting the pickets G and G′, each of which posts a vedette at the crossings R and S respectively. E′ is a main guard of 1 company, supporting the pickets G″, which post one vedette at T and one at a crossing above, and G‴, which posts a vedette at V. The pickets G, G′, G″, G‴, each consist of a platoon. K is a picket, consisting of a company which posts two vedettes near the village I, and patrols the road beyond. M is a distant patrol, of one company, detached from the reserve to find the enemy. O is a picket belonging to the detachment B, which posts a vedette at the crossing Q.

Scale of miles.

▬▬ Infantry.
▭▭ Cavalry.

2. Until the enemy arrives at the village N, the outposts will keep only independent pickets at the crossings of the stream P, at R, S, T, U, and V; the main guards to be companies near F, I, and L; in order to observe the enemy better, one company will be sent through the village N, to keep on until it finds the enemy; the remainder of the cavalry and the guns will be posted in reserve near the village D. Near patrols will be sent out, as usual, from all the pickets, in the direction of the villages N and W, and distant patrols to keep on until they find the enemy.

To carry out these instructions, the outposts may be arranged as shown in fig. 10.

§ 442. If the line observed by the independent pickets is very far from the camp, and it is not intended to defend it, but they are restricted to observation and giving notice of the enemy's approach, then this line is occupied by cavalry alone, according to the rules for independent pickets.

§ 443. But if the line is near the camp, or for other reasons it is necessary to defend as well as observe it, then it should be occupied by infantry in force proportionate to the importance of the case, or the possibility of holding it long enough to permit other troops to arrive.

§ 444. Such posts are called *independent defensive posts*.

If an independent defensive post is far from camp, and it is only intended to delay the advance of the head of the enemy's column, and then fall back on the other troops, cavalry should occupy it in preference.

§ 445. In such cases mounted riflemen are of great use, because they repulse the enemy by acting as infantry, and can retreat with the rapidity of cavalry when it becomes necessary; and, when covering the retreat of other troops, they can act sometimes as infantry, sometimes as cavalry, according to the nature of the ground and the necessity of the case.

§ 446. In an independent defensive post, the party on duty dismounts and occupies the point to be defended as infantry; the rest of the men repose near the horses, observing the precautions prescribed for main guards; they are placed in rear of the men acting as infantry, and keep the horses bitted.

§ 447. In all the cases mentioned in this chapter, precise instructions are given to the commander of each party as to what is to be done in the event of the appearance of the enemy.

§ 448. As a conclusion to this chapter, it may be stated that, although the disposition of the outposts, according to the nature of the ground, is of the utmost importance, for the reason that success in watching the enemy depends neither on the number nor strength of the outposts, but on their skilful arrangement, all that can be said on the subject is limited rather to an explanation of the general importance of objects than to laying down any precise rules. In all cases theory must yield to the judgment of the commander, for a blind and unconditional following of rules may result in injury rather than advantage.

From all that precedes, it appears that troops may be guarded either by continuous chains with lines of supports, or by independent posts, or by patrols, or, finally, by all three methods combined.

But there is no doubt that, if we carefully conform to the principles laid down for each of these arrangements, one of them will often suffice; while, on the contrary, if we neglect these principles, the employment of all three may be insufficient.

CHAPTER VIII.

PRECAUTIONS TO BE OBSERVED IN THE CAMP OF THE MAIN BODY.

§ 449. To avoid fatiguing the troops by keeping all of them constantly ready for a movement and combat, but at the same time to secure them against attack, and be able to afford prompt assistance to the outposts, a portion of the main body is detailed as an *inlying picket*.

§ 450. The inlying picket must always be ready for action on the first order or signal. The men should therefore always be to the front, and be dressed both by day and night; their arms should be loaded, and their horses saddled but unbitted and picketed; they are taken to water by turns, in parties. In the artillery, the men of the inlying picket are always dressed, the horses have their collars on, and are taken to water only by piece or by section.

§ 451. It rests with the commander of the main body, according to the news he has of the enemy, whether to direct additional precautions on the part of the inlying picket; for instance, that the men should wear their accoutrements, &c.

§ 452. The strength of the inlying picket is regulated by the commander of the detachment, or army, in conformity with the degree of danger, the proximity of the enemy, and his means of turning our position. Approximately, the inlying picket is $\frac{1}{5}$ or $\frac{1}{6}$ of the whole force.

§ 453. In small detachments from which it is impossible to

send out many men on outpost duty, and in general near the enemy, the whole detachment sometimes forms a kind of inlying picket; in this case only a small number are relieved at a time, according to the judgment of the commander, but the greater portion remain in readiness for action.

§ 454. Upon receiving from the outposts news of the approach of the enemy, the inlying picket at once moves to the front to receive the outposts and afford the other troops time to prepare.

§ 455. For greater security, the inlying picket is sometimes posted a little to the front, and then picket their horses somewhat in advance of the general camp. This is done whenever there is any thing immediately in front of the camp to cause delay.

§ 456. The commander and all the officers of the inlying picket will strictly superintend the observation of all the precautions required.

§ 457. To prevent confusion in the camp in case of an alarm or an attack, it is necessary to watch—

1. That all parts of the troops are arranged in conformity with the movements they are to make, so that they can form in order of battle without confusion, and without crossing each other's paths.

2. That all commanders, down to those of regiments and batteries, inclusive, know the places their commands are to occupy in the general order of battle, if it is determined to accept battle at or near the camp.

3. That all impediments to the free communications and movements of the troops are removed in season as far as practicable.

4. That the commander of the train is always informed whither to direct it, in case of leaving camp suddenly.

5. That the parties of troops, from whom mixed detachments are sent out for forage and other necessaries, are formed immediately after their departure, to count and organize those remaining.

§ 458. The commander of the main body should be well informed in regard to all the country in the vicinity of his position, and especially as to the roads and crossings of streams in the direction in which he expects to move.

§ 459. In camps of the main body, the inlying picket posts camp and quarter guards immediately after reaching camp; this is done as in time of peace.

§ 460. It is the duty of the sentinels of the camp and quarter guards to see that no one leaves camp between evening twilight and reveille without a special permit from the commander, unless on duty.

Men who are not known, and do not belong to the troops, or who have not the necessary permission, are allowed to leave camp neither by day nor night, but are stopped by the sentinels and sent to the guards, by whom they are sent to the inlying picket.

§ 461. In the night the sentinels of the camp and quarter guards challenge all who approach from the exterior, and act as prescribed for vedettes.

§ 462. In general, all the rules laid down for camp and garrison service in time of peace are carried out as far as possible in the camps of the main body.

CHAPTER IX.

PRECAUTIONS TO BE OBSERVED FOR THE SECURITY OF CANTONMENTS.

ARTICLE 1.

Of advanced detachments.

§ 463. Troops in cantonments, being scattered over a great space, and requiring much time to assemble, are not covered by a continuous chain of outposts. In this case, the arrangements for the early discovery of the approach of the enemy are made entirely by the cavalry, who must, by means of their outposts, patrols, and parties, watch the whole space in front of the cantonments towards the enemy.

§ 464. These outposts consist entirely of independent posts, whose arrangement depends altogether upon circumstances. It can only be said that, as they are sent out to discover the enemy, they are posted in preference on the main roads, at the junctions of roads on which the enemy must move, and in places favorable to defensive operations. If there is any place on the flank of the cantonments offering advantages to the enemy, it must be occupied.

§ 465. The posts should be strong in proportion to the importance of the road on which they are placed, their distance from the cantonments, and the facility for defence offered by the ground.

§ 466. The precautions to be observed by these posts have a twofold object: (*a*) their own safety; (*b*) to afford timely information of the approach of the enemy. In this matter they conform to what is prescribed in Part II., Chapter I., Article 6, of these regulations.

§ 467. The more extensive the space over which the outposts are scattered, the more are they left to their own resources, and the more must their success depend upon the good sense of the commander of each party. His only means of obtaining news of the enemy are his own eyes, sentinels, vedettes, patrols, and information from travellers and the inhabitants; but it depends upon his own sagacity to apply them with the greatest success.

§ 468. To support the independent pickets, there may be sent out main guards, and on the most important points of all the roads leading towards the enemy *main advanced detachments*.

§ 469. These last, being intended not only to support the cavalry outposts and parties, but also to check the enemy long enough to enable the troops in the cantonments to assemble at the designated rendezvous, should possess a certain independent strength; therefore they should consist of all three arms, according to the importance of the point.

§ 470. These detachments are pushed one or two marches from the cantonments, and occupy strong positions, which they may sometimes strengthen by field works.

§ 471. If the intervals between them are considerable, smaller posts are placed between them, to keep up the communication and secure the cantonments from being alarmed by light detachments of the enemy.

§ 472. The commander of a main advanced detachment must make himself well acquainted with the country in the vicinity, examine all the approaches by which the enemy may arrive, and take all measures to discover his movements betimes, as well as to secure the best possible defence of the post.

§ 473. All the outposts are subordinate to the commander of the main advanced detachment; he arranges their movements, and receives from them all news of the enemy.

§ 474. The main advanced detachments post camp and quarter guards. All the men should be in readiness for action; therefore the horses are saddled at the picket-ropes, arms loaded, accoutrements close at hand, and they do not undress at night; their inlying pickets keep their horses bridled and accoutrements on. The guns in position should be loaded, artillery horses with their collars on, the detachments close to their pieces.

§ 475. All the posts mentioned in this article guard themselves by the various dispositions for outpost service; that is to say, they detach independent posts or surround themselves by chains, according to their distance from the enemy. They send out patrols and flying detachments as far as the position of the enemy, and also patrols to keep up their communication with each other and with the cantonments.

§ 476. In order to embarrass and retard his approach, preparations are made betimes to take up the bridges, destroy the causeways, &c., in the direction of the enemy, so that the advanced parties may accomplish the purpose immediately upon their retreat across them. But the communications with the cantonments should be perfectly open; therefore all obstacles should be removed betimes.

§ 477. If the commander of a main advanced detachment receives news of the enemy, he at once reports it to the commander-in-chief, and, if necessary, to the commanders of the nearest posts and detachments. In such cases it is necessary to be unusually circumspect with regard to reports; and in case of the appearance of the enemy, to endeavor to ascertain his force and designs, in order to avoid alarming the cantonments without cause.

§ 478. That the commander-in-chief may be constantly informed of what is going on at the outposts, the commanders of the main advanced detachments send reports to him at the hours he may specify, several times a day, even if nothing of importance has been observed.

§ 479. Signal stations, telegraphs, &c., are established at convenient points to convey prompt information of the approach of the enemy.

§ 480. If a main advanced detachment is attacked, its movements must depend upon the orders it has received from the commander-in-chief.

§ 481. Only their wagons of the 1st class, with a part of those of the 2d, are with the main advanced detachments.

If the enemy advances, the wagons at once move to the rear, so as not to impede the movements of the troops if they are forced to retreat.

§ 482. On account of the fatiguing nature of the outpost duty, the troops should be relieved from time to time, according to the judgment of the commander-in-chief.

ARTICLE 2.

Precautions to be observed by the main body in cantonments.

§ 483. In addition to the outposts and advanced detachments for guarding the cantonments, certain measures of precaution are taken by the main body itself, especially in reference to the rapid assembly of the troops in the event of an attack. These measures are regulated by the commander-in-chief, according to the proximity of the enemy and the degree of the danger.

§ 484. The troops nearest the enemy, being most exposed to attack, are placed in crowded quarters to secure a prompt assembly; the others may be placed farther apart and in more roomy quarters, for the greater facility of obtaining supplies.

§ 485. In the distribution of the troops, their position in the cantonments must correspond, as nearly as possible, with their position in the order of battle. The artillery is placed near the points where it is destined to act, the men and horses being in the same villages with the parks.

§ 486. If it is necessary, inlying pickets are detailed in the villages nearest the enemy; the state of preparation in which they are kept is regulated by the commander-in-chief according to circumstances. If necessary, distant patrols are sent out by these inlying pickets.

§ 487. In addition to the guards at regimental head-quarters, and in the different parts of large villages, infantry guards are posted at the outlets of the villages on the side of the enemy. These guards post sentinels, and are ordered to prevent the passage of people without the countersign at night, or both by day and night, according to circumstances.

§ 488. Signal stations and telegraphs must be arranged in the cantonments. The signals to turn out and form must be explained to the troops.

§ 489. That the troops may meet the enemy in force if he attacks, points of rendezvous must be designated near the quarters for regiments, divisions, and other parties.

§ 490. In addition to the general rendezvous, there is a special one for the troops in each village. This is chosen outside of the village, on the side nearest the general rendezvous; and measures are taken betimes that all the roads leading to the rendezvous may be open and free from obstacles.

§ 491. When the troops march to the rendezvous, only the wagons of the 1st class accompany them; special rendezvous are given for the other wagons, so that the troops may not be delayed or embarrassed by them either when moving to the rendezvous or in case of retreat.

§ 492. For the march of the troops to the rendezvous, roads are chosen for each party, so that they may neither cross nor delay each other on the march.

The roads should be examined and repaired betimes.

PART III.

OF THE PRINCIPAL OPERATIONS OF SPECIAL DETACHMENTS.

CHAPTER I.

OF SUDDEN ATTACKS UPON THE ENEMY.

§ 493. Sudden attacks upon the enemy are made with several objects:
1. To alarm his posts;
2. To capture one or more of them; and,
3. To attack his quarters.

§ 494. For all such enterprises, cavalry are chosen in preference. Mounted rifles, or dragoons, uniting the defensive force of infantry with the velocity of cavalry, may be of particular advantage in the last two cases, especially in passing to the defensive and covering a retreat, in case of a failure in the enterprise.

§ 495. The principal conditions of success in all enterprises of this kind may be stated to be: 1. Complete knowledge of the ground, and positive information as to the force and distribution of the enemy; 2. A concealed approach to the point on which the attack is to be made; 3. Rapidity of movement, seconded by the secrecy and unexpectedness of the attack; and, 4. To keep the movements of the different parties as closely united as possible until the last moment, so that no one of them may be delayed by unexpected obstacles, or discovered by the enemy on account of having separated too soon; finally, the whole force must be perfectly ready for action at a moment's notice.

§ 496. In accomplishing a concealed approach to the point on which the attack is to be made, we will be assisted by selecting the time when the enemy least expects an attack,—that is, in the night, or thick weather; by choosing the route affording the best cover; by announcing an enterprise of an entirely different nature; and, sometimes, by starting in the opposite direction, that after having made a considerable circuit we may finally come out in the real direction.

§ 497. Besides the general conditions specified, there are also particular conditions, relating to each of the cases specified in § 493, which are discussed in the following sections.

§ 498. Attacks upon the enemy's outposts are undertaken either to harass him, by obliging him to be in constant readiness for action, or to divert his attention, in order to cover some movement favorable to us.

In this and the other cases, we should endeavor to extend the alarm over the greatest possible space with the fewest possible men.

For this, it is advantageous to divide the party into several sections, which, attacking at several points, either simultaneously or successively, break through the chain, gallop up to the main guards, and, having alarmed them, at once fall back; if successful, they seize some vedettes or even pickets. In such an attack every section exerts itself to appear as strong as possible; they therefore scatter, and generally keep up a warm firing and great noise.

§ 499. Besides harassing the enemy, which is the direct object of these attacks, they may procure the advantage of making the enemy careless if they are frequently repeated, and thus facilitate the success of more important operations.

§ 500. In making an attack for the purpose of capturing a post of the enemy, it is well to divide the detachment detailed for the service into three parts: one moves to the rear of the post, on its road of retreat and reinforcement; another part makes the direct attack; the third is held in reserve to support the attack, or, in case of failure, cover the retreat of the other parts. If possible, it is well to conceal the reserve until the moment when the enemy is allured to pursue the repulsed party; then the reserve, acting as an ambuscade, endeavors to take the enemy in flank or in rear, and seize the abandoned post.

§ 501. If the post attacked is in a village, the place of assembly should be ascertained, and a party of men sent there to seize the enemy as they arrive singly upon the alarm.

§ 502. In general, in attacking a post with the design of taking possession of it, the greatest silence should be observed, and the firing commenced only when the attacking party has been already discovered; then rapidity and decision are necessary, so that the enemy may not have time to recover; rapidity and audacity in the attack usually command success.

§ 503. If the enemy retreats, then on the return march the reserve usually marches in front with the prisoners; the attacking party follows; the party which moved on the enemy's rear acts as a rear guard.

§ 504. If the ground permits, the attack may be combined with an ambuscade. For this purpose veteran troops are detailed, who are concealed with the object of falling suddenly upon the enemy when he has been decoyed to their position. In this case, success depends much upon the conduct of the troops who act openly, and who should endeavor to decoy the enemy into an imprudent pursuit, and draw him into the ambuscade.

§ 505. The success of the ambuscade itself depends chiefly upon seizing the proper moment for action. As a general rule, it should not begin to act too soon, lest the enemy retreat without loss. It is best to allow his leading parties to pass so far by that he may be attacked in flank, or, still better, in rear and his retreat cut off.

§ 506. Apart from the object of seizing important points, attacks are sometimes made upon the enemy's posts with the special object of encouraging the military spirit of our own troops, and increasing their boldness and self-confidence by partial successes.

In this case prudence requires progression in the undertakings; beginning with those that require small numbers and at the same time promise full success, such as capturing single vedettes; then, upon success, to undertake the capture of pickets, and finally to pass to more important enterprises. Inital successes in a campaign are of particular importance; they produce favorable impressions upon our own people, and depress the courage of the enemy.

If the enemy is at all negligent in guarding his horses, small parties may accomplish important results by stampeding them at night.

§ 507. The object of attacks upon the cantonments of the enemy may be to alarm him, to capture important points, or to profit by his dispersion and attack in force so as to defeat him in detail.

§ 508. In the first two cases the operations, although on a larger scale, will be nearly like those for attacking the outposts.

In the last case, when the detachment making the attack succeeds in carrying any important point, it should be at once supported by the co-operation of other troops. Thus, not being delayed by the first success, it can at once move on, and, taking advantage of the dispersion of the enemy, endeavor to capture his troops before they are assembled and ready for action, trusting to the troops in rear of it for a safe retreat.

§ 509. It is evident that the strength of detachments detailed for sudden attacks must vary very much; to capture a vedette 3 or 4 men are enough,—the fewer the better. To capture a picket, and generally to attack the enemy's outposts, parties of our own advanced troops may be employed; to attack posts of importance, detachments of considerable strength may be sent out; while to attack the cantonments of the enemy, the whole of the main body is sometimes employed.

CHAPTER II.

OF RECONNOISSANCES.

§ 510. A reconnoissance—that is, an ocular examination—should precede every military enterprise. It is always necessary to know beforehand with what troops we have to deal, and the nature of the country in which the operation is to be effected; this information can be fully obtained neither by interrogation nor from maps; there is no other way than by a reconnoissance.

§ 511. Information obtained by a reconnoissance is preferable to that by interrogation, as being more full, and generally obtained with less delay.

§ 512. If the enemy is so near that our own chain can see every thing, the reconnoissance is made under its protection. In such a case the reconnoitring officer either takes no escort, or a very small one, and, for greater secrecy, leaves even that at some distance.

§ 513. If the enemy is at some distance, distant patrols are detailed for the reconnoissance; the duty is, according to its importance, intrusted either to the commander of the patrol or to a special officer (sometimes an officer of the staff) to whom the patrol is given as an escort.

§ 514. If it is necessary to make a close reconnoissance of the position and arrangements of the enemy, detachments of considerable strength must be employed. Their composition must be such that they can drive in the enemy's outposts, break through his lines to the required distance, and remain long enough to gain satisfactory information. Such reconnoissances made openly and in force are called *forced reconnoissances*. Their object is sometimes not only to examine the ground and the arrangements of the enemy, but also to ascertain his strength; consequently, to alarm him to such a degree as to make him show the parties at first concealed.

§ 515. To insure the success of a reconnoissance, whatever its object may be, it is necessary to attack suddenly and have a secure retreat.

§ 516. Small reconnoitring parties usually consist of cavalry alone; but if a certain effort is required to seize any point, or if we must leave it occupied while we pass beyond it, then artillery and infantry must be added. Here, as in all cases when it is necessary to combine rapidity of movement with some defensive strength, mounted rifles may be advantageously employed.

§ 517. The strength of a reconnoitring party can only be

determined by its object and the obstacles it may be expected to encounter, not only from the greater or less force of the enemy, but from the nature of the ground, the distance of the place to be examined from our main body, the degree of security of the retreat, &c. If the affair consists merely in driving in an independent picket and holding its position long enough to make an examination, a strong patrol will be sufficient; but if it is necessary to examine a large portion of the enemy's position, or to ascertain his strength, a considerable force may be required. But every thing stated in this chapter relates more particularly to reconnoissances made with small detachments.

§ 518. Whatever may be the object of the reconnoissance and the composition of the detachment, the first thing is to determine the point from which the examination can be best made, and the principal effort must be directed to the occupation of this point. This effort should not be limited to a direct attack, but should be aided by several simultaneous attacks upon other points, in order to distract the attention of the enemy, divide his force, and throw him into irresolution. Such operations will be particularly useful if the object is to ascertain the strength of the enemy, for the partial attacks force him to show his whole force.

§ 519. Having occupied the point from which the reconnoissance is to be made, we should not be enticed into a pursuit of the beaten enemy, but proceed at once to strengthen ourselves in the position; that is, we should take measures for meeting the enemy with advantage when he returns to the attack: with this view, the safety of the flanks must be particularly attended to, to prevent the enemy from endangering the retreat of the detachment by turning the position.

§ 520. If the enemy makes a resolute attack before the reconnoissance is completed, the degree of defence must depend upon the importance of the object, that the sacrifice may be in proportion. A retreat commenced at the wrong time may encounter peculiar difficulty: to commence the retreat before the completion of the reconnoissance, is to abandon the work when nearly finished; remaining too long in position may expose us to useless loss. Therefore, if the object is to ascertain the strength of the enemy, the retreat should be commenced at once, because the enemy will soon recover from the first attack and gain the means of assuming the offensive.

§ 521. When a party has made a reconnoissance, its arrangements during the retreat present nothing unusual; it should carefully guard its flanks by strong parties or patrols, and always expect to be violently attacked.

§ 522. This is particularly to be anticipated when the object was to ascertain the strength of the enemy, and the retreat was commenced late. In such cases, prudence demands that we should place, beforehand, on the road of retreat, separate supports of sufficient strength to stop the pursuit and cover the retreat of the party.

§ 523. When the supports of the reconnoitring party are shown, and the enemy is near, it is prudent to have a considerable part, if not the whole, of the main body ready for action. For it may easily happen that the enemy, having been alarmed by the reconnoissance, and afterwards excited by its repulse and pursuit, may change his operations into a general attack, especially if he observes the slightest negligence on our part; in this case, all the advantage would be on his side.

Remark.—There are two kinds of reconnoissances: those to ascertain the general nature of the country, position and movements of the enemy, &c.; and those immediately preceding an action. The first should be made with extreme minuteness, and as much time given to them as possible; they may be well done by a man with but little genius and of a careful, business turn of mind. The second require the highest order of military genius, a rapid and unerring *coup-d'œil*, an accurate and instinctive knowledge of the tactics of all arms; they must be made with extreme rapidity, and acted upon at once.

There have been innumerable instances in military history, and not a few in our own, where, on the one hand, invaluable time and opportunity have been lost by the system of slow and minute reconnoissances in front of the enemy,—obtaining the horizontal curves of a field of battle; on the other hand, plunging headlong into action without a proper knowledge of the ground.

The important points are: the strength of the enemy, the key-points of his position, the nature of the ground between your own position and his; that is, is it passable, and for what arms? Let the subordinate commanders attend to minor obstacles. As soon as the proper information is obtained on these points, act. The mere moral effect of a rapid and unhesitating movement is very great. During the ordinary marches and intervals of rest, the cavalry and staff officers should collect every possible item of information; nothing is too trifling to be worth knowing; if they have done their duty properly, no general need hesitate more than a few minutes when he finds himself in presence of the enemy.

CHAPTER III.

OF CONVOYS.

Article 1.

The defence of convoys.

§ 524. The rules for escorting trains, and the arrangements for securing them against attack, were explained in Part I., Chapter I., Article 5; in the present article will be explained the manner of defending the convoy when attacked.

§ 525. The immediate defence of a very large train is, if not wholly impossible, at least very difficult; for it involves an injurious division of force.

§ 526. The following rules are laid down as the most important: to keep the force as much concentrated as possible, in order to act offensively, leaving with the wagons only the number of men absolutely necessary; if this is impossible, an effort should be made to keep the enemy away from the train as long as possible.

§ 527. In accordance with this, on the approach of the enemy, if the force of the escort is at all in proportion to that of the attacking party, it is best to move out to meet the enemy with the greater part of the escort, overthrow him, and clear the country in the direction of the march of the train. Even if the escort is much weaker than the enemy, it should move out to meet him, but must limit its subsequent operations to the defensive, endeavoring to keep the enemy away from the train long enough for it to gain a good defensive position.

§ 528. In the latter case, the train is, if possible, parked in square, or corralled. The escort, having kept off the enemy long enough to permit this, retreats upon the train; the defence, facilitated by the diminution of the space occupied, is now conducted in accordance with the general rules for the defence of the ground occupied, taking advantage of the obstacle presented by the wagons.

§ 529. If the attack is altogether by surprise, and is made on several points at once, so that it is impossible to collect all the wagons in one place, then each section of the train should be formed into a separate column, square, or corral.

§ 530. Any wagons loaded with powder or combustibles should be placed by themselves inside the square, or else formed into a separate park outside, placing them under cover of some defensible object.

§ 531. In these cases, it is very necessary to watch the movements of the wagons, which should move to their places at such a gait as to render confusion impossible.

Remarks.—At the commencement of the expedition, the commander of the convoy should issue detailed instructions as to the manner of forming square or corral in case of attack. In square, the hind wheels of the wagons should be towards the exterior, the wagons should be fastened together by the lock-chains, and in all cases intervals should be left for the passage of the escort at proper points; these intervals should be closed by chevaux-de-frise, chains, &c.

The train is most readily corralled when moving in two columns by file and abreast. The leading wagons halt at a suitable distance apart, the others oblique outwards, each wagon moving to the front as soon as it clears the wagon next in front of it; each wagon then halts with its inner hind wheel close to the outer fore wheel of the wagon which preceded it in the column, and these wheels are chained together; any desirable shape may be given to the corral by throwing the pole of each successive wagon more or less inward.

§ 532. If there is a reasonable probability of saving the train by the operation, it is best to concentrate it in a favorable position, and await assistance; if the escort is altogether inferior in force, it may be best to save the train by a retreat.

§ 533. When the wagons are formed in column, square, or corral, their defence devolves upon the infantry portion of the escort; the cavalry, remaining outside the park, can only co-operate by endeavoring to take the enemy in flank, &c.

§ 534. The enemy may send out small detachments with the object of alarming the convoy and delaying its march by forcing it to halt and form. Such parties should be driven off by detachments from the escort, without assembling the train, which should be parked only when the enemy attacks decisively and in considerable force. Therefore patrols should be sent out as far as possible, to discover the approach of the enemy and ascertain his force betimes.

§ 535. Having repulsed the enemy, the escort must not be induced to pursue him too far from the wagons; it is only necessary to take measures to allow the train to pursue its march.

§ 536. If the convoy is attacked when halted, the defence is conducted as already prescribed; but in this case the defence is easier, because the wagons are already formed and the escort in position. Even here it is best to try to keep the enemy at a distance, or, if the forces are at all equal, to defeat him, and then return to the train.

§ 537. The selection of the positions for rests and camps will have a great influence upon the success of the defence of the convoy. In the selection, preference will be given to those places which are favorable to the action of the troops composing the escort, or the greater part of it. For parking the train, places must be chosen at a distance from objects which would conceal the approach of the enemy, and enable him to hold a position dangerously near; on the other hand, it should be surrounded by objects preventing easy access, but not interfering with observation.

§ 538. At the park, the troops of the escort are posted as follows: the infantry and artillery bivouac inside the square; the first places its parties along the faces they are respectively detailed to defend, and posts guards and a chain of sentinels around the park; the guns are placed at the angles, and generally at the weakest points, or where it is easiest to sweep the ground in front.

The cavalry, bivouacked outside the park, places outposts and sends out patrols according to the rules for outpost service.

The draught-animals should be collected in the centre, so as not to interfere with the defence of the sides.

Article 2.

The attack of convoys.

§ 539. An attack upon a convoy may be intended either to capture it, to destroy it, or merely to alarm and delay it.

Independently of other considerations, the composition and force of the attacking party must depend upon the object in view.

§ 540. The general conditions for success in the attack of convoys are usually the same as for sudden attacks. The most favorable moment for attacking a convoy is when it is passing a defile, crossing hills, streams, &c.

§ 541. The main effort of the attack should be directed against the escort, especially if it is marching in one body, not only to occupy its attention, but also to separate it from the train if possible. At the same time, small parties should move upon different parts of the train, to prevent it from parking, carry it off, or destroy the wagons. A part of the troops must be held in reserve.

§ 542. If the train succeeds in parking, the operations against it become difficult for cavalry alone; in that case, the infantry and artillery must act.

§ 543. If the train or a part of it is captured, and it is possible to carry it off, the operations of the detachment change; it then escorts the wagons, as directed in Part I., Chapter I., Article 5, and acts as is laid down in the preceding article.

§ 544. When the attacking detachment is sent out merely to delay and annoy the convoy, it passes in advance of it, destroys the roads, ruins the crossings of streams, and alarms the convoys by partial attacks, particularly during the night and at well-known places.

CHAPTER IV.

OF FORAGING, AND ATTACKS UPON FORAGERS.

ARTICLE 1.

Of foraging.

§ 545.[1] **Under** the head of foraging are included the operations of parties detailed to obtain not only forage, but supplies of all kinds.

§ 546. Foraging is effected sometimes where there is no danger from the enemy, sometimes in places where an attack may be expected, and, in cases of extreme necessity, sometimes in places actually occupied by the enemy. The manner of conducting the operation is somewhat different in the three cases.

Remark.—If the enemy is so near that an attack may be expected, the artillery send out no foragers, so as not to break up the detachments with the guns and interfere with their readiness for action. In such cases, if it is not possible to supply the batteries from the temporary magazines, their foraging is imposed upon the cavalry.

§ 547. Foraging out of all danger from the enemy is effected as follows: a space for foraging is assigned to each party of the troops, and, if it is expected to remain some time in the same position, the villages are occupied by safeguards sent by the party in whose ground each falls. The foraging is commenced at the places nearest the enemy, falling back, as he approaches, to those immediately in our front, and finally to those in rear.

§ 548. For foraging, parties of men, with the proper number of officers, are detailed, and the necessary wagons sent with them; if the forage is to be packed on the troop horses, this is done as shown in figs. 11, 12. If the foraging is to be effected in villages, severe measures must be taken to prevent disorder and plundering on the part of the foragers.

§ 549. In this case, it is best not to take the party into the

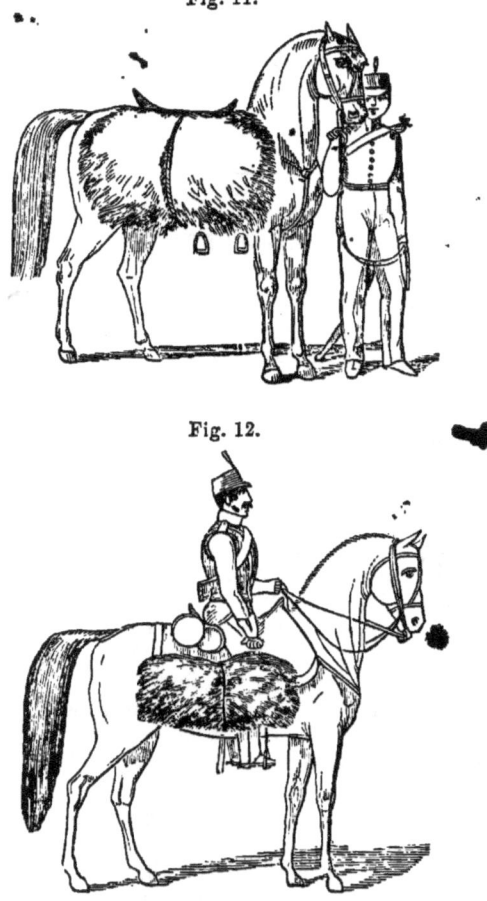

Fig. 11.

Fig. 12.

village, but to send for the chief persons and stipulate with them that the inhabitants shall bring the required forage and other stores out to the troops. If the inhabitants do not promptly comply with this moderate command, it is necessary to take the party in.

§ 550. In this event, all possible means must be taken to prevent disorder, as, for instance:

1. A certain number of houses are assigned to each company, so that the commander of the detachment may hold each company responsible for the disorders committed within its limits.

2. Guards are posted and patrols sent out, who arrest any foragers guilty of disorder.

3. If the form of the village permits, a part of the detachment remains at the centre to pack the hay and load the wagons as fast as the other men bring the forage from the houses.

§ 551. In places where an attack may be expected, the foraging is conducted as follows: Either fatigue parties are sent with wagons, or parties of cavalry with their own horses; in both cases a special escort is added for the protection of the foragers.

§ 552. In all cases, the strength of the escort depends upon the degree of danger, the space over which the foraging is to extend, and the distance from the enemy.

§ 553. During the march of foragers to and from the foraging-ground, if they consist of a fatigue party with wagons, an escort is added, which acts in conformity with the rules for escorting convoys.

If the foragers consist only of cavalry with their own horses, then on the outward march they move in one body, observing the precautions prescribed for movements near the enemy; on the return march, if the horses of the foragers are packed and led, the detachment acting as escort should not pack more than 40 pounds on their horses, so that the load may not prevent them from acting against the enemy.

Remarks.—Hay is packed as shown in figs. 11, 12.

One hundred and twelve pounds may be packed on a horse, as shown in fig. 11, and the horse must be led; 56 pounds are packed as shown in fig. 12, in two trusses.

§ 554. Sometimes the escort, or a part of it, may be sent out early to the foraging-ground, to take measures for the security of the foragers before they arrive.

§ 555. For the safety of the foragers when at their work, the escort is divided into two or three parts, according to circumstances: one part places a chain of outposts and sends out patrols, to guard the whole ground; another furnishes the supports of the outposts, and if there are infantry or mounted rifles with it they occupy the points which cover the approaches; the third part is placed in reserve near the centre of the ground, that it may easily reach any point attacked.

§ 556. If the enemy attacks while the foraging is going on, the escort should go to meet him or defend itself in position, endeavoring to stop him until the foragers have finished their work, and are drawn out on the road for their return march;

then the escort commences its retreat, acting as a rear guard, and endeavoring to keep the enemy as far from the foragers as possible. If it is impossible to hold the enemy in check long enough to finish the work, they should at least send forward and protect all the foragers who have packed their horses or loaded their wagons; the rest join the escort. If there is a probability of driving off the enemy by uniting all the foragers to the escort, it is best to abandon the forage already packed, and to begin foraging anew after having repulsed the enemy. It is permitted to abandon the forage entirely only in extreme urgency, when there is absolutely no other way of saving the foragers.

§ 557. If the enemy is repulsed, we must not be induced to pursue him any farther than enough to prevent a renewal of the attack, but must endeavor to complete the foraging.

§ 558. The foraging must not be extended over any ground not guarded by the escort. If the escort is too weak to cover the whole space designated for foraging, the ground is divided into parts, and the foraging effected in the different portions successively.

§ 559. If the foragers are attacked on their march, the defence is conducted as prescribed in the preceding chapter.

§ 560. If the foraging-ground is at a considerable distance from the camp, it will be a proper precaution to post a special detachment in support half-way.

§ 561. Foraging in places occupied by the enemy is undertaken only upon the entire exhaustion of the ground occupied by our own troops. Such foraging is covered by offensive operations, so that, having driven in the enemy's advanced troops or other parties, we may rapidly seize all the supplies to be found in the vicinity. This is called *forced foraging*.

§ 562. The strength and composition of a detachment for forced foraging must be such that it can overwhelm the enemy's troops, and remain long enough in position to enable the accompanying detachment of foragers to complete their work and retreat out of danger.

§ 563. The main conditions of success in such an enterprise are suddenness, rapidity, and determination in the attack, promptness in the work of the foragers, and tenacity in holding the positions taken from the enemy as long as necessary. Success will be greatly facilitated by partial attacks made upon different points of the enemy's position while the foraging is going on.

Article 2.

Of attacks upon foragers.

§ 564. Attacks upon foragers should be sudden and rapid, in order, by not giving the escort time to defend the points attacked, to produce confusion among the foragers and thus prevent them from working.

§ 565. The approach of the attacking party should be concealed, rapid, and compact; that is, it should not send out parties to any great distance in front or on the flanks, and, as a general rule, should not divide its force prematurely, but only the moment before the attack.

§ 566. The force of the detachment sent to attack foragers depends chiefly upon the object of the attack; that is, whether it is designed to capture the foragers, or only to prevent them from foraging by alarming them, or to prevent them from carrying off forage already packed.

§ 567. It is in all cases advantageous to begin with several simultaneous false attacks by small parties, to perplex the enemy and oblige him to divide the escort; then to direct the main party of the detachment upon the principal point of the enemy's arrangements, overthrow his weakened escort, and penetrate to the road of retreat, so as either to cut off and destroy a part of the escort and foragers, or to force them to abandon their work and fly, by threatening to cut them off.

§ 568. If from the disproportion of force it is impossible to prevent the foraging entirely, the attacking party confines itself to delaying the work: its operations, therefore, should consist in partial attacks upon several points, in order to alarm and disperse the foragers by breaking through the outposts at several points. Upon meeting a considerable force of the enemy, these attacking parties should at once retreat, and renew the attack in a different place. In such operations a portion of the attacking detachment should be kept together and held in reserve, as a support and rallying-point for the small parties.

§ 569. If they do not succeed in preventing the foraging, they may try to attack the foragers on the return march; observing in this case the rules laid down in the preceding chapter for attacks upon convoys.

CAVALRY TACTICS.

BASIS OF INSTRUCTION.

CAVALRY TACTICS.*

BASIS OF INSTRUCTION.

ARTICLE FIRST.

FORMATION OF A REGIMENT OF FIVE SQUADRONS IN ORDER OF BATTLE, (OR IN LINE.)

The squadrons of a regiment in order of battle are distinguished by the denomination of 1st, 2d, 3d, 4th, and 5th; they are formed on the same line, in the order of these numbers, commencing on the right, and with an interval of 12 paces.

This is the primitive and habitual order of the squadrons in regiments.

Each squadron is composed of four platoons, distinguished by the denomination of 1st, 2d, 3d, and 4th, commencing on the right.

The 1st and 2d platoons form the first division, the 3d and 4th form the 2d division.

The formation is in two ranks; the oldest soldiers in each platoon are placed in the front rank, and from right to left in each rank.

When the squadron is to be exercised, it is composed habitually of 48 files; consequently, each division is composed of 24 files, and each platoon of 12; if the squadron is increased to 64 files, the platoon is then divided into 2 sections; that on the right is the first, and that on the left the second.

That which is prescribed for the formation when mounted is applicable to the formation on foot.

Posts of the Officers and Non-commissioned Officers of the Field and Staff of a Regiment in Order of Battle.

(Plate 1.) The colonel 25 paces in front of the centre of the regiment, having a chief bugler behind him.

---

* The Nos. in this Basis of Instruction refer to paragraphs in the Authorized Cavalry Tactics, and should be thus consulted.

The lieutenant-colonel 12 paces in advance of the centre of the right wing.

The major 12 paces in advance of the centre of the left wing.

The colonel moves wherever his presence may be necessary.

The lieutenant-colonel and major move wherever the colonel may think proper to direct them.

The adjutant on a line with the front rank, 2 paces from the right of the regiment. When the regiment marches in line with the guide right, it is his duty to give the points of direction, and superintend the guides and the direction of the march.

The sergeant-major on a line with the front rank, 2 paces from the left of the regiment. He is charged with the same functions as the adjutant, when the march is in line with the guide left.

The adjutant, assisted by the sergeant-major, is also charged with the tracing of the lines.

The standard-bearer is placed at the last file but one from the left of the front rank of the platoon on the right of the centre of the regiment.

General staff officers serving with the regiment, 25 paces in rear of the right of the 1st squadron, according to rank.

The quartermaster-sergeant behind the adjutant, on the line of the rear rank.

The general guides of the right and left are placed in the rank of file-closers, in rear of the sergeant-major and quartermaster-sergeant.

The trumpeters, formed in two ranks, are posted 25 paces in rear of the centre of the regiment.

The trumpeters of a squadron acting separately are posted in the same manner, but in one rank.

Posts of the Officers and Non-commissioned Officers of a Squadron in Line.

The captain commanding is posted at the centre of the squadron, the croup of his horse 1 pace in front of the heads of the horses of the front rank.

The 2d captain 3 paces in rear of the centre of the squadron. He is charged with the alignment of the rear rank and file-closers.

The senior 1st lieutenant commands the 1st platoon; the other 1st lieutenant commands the 4th platoon.

The senior 2d lieutenant commands the 2d platoon; the other 2d lieutenant commands the 3d platoon.

Each of these officers is posted at the centre of his platoon, with the croup of his horse 1 pace in front of the heads of the horses of the front rank.

The senior sergeant is posted behind the 3d file from the right of the 1st platoon; he is the principal guide when the column of squadrons is left in front.

The 2d sergeant behind the 3d file from the left of the fourth platoon; he is the principal guide when the column of squadrons is right in front.

The 3d sergeant is posted on the right of the front rank of the squadron; he is not counted in the rank.

The 4th sergeant on the left of the front rank; he is not counted in the rank.

The 5th sergeant on the left of the 1st platoon.

The 6th sergeant on the right of the 2d platoon.

The 7th sergeant on the right of the 3d platoon.

The 8th sergeant on the right of the 4th platoon.

The heads of the horses of all the file-closers are at 1 pace from the croups of those of the rear rank.

The corporals are posted in the front rank, on the right and left of their respective platoons, and supply the places of sergeants when necessary.

When guidons are used, they are carried by the non-commissioned officers on the left of the 1st and 3d platoons.

Posts of Officers and Non-commissioned Officers of a Company acting singly.

The captain in front of the centre, 1 pace distant from the front rank.

The 1st lieutenant in rear of the centre, in the rank of file-closers.

The 2d lieutenant commands the 1st platoon; in the absence of a 3d lieutenant the 2d platoon is commanded by the senior sergeant. The chiefs of platoons are posted 1 pace in front of the centre of their respective platoons.

The 1st sergeant in rear of the right, in the rank of file-closers.

The 2d and 3d sergeants on the right and left of the troop not told off.

A non-commissioned officer is posted on the left of the 1st platoon, and on the right of the 2d.

Corporals, next to the sergeants who are on the flanks of platoons.

The saddler and farrier, in rear of the left of the troop, 8 paces retired from the line of file-closers; and the buglers, 20 paces in rear of the centre.

Assembly of a Regiment mounted.

When a regiment is to mount, *boots and saddles* is sounded; at this signal, the horses are saddled, bridled, and prepared to be led out.

At the signal *to horse*, the 1st sergeants direct the men to lead out.

The sergeants, corporals, and privates being in two ranks, in the order of their platoons, at the heads of their horses, the orderly sergeant calls the roll.

The captain directs them to call off by fours and to mount, and, on reaching the regimental parade, reports all absentees to the adjutant through his orderly sergeant.

The colonel detaches the troop which is to escort the standard; if the standard is too far from the parade-ground, the colonel detaches this troop before the regiment mounts.

In camps, or when the colonel lodges in the barracks, the standard-bearer goes for the standard escorted only by two sergeants.

In case of alarm or surprise, *to horse* is sounded; the men then saddle, pack up, bridle, and mount with the utmost celerity, and repair to the place of assembly, which is always previously designated.

Assembly of a Regiment dismounted.

When a regiment is to turn out under arms on foot, *to arms* will be sounded; at this signal, the men are formed and inspected, and the reports are made as is prescribed.

Formation of the Escort of the Standard.

(Pl. 2, *fig. A.*) The squadrons of a regiment, commencing with the first, furnish in turn the escort of the standard.

The captain commanding and the 2d captain alternate in the command of this escort.

It is composed of two platoons.

Each squadron, successively, furnishes first its two first platoons, and then its two last.

The 1st platoon of the escort furnishes the advanced guard, composed of two men in front *with the carbine advanced or pistol raised*, (according to the corps;) a corporal and four men with drawn sabres (or lances at *a carry*) march 10 paces from them.

The trumpeters, formed by fours and conducted by the adjutant, march 10 paces from the four men who precede.

The rest of the platoon, with drawn sabres, (or lances at *a carry*,) having the lieutenant at its head, marches by fours 10 paces from the trumpeters.

The standard-bearer follows immediately after, between two sergeants.

The 2d platoon, with drawn sabres, (or lances at *a carry*,) having the 2d lieutenant at its head, follows the standard-bearer, marches by fours, and furnishes the rear guard, composed of a corporal and two men, who march with drawn sabres, (or lances at *a carry*,) 10 paces in rear of the 2d platoon.

Two other men, *with the carbine advanced or pistol raised*, (according to the corps,) march 10 paces in rear.

The captain marches 4 paces from the left flank opposite to the standard-bearer.

This detachment having arrived where the standard is kept, without sounding the trumpets, is there formed into line.

The adjutant dismounts, takes the standard, and gives it to the standard-bearer.

Reception of the Standard.

As soon as the standard appears, the captain orders the sabres to be presented; the trumpets sound *to the standard*.

After this signal has been twice repeated, the captain orders the sabres to be carried, and breaks in the same order in which he came; the trumpets sound the *march*.

When the standard arrives, the colonel orders the sabres to be drawn; the trumpets cease to sound, and, with the escort, take their place in line, passing behind the regiment.

The standard-bearer, accompanied by the two sergeants, moves toward the centre of the regiment, parallel to the front, and halts before the colonel, fronting the regiment; the colonel then orders the sabres to be presented, and the trumpets to sound *to the standard;* he salutes with the sabre. The standard-bearer then takes his place in line, and the colonel orders the sabres to be carried.

The field officers salute with the sabre when the standard passes before them.

The standard receives the same honors on its departure as on its arrival, and it is escorted to the colonel's quarters in the order prescribed above.

On foot, the escort is composed in the same manner, and the standard receives the same honors.

Salute with the Standard.

When the standard is to pay honors, the standard-bearer salutes in the following manner, in two times:

1. At 4 paces from the person who is to be saluted, lower the lance gently to the front, bending as near to the horizontal line as possible.

2. Raise the lance gently when the person saluted has passed 4 paces.

Salute with the Sabre.

When the superior and other officers are to salute, whether on horseback or on foot, at a halt or marching, they do it in four times:

1. At 4 paces from the person to be saluted, raise the sabre perpendicularly, the point upward, the edge to the left, the hand opposite to and one foot from the right shoulder, the elbow 6 inches from the body.

2. Lower the blade, extending the arm to its full length, the hand in quarte, until the point of the sabre is near the foot.

3. Raise the sabre quickly, the point upward, as in the first time, after the person saluted has passed 4 paces.

4. Carry the sabre to the shoulder.

ARTICLE SECOND.

FORMATION OF A REGIMENT OF FIVE SQUADRONS IN COLUMN.

Order in Column by Twos or by Fours.

(Pl. 2, *fig. B.*) In this order the squadrons preserve an interval of 12 paces (12 yards) between each other, equal to their interval in line.

This distance is measured from the croups of the horses of the last files of one squadron, to the heads of the horses of the first files of the next squadron.

The colonel marches at the centre of the regiment, on the side of the guides, 25 paces from the flank of the column, having behind him a chief bugler. He moves wherever his presence may be necessary.

The lieutenant-colonel, on the side of the guides, 12 paces from the flank of the column; he marches habitually on a line with the lieutenant commanding the 1st platoon of the 1st squadron.

BASIS OF INSTRUCTION. 129

The major marches in the direction of the lieutenant-colonel, and on a line with the particular guide of the left of the 5th squadron.

The adjutant marches on the side of the guides, 2 paces from the flank, and on a line with the first files of the column, to observe the guides and the direction of the march.

The sergeant-major marches on the side of the guides, 2 paces from the flank of the column, and on a line with the particular guide of the left of the 5th squadron; if the left is in front, he executes on the side of the guides what is prescribed for the adjutant when the right is in front.

The quartermaster-sergeant, having the general guide of the right behind him, marches on the side opposite to the guides, 2 paces from the flank, and on a line with the first files of the column.

The captains commanding march on the side of the guides, and 4 paces from the flank, and abreast of the centre of their squadrons.

The second captains march on the side opposite to the guides, 4 paces from the flank, and abreast of the centre of their squadrons.

The 1st lieutenant of each squadron marches at the head of the 1st platoon, 1 pace in advance of the first files, having the particular guide of the right on his right.

The chiefs of the other platoons march on the side of the guides, 1 pace from the flank of the column, and abreast of their first files; the file-closers march on the side opposite to the guides, 1 pace from the flank, and on a line with the centre of their platoons.

They all march in a similar manner on the flanks of the column when the left is in front; and, in this case, it is the junior 1st lieutenant who marches in the column at the head of the 4th platoon of each squadron.

The particular guide, who in line is posted on the left of the squadron, marches behind the last files of the squadron; when the column is left in front, he takes post on the left of the officer commanding the 4th platoon, 1 pace in front of the left file.

When the nature of the ground obliges the officers and file-closers to enter the column, the movement is made successively; the superior officers, the captains commanding, and the chiefs of platoons, place themselves at the head; the second captains, and the file-closers, in rear of their respective troops.

The major marches in rear of the column; and also the sergeant-major.

The primitive order is resumed as soon as the nature of the ground will permit.

Order in Column of Platoons.

(Pl. 3, *fig. A.*) In this order, the distance from one platoon to another, measured from the men of one front rank to those of another front rank, is equal to the front of a platoon; that is to say, it is 12 paces if the platoons are of twelve files. Subtracting the depth of two ranks, which is 6 paces, there remains 6 paces from the croups of the horses of the rear rank of one platoon to the heads of the horses of the front rank of the next platoon, a distance which is equal to half of the front of a platoon.

The colonel marches at the centre of the regiment, on the side of the guides, 25 paces from the flank of the column, having behind him a chief bugler; he moves wherever his presence may be required.

The lieutenant-colonel marches habitually on the side of the guides, 12 paces from the flank of the column, and on a line with the lieutenant commanding the 1st platoon of the 1st squadron.

The major marches in the direction of the lieutenant-colonel, and habitually abreast of the file-closers of the last platoon of the column.

The adjutant marches behind the left file of the 1st platoon, to direct the guide of the column; he should occasionally place himself in front of this file, to satisfy himself that the guides of each platoon preserve the same direction.

The sergeant-major marches on the side of the guides, 2 paces from the flank of the column, and abreast of the file-closers of the 4th platoon of the 5th squadron; and, if the left is in front, he executes on the side of the guides that which is prescribed for the adjutant when the right is in front.

The quartermaster-sergeant, having the general guide of the right behind him, marches on the side opposite to the guides, 2 paces from the flank of the column, and on a line with the front rank of the 1st platoon.

The captains commanding march on the side of the guides, 4 paces from the flank of the column, and habitually abreast of the centre of their squadrons.

The second captains march on the side opposite to the guides, 4 paces from the flank of the column, and abreast of the centre of their squadrons.

The 1st and 2d lieutenants march at the centre of their platoons, 1 pace from the front rank; those who command the platoons at the head of squadrons preserve, besides their distance, the ground necessary to enable each squadron, in wheeling into line, to maintain its interval.

The sergeants, who are file-closers, march on the side opposite to the guides, behind the third file of their platoons.

When the column marches right in front, the particular guide of the right of each squadron marches on the right of the 1st platoon; and the particular guide of the left places himself as file-closer behind the 2d file from the left of the 4th platoon.

The posts of these sergeants are the reverse when the left is in front.

(Pl. 3, *fig. B.*) The squadron being composed of 64 files, when it is broken into sections, the 1st lieutenant of each squadron marches at the head of the 1st section of the 1st platoon; the chiefs of the other platoons remain on the side of the guides, 1 pace from and on a line with the front rank of their 1st section.

The file-closers who command the 2d sections march on the side opposite to the guides, 1 pace from and on a line with the front rank.

The posts of the commandants of sections are the reverse when the left is in front.

Order in Column of Divisions.

(Pl. 3, *fig. C.*) The colonel, lieutenant-colonel, major, and adjutant, are posted as in the column of platoons.

It is the same for the captains commanding and the second captains.

The senior 1st lieutenant commands the 1st division, the other 1st lieutenant the 2d; they remain, however, at the centre of their platoons.

All the other officers and sergeants of each division are posted as prescribed in the order in column of platoons, the file-closers remaining in their places, on whatsoever side the guide may be.

Order in Close Column.

Pl. 4.) In this order, the distance from one squadron to another, which is 12 paces, (12 yards,) is measured from the croups of the horses of the rear rank of one squadron, to the heads of the horses of the front rank of the next squadron.

The colonel, lieutenant-colonel, and major are posted as in column of platoons.

The adjutant marches behind the left guide of the 1st squadron, on the alignment of the file-closers, to superintend the direction of the march.

The sergeant-major is posted as in column of platoons, and, when the left is in front, he performs the same duties as the adjutant when the right is in front.

The quartermaster-sergeant marches on the side opposite to the guides, as in column of platoons.

The particular guide of the left wing of the 1st squadron moves to the front on the alignment of the officers; he is replaced by the sergeant file-closer of the 4th platoon. If the left is in front, the particular guide of the right of the 5th squadron places himself on the alignment of the officers to serve as guide; he is replaced by the sergeant file-closer of the 1st platoon.

All the officers of the squadron and the file-closers remain posted as in order of battle, except the captains commanding, who march on the side of the guides, 4 paces from the flank, and on a line with the officers of their squadrons.

Compliments by Cavalry under Review.

The regiment being in line, the captains 1 pace in advance of the centre of their companies, the lieutenants commanding platoons 1 pace in advance of the centre of their platoons, the colonel commands:

1. *Attention.*
2. *Prepare for review.*
3. *Rear rank, open order.*
4. MARCH.
5. *Right*—DRESS.
6. FRONT.

At the fourth command, the ranks are opened after the principles prescribed No. 436, all the officers in the rank of the file-closers advancing to the front, and placing themselves on the line of officers, opposite to the positions they before occupied. The staff officers place themselves on the right of the rank of company officers, according to their relative rank, 1 pace from each other. The quartermaster-sergeant and the sergeant-major are on the right of the front rank of the regiment.

The colonel, lieutenant-colonel, major, and adjutant are posted as in order of battle.

The music is formed at the same time in one rank on the right of the regiment, and 10 paces from it.

After the ranks are opened, the colonel commands:

1. *Attention.*
2. *Draw*—SABRE.

In this parade order, the regiment awaits the approach of the personage who is to review it; for whose guide a camp-color will have been placed 80 or 150 paces in front of the centre, according to the extent of the line and the plain in front of it.

When the reviewing personage is midway between the camp-color and the colonel, the latter turns his horse to the right about on his ground, and commands:

    1. *Attention.*
    2. *Present*—SABRE.

And resumes immediately his proper front. The officers all salute.

When the reviewing personage, who has halted until the proper compliments are paid, advances, the colonel brings his sabre to a carry, turns about as before to the line, and commands:

    1. *Attention.*
    2. *Carry*—SABRE.

When the whole line remains perfectly steady, except the colonel, who resumes his proper front.

The reviewing personage now turns off to the right of the regiment, passes thence, in front of all the officers, to the left, around the left, and behind the rank of file-closers, to the right again. While he is passing around the regiment, no matter what his rank, the music will play; and when he turns off to take his station near the camp-color, the music will cease.

When the music ceases, the colonel turns about, and commands:

    1. *Attention.*
    2. *Rear rank, close order.*
    3. MARCH.

At the command MARCH, all the officers from the rank of file-closers return to their position in that rank.

The reviewing personage having taken a position near the camp-color, previously placed at a proper distance, the colonel causes the regiment to break into column of companies, right or left, in front, and commands:

    Pass in review.

At this command, the band and trumpeters repair to the head of the regimental column, 6 paces in front of the colonel. The quartermaster-sergeant places himself 10 paces in front of the colonel, 2 paces from the flank opposite to the guides.

The quartermaster, surgeon, and assistant surgeon are in one rank, in the order in which they are named, 4 paces in rear of the last division.

The colonel is 6 paces in front of the captain of the leading company.

The lieutenant-colonel on a line with the first company, 6 paces from the flank opposite to the guide.

The major on a line with the last company, 6 paces from the side opposite to the guide.

The adjutant on a line with the second company, 6 paces from the flank opposite to the guide.

The sergeant-major on a line with the company next to the rear, 6 paces from the flank opposite to the guide.

Captains, 2 paces in advance of the centre of their companies.

Chiefs of platoons, 2 paces in advance of the centre of their platoons.

Officers of the rank of file-closers, on the side opposite to the guide, on a line with the chiefs of platoons.

The column is then put in march, at a walk, with the guide on the side next to the reviewing personage.

The column first passes at a walk, and afterward, if required, at a trot.

The regiments take, in marching, intervals of about 40 paces from each other.

When the head of the column arrives within 50 paces of the reviewing personage, the music commences to play.

The band having passed, the chief musician causes it to wheel out of the column and take position opposite to the reviewing personage; the music continues to play, until the last company has passed, when it ceases, and follows in the rear.

Passing at a walk, the colonel and all the officers salute with the sabre as they successively arrive within 6 paces of the reviewing personage, turning the heads toward him.

The standard does not salute, except to the President or Vice-President of the United States, Governors of States, heads of Departments, or the commander-in-chief; when the trumpets are to flourish in passing, the band ceases playing, and resumes the same air or march when the flourishes have ceased.

The guides and the men keep the head well to the front in passing in review.

Form and Course of Inspection.

The regiment being in line as prescribed for a review, on an intimation from the inspector, the colonel causes the companies to wheel to the right. He then orders the ranks to be opened; at which the standard-bearers, under the direction of the adjutant, are posted about 20 paces ahead of the column.

The colonel, seeing the ranks aligned, commands: 1. *Officers and non-commissioned officers.* 2. *To the front of your companies*—MARCH, on which the officers form themselves in one rank, 12 paces, and the non-commissioned officers in one rank, 6 paces, in advance, along the whole front of their respective troops, in the order of rank, the highest on the right, and the lowest on the left; the trumpeters of each company, at the same time, take post on the alignment of the front rank, 6 paces from the right; and the farriers in the rear on the alignment of the rear rank.

Seeing the last order in train of execution, the colonel commands: 1. *Field and Staff.* 2. *To the front*—MARCH. The commissioned officers thus designated form themselves in one rank, 12 paces in front of the standards, in the following order, beginning on the right: lieutenant-colonel, major, adjutant, quartermaster, surgeon, and assistant surgeon. The non-commissioned staff in a similar manner, 6 paces in rear of the preceding rank. The band is formed in one rank, 10 paces in rear of the column, the chief musician 4 paces in front of it.

The colonel now takes post on the right of the lieutenant-colonel; but such of the field officers as may be superior in rank to the inspector do not take post as above.

The inspection commences in front. After inspecting the dress and general appearance of the field and commissioned staff, the inspector, accompanied by these officers, passes down the column, looking at every rank, in front and in rear, with a view to the same objects. He afterward, in a like manner, passes and inspects the arms; as he successively approaches each company for this purpose, its captain commands: 1. *Attention.* 2. *Inspection—(of)* ARMS, which is executed as prescribed No. 405.

The inspector then dismounts with the field and commissioned staff, for the purpose of inspecting horse furniture, and valises, preparatory to which, the colonel causes the column to dismount. The men being then in the position of *stand to horse,* the colonel commands: REST, for the whole column; when the inspector proceeds to make a minute inspection of the several ranks, in succession, commencing in front.

On approaching the non-commissioned staff and the band, the adjutant gives the necessary orders for the inspection of boxes and valises; and in a like manner as to the standard-bearers. To enable the latter to display their valises, after dismounting, the standards are planted firm in the ground. This division being inspected, the adjutant may direct the standard-bearers to link and to disperse, until the standards are to be escorted back to the place from which they were taken. The non-commissioned staff may be dismissed as soon as inspected.

As the inspector successively approaches the companies, each captain commands: 1. *Attention.* 2. *Unstrap valises.* 3. *Open boxes;* when the valises are placed at the feet of the men, with the flaps from them. In this position the inspector may examine the contents of all the boxes and valises, or of as many as he may think necessary, beginning again with the non-commissioned officers, noticing, in passing, the tools, &c. of the farriers, and the trumpets of the musicians.

As the inspector passes each company, the captain orders the valises to be repacked and restrapped, and the men to file off to their tents or quarters, except the company which is to escort the standards, which awaits the orders of the colonel.

In an extensive column, some of the rearmost companies, when dismounted after the inspection of dress, general appearance, horses, and arms, may be permitted to *link*, awaiting the approach of the inspector. In this case, such companies resume the position above supposed, before the minute inspection.

ARTICLE THIRD.

DUTIES OF INSTRUCTORS.

The colonel is responsible for the instruction of the regiment, and he shall not change, under any pretext, the dispositions contained in this book.

He will be present, as often as his other duties permit, at the theoretical and practical instructions, and especially at that of the officers assembled together.

The lieutenant-colonel and major are especially charged with the supervision of the instruction of their respective wings.

Individual instruction being the basis of the instruction of squadrons, on which that of a regiment depends, and the first principles having the greatest influence upon this individual instruction, the classes of recruits should be watched with the greatest care.

The instructors place themselves habitually at such a distance that they can see their whole troop at a glance, and make themselves distinctly heard by it. They leave their place as seldom as possible, and only to make the corrections which are indispensable in the position of the men and the execution of the movements.

They repeat, in a few clear and precise words, the explanations which have not been well understood; and, not to overburden the memory of the men, they always use the same terms to demonstrate the same principles.

They should often join example to precept, should keep up the attention of the men by an animated tone, and pass to another movement as soon as that which they command has been executed in a satisfactory manner. In fine, they should become every day more exacting in regard to precision and unity.

When at rest, the instructor questions the men, to satisfy himself that their lessons have been well understood. In the theoretical instruction, he requires the commands and explanations to be given as if they were on the ground.

ARTICLE FOURTH.

DIVISION, ORDER, AND PROGRESSION OF INSTRUCTION.

As instruction cannot be established on a solid basis without joining theory to practice, there is in each regiment a theoretical instruction, independent of the exercises in the field.

From the first of November to the first of May, the colonel assembles the officers at least twice a week, for the theory of the different parts of their instruction.

The major and adjutant assemble, in a like manner, the sergeants and corporals.

From the first of May to the first of November, these theoretical exercises occur once a week for all, and oftener if necessary.

The practical instruction is divided into instruction on foot and instruction mounted.

The instruction on foot, as well as the instruction mounted, includes the school of the trooper, the school of the platoon, and the school of the squadron.

The school of the trooper is divided into four lessons, and each lesson into two parts.

The school of the platoon is divided into four articles.

The school of the squadron is divided into four articles.

Instruction.

Each lesson lasts one hour and a half, without including the rests.

When the weather is bad, the men are exercised in the riding-house. They are conducted to the riding-ground whenever the weather will permit.

The horses of the orderly sergeants and trumpeters cannot

be excused on any pretext from participating in the different classes of instruction.

The horses which have not been trained are sent out with a snaffle-bridle at least three times a week; and, as far as possible, they are all saddled and ridden.

The colonel causes the squadrons, divisions, and platoons to be commanded by all the officers in turn, in order to satisfy himself of their instruction, and to instruct those who are not already sufficiently instructed.

During the summer, and until the end of October, the regiment is exercised alternately at the evolutions and in the details of the service in war. For this purpose, whenever it is practicable, the colonel takes the regiment into the country, in order to accustom it to pass over all kinds of ground, and to apply the evolutions to the different localities.

The remount horses are sent out every day for two hours, saddled and bridled, with a snaffle.

The non-commissioned officers and privates, who are negligent in the different exercises, either on foot or mounted, are put back into the lower classes.

When the regiment is assembled, the colonel should direct the superior officers to command, occasionally, in the different evolutions, in order to judge of the progress of their instruction. He should also require the other officers to exercise a command superior to that of their grades, when the instruction is sufficiently advanced.

ARTICLE FIFTH.

GRADATION OF INSTRUCTION.

Recruits.

The recruit commences his instruction on foot. The first week after his arrival at the regiment is employed exclusively in instructing him in all the details of discipline, police, and interior service, and in those relating to his dress and the grooming of his horse.

He is taught to mount without saddle, on both sides of the horse.

He is taught the name and use of the principal parts of the arms and equipments, and the manner of keeping them clean; the manner of rolling the cloak, of folding the effects, and of placing them in the valise.

BASIS OF INSTRUCTION.

These different instructions are given by the corporal of the squad, under the superintendence of the sergeant and officer of the platoon.

At the end of this week, the recruit commences the first lesson on foot; he continues to be instructed in the above-mentioned details.

The recruits are drilled on foot twice a day, when possible, and an hour and a half each time. Half an hour of this time is employed in teaching them the duties of guards.

At the end of six weeks, or two months at most, the recruits should be able to mount the quarter guard, and, consequently, they should have commenced the fourth lesson on foot.

Before the recruit mounts guard, he learns the different parts of a complete equipment, and the means of preserving it; and also the manner of saddling, bridling, unsaddling, and unbridling, and of packing his effects on the horse.

After he has mounted his first guard, his instruction on horseback is commenced, care being taken to give him a gentle and well-trained horse.

Recapitulation of the Time necessary to instruct a Trooper to the School of the Platoon Mounted, inclusive.

DISMOUNTED.

School of the Trooper.

1st lesson	{ 1st part, 4 lessons	}	12 lessons.
	{ 2d " 8 "		
2d "	{ 1st part, 6 "	}	18 "
	{ 2d " 12 "		
3d "	{ 1st part, 5 "	}	10 "
	{ 2d " 5 "		
4th "	{ 1st part, 15 "	}	30 "
	{ 2d " 15 "		
Total..........................			70 lessons.

School of the Platoon.

NOTE.—As the school of the platoon dismounted should progress conjointly with that of the trooper mounted, the number of lessons will be such as may be judged necessary.

MOUNTED.

School of the Trooper.

1st lesson	{ 1st part,	5 lessons	}	20 lessons.
	2d "	15 "		
2d "	{ 1st part,	20 "	}	40 "
	2d "	20 "		
3d "	{ 1st part,	15 "	}	30 "
	2d "	15 "		
4th "	{ 1st part,	15 "	}	30 "
	2d "	15 "		

Total............................ 120 lessons.

School of the Platoon.

1st article,........................... 15 lessons.
2d   "   15   "
3d   "   15   "
4th   "   15   "

Total........................ 60 lessons.

It results from this gradation, that the trooper, after 180 lessons or days of instruction, should be able to enter the school of the squadron.

Corporals.

The corporals should be capable of executing all the lessons mounted and dismounted, and should be qualified to teach at least the two first lessons dismounted, and the first lesson mounted.

Their theoretical instruction should include, in addition to these lessons, all the details relative to the functions of their grade in the interior service, both in garrison and in campaign.

The colonel selects, in each squadron, a certain number of privates, who may be admitted to the theoretical instruction of the corporals.

Sergeants.

The sergeants should be capable of executing, dismounted and mounted, all that is prescribed by this book; and should be able to teach the lessons of the school of the trooper. They should likewise know all the details of the service, so as to have it in their power to conduct their troop and replace the chiefs of platoons if necessary.

The theoretical instruction of the sergeants should include the basis of instruction, the school of the trooper, the school of the platoon, and the school of the squadron; also, the regulations for the interior service in garrison and in campaign, so far as their grade is concerned.

The colonel selects, in each company, those among the corporals whom he judges fit to be admitted to the theoretical instruction of the sergeants.

Officers.

Every officer, from the colonel to the 2d lieutenant, should be able to command according to his rank. No one will be considered fully instructed unless he can also explain and execute all that is contained in this book.

The *theory* of the officers should include this book and all the regulations which prescribe their duties in their different positions, either in peace or war.

Every officer who joins the regiment for the first time must be examined on his theoretical and practical instruction by the colonel.

If the faults committed on drill by an officer of any rank whatsoever arise from negligence or want of instruction, the commandant of the regiment shall cause him to be immediately replaced.

If the colonel thinks proper, he may excuse from the theory, every other time, those officers whose instruction is completed.

ARTICLE SIXTH.

INSTRUCTION TO MOUNT WITHOUT SADDLE, TO PACK UP, TO SADDLE, AND TO UNSADDLE.

Manner of Vaulting.

Seize the mane with the left hand, hold the reins of the snaffle in the right hand, and place it on the withers, the thumb to the left, the fingers to the right; raise yourself lightly on the two wrists, the body straight; pass the right leg, extended, over the croup of the horse, without touching him, and seat yourself gently on horseback.

To dismount, pass the left rein of the snaffle into the right hand; place this hand on the withers; seize the mane with the left hand, raise yourself gently on the two wrists; pass the right leg extended over the croup of the horse, without touching him; bring the right thigh near the left, the body straight, and come to the ground lightly on the toes, bending the knees a little.

Manner of packing up the Effects.

The uniform pantaloons, folded the length of the valise, should be well spread out in the bottom.

The white pantaloons, folded in the same manner, placed on the uniform pantaloons.

The shirts, unfolded, are laid on the white pantaloons.

The soldier's book on the shirts.

The cap-cord on the book.

The shaving-case, the pocket-handkerchiefs, the gloves, and the socks, divided equally in the ends.

The second pair of boots under the flap of the valise.

The plume in its case, along with the boots.

The stable-jacket in the valise-wallet; and also the forage-cap, which is placed in the middle.

The stable-frock, rolled the length of the cloak, in the forage-sack.

The things used in grooming, the brushes, grease-box, and other cleaning-utensils, in the holster-pouch.

Manner of rolling the Cloak.

The cloak being entirely unfolded, the sleeves are laid flat and extended parallel to the two front edges of the cloak; each one is then turned up and folded near the elbow, so as to give a length of 3 feet 6 inches from one elbow to the other, the middle of the cloak remaining uncovered. The cape is then turned down over the sleeves, in such a manner that the front edge may exactly cover those of the cloak.

The lower extremity of the cloak is turned up about 10 inches; the skirts are likewise turned toward each other, so that they may touch the fold of the sleeves, and that, being folded a second time upon themselves, they may give to the cloak the form of a rectangle; the lower extremity of the cloak is then turned up about 7 inches, and it is rolled as tightly as possible, commencing at the collar and pressing the knee upon it as it is rolled, to hold it. The part of the cloak which is rolled is then introduced into the sort of pocket formed by the part which is turned back.

Manner of adjusting a Saddle.

HEAVY CAVALRY.	LIGHT CAVALRY.
The saddle should be placed on the horse without a blanket, in order to see clearly whether its shape agrees with that of his back.	The saddle should be laid on the horse without a blanket, in order to see clearly whether its shape agrees with that of his back.
In order that the saddle may be well placed, it is necessary that the point of the bow should be three fingers in rear of the point of the shoulder; that the gullet leave sufficient room on the withers and loins to permit the hand to be passed easily between these parts and the saddle when the trooper is mounted; that the front part of the gullet be sufficiently wide to prevent the pad from pressing on the side of the withers; that the bars bear equally upon all parts without touching the back-bone, and that the points of the bow do not press upon the back. The breast-strap should be placed above the point of the shoulders, so as not to interfere with their movements, and the crupper should not be stretched, for fear of wounding the horse under the tail.	In order that the saddle may be well placed, it is necessary that the front end of the bars should be three fingers in rear of the point of the shoulder; that the bows be sufficiently elevated above the withers and loins to allow the fist to be passed under the rear bow, and almost as much under the front one, when the trooper is mounted; that the ends of the bars do not bear upon the back, and that the finger can be passed under them; that the rest of the bars bear flatly on the back, in such a way, however, that the finger may be passed between their upper edge and the back, and that they may be at least two fingers' breadth from the backbone. The breast-strap should be placed above the point of the shoulders, so as not to interfere with their movement. The leathern heart should be in the middle of the breast, and the crupper should not be stretched, for fear of wounding the horse under the tail.

To attach the stirrups to the saddle, run the stirrup-leather through the eye of the stirrup, pass it through the loop, and draw it up until the loop touches the eye of the stirrup: then, holding the stirrup-leather in such a manner that the buckle may be turned toward the horse, run it through the hole or staple in the saddle from above, and draw it down; fasten it at the proper length by means of the buckle, run it through the loop which is under the buckle, and pass the end twice through the same loop.

When the stirrup is arranged in this manner, and hangs naturally, the buckle will be on the inside next the horse.

Manner of Saddling.

HEAVY CAVALRY.

Approach the horse on the left side, and lay the blanket, folded in 4 equal parts, on his back; the edges on the left side, the large fold on the withers.

Seize it, then, with the left hand on the withers, and with the right on the loins; slide it once or twice from front to rear, to smooth the hair, taking care to raise it in carrying it forward, so as not to brush up the hair.

The blanket should be so arranged as not to project beyond the bars in rear.

Throw the girths over the seat of the saddle, and also the crupper, which is held with the left hand.

Seize the saddle with the same hand at the pommel, the right hand under the cantle, place it gently on the horse's back, bringing it from the direction of his croup, in order not to frighten him, and place it a little in rear, that the crupper may be put on without drawing it back. Let down the girths and crupper, step behind the horse, seize the tail with the left hand, and twist the hair around the dock with the right hand, which then seizes the crupper and passes the tail through it, taking care that none of the hair remains under it, which would hurt the horse.

LIGHT CAVALRY.

Approach the horse on the left side, and lay the blanket, folded into 12 or 16 thicknesses, on his back; the edges on the left side.

Seize it, then, with the left hand on the withers, and with the right on the loins; slide it once or twice from front to rear, to smooth the hair, taking care to raise it in carrying it forward, so as not to brush up the hair.

The blanket should be so arranged as to project one finger's breadth beyond the bars in rear.

Seize the saddle at the pommel with the left hand, at the cantle with the right hand, and place it gently on the horse's back, bringing it from the direction of his croup, in order not to frighten him, and place it a little in rear, that the crupper may be put on without drawing it back. Let down the girth, breast-strap, and crupper; step behind the horse, seize the tail with the left hand, and twist the hair around the dock with the right, which then seizes the crupper and passes the tail through it, taking care that none of the hair remains under it, which would hurt the horse.

Step to the right side of the horse, and, seizing the saddle at the cantle with the left hand, and at the pommel with the

Step to the right side of the horse to let down the right stirrup, return to the left side, raise up the saddle, carry it forward, taking care that the blanket is smooth, and that it does not compress the withers, which is avoided by raising it up over this part; see that there are no straps caught under the saddle; begin by fastening the first girth, which is passed through the loop of the breast-strap; the second girth less tight than the first girth and surcingle, because it is the one which most impedes the respiration of the horse; then buckle the breast-strap and let down the left stirrup.

right hand, raise it and carry it forward, without moving the blanket; see at the same time that there are no straps caught under the saddle; place the girth flat, and pass it through the loop of the false martingale; return to the left side by the head of the horse; run the left hand between the withers and the blanket; raise it up a little so that it will not compress the withers; buckle the girth and the breast-strap.

Manner of packing the Effects on the Horse.

HEAVY CAVALRY.

The schabraque being on the saddle, the front part turned back on the seat, and the packing-straps run through their holes, fasten the cloak and the forage-sack containing the stable-frock, drawing the middle-strap very tight, that the cloak may be on the pommel. With the cloak-straps, fasten the ends of the cloak and forage-sack in such a manner that the ends shall not project beyond the schabraque. Place the pistol in the holster in front of the cloak, and fasten the strap in the ring of the butt. Place the hatchet in its case, and turn down the front of the schabraque.

Extend the right and left

LIGHT CAVALRY.

The schabraque being on the saddle, the front part turned back on the seat, the surcingle passed through the loop of the false martingale, the packing-straps run through their holes, fasten the cloak and the forage-sack containing the stable-frock, drawing the middle-strap very tight, that the cloak may be in front of the pommel, falling down in front of the holsters. With the cloak-straps, fasten the ends of the cloak and forage-sack in such a manner that the ends shall not project beyond the schabraque. Place the pistol in the holster inside of the cloak, and fasten the strap in the ring of the butt. Place the packing-straps upon the croup; place the wallet flat upon the pillion; lay the middle packing-strap over the wallet; place the valise with the buckles toward the saddle; fasten it tightly with this strap; fasten the wallet and valise together with the side-straps; then attach the forage-cord, rolled and twisted into a circle, to the left pack-strap, under the schabraque; in the same manner, attach the watering-bridle on the right side; see that there is no fold in the valise, and that it lies flat.

When nose-bags are used, they will be attached to the pommel, on the off side.

hatchet in its case, turn down the front of the schabraque, and pass the gun-strap through its hole.

Extend the right and left packing-straps upon the croup; place the wallet flat against the cantle; lay the middle packing-strap over the wallet; place the valise with the buckles toward the saddle; fasten it tightly to the peak with this strap; fasten the wallet and valise together with the side-straps; then attach the forage-cord, rolled and twisted into a circle, on the left side, under the schabraque; in the same manner, attach the watering-bridle on the right side to the straps which are fixed to the saddle for that purpose; see that there is no fold in the valise.

Fasten the lock-cover to the cloak-strap on the right side, the buckles against the schabraque.

When blankets are used instead of schabraques, they will be folded twice, with the edges placed on the off side.

To have the effects well packed, the three straps must be tightly buckled, and must come up straight three inches from each other; the three buckles on the same line in the middle of the valise; the valise and wallet square, so that both can be seen from behind. (*Light Cavalry*, the wallet placed in such a manner that it cannot be seen from behind.)

The valise and wallet should not incline to either side.

The cloak and other articles in front should be so arranged as to raise the bridle-hand as little as possible.

Nothing should project beyond the schabraque.

If a bundle of forage is to be carried, it is placed on the valise, a little to the rear, and tied to the packing-straps.

When the carbine is in the boot, it is so placed that its end may be 4 or 5 inches from the horse's shoulder, without projecting beyond it; it is fastened to the saddle by the gun-strap, which makes two turns round the small of the stock. The carbine must never be left in the boot when the horses enter or go out of the stable.

Manner of Bridling.

Stand on the left side of the horse, the reins of the snaffle and of the curb-bridle in the bend of the left arm, the top of the headstall on the forearm. Seize the curb-bridle and the snaffle by the top of the headstall with the right hand, the nails downward; pass the arm over the horse's neck, so that the hand may be in front of his head; seize the snaffle-bit with the left hand near the ring, and the curb-bit near the boss, taking care that the snaffle-bit is above the curb-bit; place them together in the horse's mouth, pressing the left thumb upon the bars to make him open it; pass the horse's ears between the front and top of the headstall, commencing with the right; run the nose-band through the square rings of the halter, so that the part of the halter over the nose may be covered, and buckle it, leaving the cheek-pieces of the snaffle outside; hook the curb, buckle the throat-strap, passing it under that of the halter; fasten the button-hole of the halter to the button on the top of the headstall; clear the forelock; pass the reins of the snaffle and curb-bridle over the horse's neck; attach the halter-strap, with the end wound up, to the holster-strap on the left side. (*Light Cavalry*, to the cloak-strap.)

If the horse is properly bridled, the buckles of the cheek-piece, and of the throat-strap, on the right side, will be at the same height, and those of the cheek-piece, throat-strap, and snaffle, on the left side, will form a kind of crow's foot; the throat-strap will not be so tight as to impede the respiration; the cheek-pieces will be in rear of the temples, and the snaffle-bit will be above the curb-bit.

Manner of Unbridling.

Unhook the curb, unbuckle the nose-band, then the throat-strap, unbutton the halter, unroll the halter-strap, and fasten the horse to the rack until he is unsaddled; bring the reins of the snaffle and curb-bridle on the top of the head, pass them over the ears, let them fall into the bend of the left arm; take off the bridle from the horse's head, beginning with the right ear; make two turns around the bridle, with the reins below the front piece, and pass them between the front and top of the headstall, so that the bridle may be hung up.

Manner of Unpacking.

Unbuckle the packing-straps, ending with the middle one; take off the valise and wallet; unbuckle the front packing-straps; take off the lock-cover; turn back the front of the schabraque on the seat; unbuckle the cloak-straps, ending with the middle one; take off the cloak and the sack; free the pistol from its strap, and take it and the hatchet out of the holsters; take off the forage-cord and watering-bridle; unbuckle the surcingle, and take off the schabraque, or blanket; double the schabraque, or blanket; lay all the effects on it, roll them up in it, and fasten them with the surcingle.

The trooper then rolls up all the straps, and unsaddles in the prescribed manner.

Manner of Unsaddling.

HEAVY CAVALRY.	LIGHT CAVALRY.
Strap up the stirrups, unbuckle the breast-strap, the surcingle, the first girth which is freed from the loop, then the second; carry the saddle a little back to free the tail from the crupper; raise the saddle, passing the left arm along the gullet; take the girths in the right hand to put them on the saddle if they are clean; if not, they will be wiped before being put up; take off the blanket, double it with the wet side inward, lay it on the saddle and fasten it there by means of the crupper, which is turned up and attached to the cloak-strap.	Unbuckle the breast-strap, pass the end of it through the holster-strap to hold it up. Unbuckle the girth; step to the right side, free the girth from the loop of the false martingale; turn up the girth and breast-strap if they are clean, and, if not, after having wiped them; then throw over the right stirrup, carry the saddle a little back to free the tail from the crupper, throw over the left stirrup and take off the saddle with both hands, the left hand hold of the pommel, the right at the cantle; take off the blanket, double it with the wet side inward; lay it on the saddle and fasten it there by means of the crupper, which is turned up and attached to the cloak-strap.

ARTICLE SEVENTH.

OF THE BIT.

(Pl. 6, *fig. A.*) The bit is composed of seven principal pieces of iron, viz.:

The *mouth-piece* (1), *the branches* (2), *the rings* (3), *the curb* (4), and *the cross-bar* (5).

The other pieces are the *S* (6), and the *hook* (7).

The *mouth-piece* is fixed to the branches by the *fonceaux* (8), and is divided into *barrels* (9), and *crook* (10).

The *barrels* act upon the bars and render the horse obedient, with the assistance of the curb.

The *crook* forms a place for the tongue.

The *branches* cause the mouth-piece and curb to act. Each one is divided into *eye of the cheek-piece* (11), *eye of the hook* or *S* (12), *banquet* (13), *bow of the banquet* (14), *tongue of the banquet* (15), and *ring-eye* (16).

The *eye of the cheek-piece* serves to pass the cheek-piece through. The *eye of the hook* or *S* serves to hold the hook or S of the curb. The *banquet and tongue of the banquet* serve to unite the mouth-piece to the branches. The *bow of the banquet* serves to strengthen the branch, and the *ring-eye* is to hold the rings for the reins.

The object of the *cross-bar* is to strengthen the bit, and to prevent the branches from hooking the reins of the other horses.

(*Fig. B.*) The *curb* is composed of *links* (1) and *rings* (2); the *links* act upon the horse's chin, and the *rings* serve to fasten the curb to the *S* and the hook; they are three in number, two on the side of the hook and one on the side of the *S*.

The *S* serves to fasten the curb to the bit, and the *hook* to hook the curb.

The *bosses* (17) are ornaments to cover the fonceaux; there are holes in them by which they are riveted to the branches.

(*Fig. C.*) The *snaffle-bit* is composed of five pieces of iron:

The *right side* (1).
The *left side* (2).
The *uniting ring* (3).
The *rings* (4), to receive the check-pieces and reins.

(*Fig. D.*) The *bit of the watering-bridle* is composed of four pieces of iron:

The *right side* (1).
The *left side* (2).

Two *rings with wings* (3), to receive the reins and cheek-pieces.

To bit the horse properly, it is necessary to understand:
1st. The effects of the bit.
2d. The horse's mouth.
3d. The conformation of the horse.

The bit is *medium* (*fig. E*) when the branches (1) are *straight*, that is, when the eye of the ring is in the prolongation of the line passing through the centre of the fonceaux and the eye of the cheek-piece; and when the mouth-piece is *mean*, that is, with the barrel (2) large and rising, and the crook not much elevated.

The bit is *mild* (*fig. F*) when the branches (1) are short and the eye of the ring in rear of the line; and when the mouth-piece is *straight*, that is, when the barrel (2) is large near the branches, slopes upward a little, and is almost without crook.

The bit is *severe* (*fig. G*) when the branches (1) are long, with the eye of the ring in front of the line; and when the mouth-piece is *powerful*, that is, when the barrel (2) is straight and small, and the crook elevated.

The position of the eye of the branch renders the action of the bit more or less powerful. If the eye is high, the bit resists the motion of the branches and produces a stronger impression on the mouth and chin. If, on the contrary, the eye is too low, the bit yields to the motion of the branches, and produces less effect.

It is necessary to consider the interior and exterior parts of the horse's mouth.

The interior parts are the *tongue*, the *canal* in which the tongue rests, the *tusks*, the *bars*, and the *inside of the lips*.

The exterior parts are the *bones of the lower jaw*, the *canal* between these bones, the *slit of the lips, the outside of the lips*, and the *chin*.

The most sensitive parts of the horse's mouth are the *bars* and the *chin;* the *tongue* and the *lips* are less so. Bars which are elevated, sharp, and without flesh, denote sensibility; it diminishes in proportion as the bars become lower, round, and covered with flesh, and as the chin becomes thick and fleshy.

When a horse is well made and free in his motions and gait, it is to be presumed that he has a good mouth.

When a horse has a heavy head and limbs, and is lazy and clumsy in his gaits, it is to be presumed that he has a bad mouth.

When a horse has long slim legs, a long body, and is loosely put together, great care is requisite in the choice of a bit, as he submits with difficulty to the action of it, not being able to endure its effects without pain, or without endeavoring to avoid them.

When a horse has the bars elevated, sharp, and without flesh, the tongue thin, and the canal sufficiently large to hold it, he should have a straight bit (*fig. F, No.* 2), that the barrel, being thicker near the branches, may press upon the tongue and lips, and ease as much as possible the other parts of the mouth. The tongue and lips, from their slight degree of sensibility, being able to sustain the bit, prevent it from producing too great an effect on the bars and pressing on them in such a manner as to cause pain.

When a horse has sensitive bars, a thick tongue, and the canal too small to hold it conveniently, he should have a medium bit (*fig. E, No.* 2), that, the tongue having a little liberty, the bit may press at the same time on the bars and tongue, without causing inconvenience. A straight bit, in such a mouth, would deprive the tongue of its liberty, and would bear entirely upon that part which is the least sensitive; the mouth would be incommoded, the horse would bear upon the hand, and would resist.

When a horse has low, round, and fleshy bars, he should have a severe bit (*fig. G, No.* 2), because bars of this kind, possessing little sensibility, can only acquire it from the action of the bit, which presses upon them.

When a horse has too large a mouth, he should have a bit with long branches.

When the horse has a small mouth, he should have a light bit; but as the small quantity of iron might be unpleasant to him, from the delicate and sensitive bars which these horses usually have, it is necessary to use the straight mouth-piece with short and mild branches.

When a horse throws out his head to the front, he should have, to prevent it, long and severe branches (*fig. G, No.* 1); if at the same time he has a sensitive mouth, which is frequently the case, he should be given a straight mouth-piece (*fig. F, No.* 2).

When a horse carries his head low, and against his breast, he should have short branches (*fig. F, No.* 1); if at the same time his mouth is not very sensitive, which is not uncommon, he must have a severe mouth-piece (*fig. G, No.* 2).

Horses which are lower before than behind are rarely well upon their haunches; they feel the extra weight which the croup throws on the shoulders, want confidence in their legs, and seek the aid of the bit. They generally have a bad mouth, and bear upon the hand. They should have a severe bit with *powerful* branches (*fig. G, Nos.* 1 *and* 2). When the mouth is very sensitive, which is rare with this kind of horses, a straight mouth-piece (*fig. F, No.* 2) is arranged with powerful branches (*fig. G, No* 1). This mouth-piece moderates the effect of the branches.

Horses which are lower behind than before generally have a fine neck and shoulders; but their proportions show little strength in the hinder parts. They are light in their fore parts, and apt to rear; they should have short and mild branches (*fig. F, No.* 1).

The bit should bear upon the bars one finger's breadth above the lower tusks: if it bore higher, it would wrinkle the lips and hurt the bone of the bar, which is sharper there; lower down, it would touch the upper tusk. In no case should the top of the mouth-piece touch the palate.

The bit should be neither wide nor narrow: in the first case, it becomes displaced and does not fit; in the second case, it compresses and wounds the mouth, and may cause the horse to contract the habit of seizing the branches with his lips, or of taking one of them between his teeth.

The curb should be arranged so as to produce its effect upon the chin, and not to compress it when the bridle-hand does not act. It should be neither long nor short: in the first case, it would permit the bit to swing, which would destroy its effect; in the second case, it would restrain the horse too much, and lead him to resist.

When young horses are bridled for the first time, a piece of leather or felt may be placed between the curb and chin, as their chins are often very sensitive. These means are no longer used after they have become accustomed to the effect of the bit.

A bit which is well adjusted should act upon all parts of the mouth, according to their sensibility.

Horses resist the bit when it causes pain; the most sensitive are the most impatient: when the bit hurts them, they rush forward to escape the pain, which they imagine to be a punishment. The more they are restrained by an unskilful hand, the greater the compression of the bars becomes; it increases the evil instead of allaying it, and gives the horse a bad mouth.

When a horse shakes his head, it is a sign that the bit incommodes him. There are horses which persist in the habit of shaking the head after the bit has been properly arranged; the hand alone can then correct this vice, and not the martingale, which is improperly supposed to be a remedy.

As a general rule, all horses should have a mild bit; and, as it is impossible that each horse in a regiment should have a particular bit, they are furnished of three different patterns: there is one-sixth of *mild bits,* four-sixths of *medium bits,* and one-sixth of *severe* bits.

ARTICLE EIGHTH.

MANNER OF TRAINING YOUNG HORSES.

The remount horses are not mounted immediately after their arrival at the regiment; they are merely led out by men mounted on trained horses; in winter, the warmest part of the day is chosen for this exercise. They must be led sometimes on the right and sometimes on the left side.

When the horses have perfectly recovered from the fatigues of the journey, they are ridden out.

They move always at a walk, the men merely requiring their horses to follow those which precede in the column.

The horses being thus habituated to carry the weight of a man, they are taught in the stables to suffer themselves to be saddled, to have the foot taken up, the shoe struck, &c.; observing always, if the horse objects, to make use of gentle means to remove his fears.

It should be borne in mind that nothing must be required of young horses beyond their strength, and that punishment is to be resorted to only at the last extremity and when well assured that the faults arise from viciousness and not from ignorance.

The horses should be gentle to mount, should march on a straight line and circular line at all paces, should back, make a few side steps to the right and left, suffer pressure in the ranks, leap the ditch and bar, and should not be alarmed at the noise of arms and drums, or the waving of standards and the flags of lances.

To avoid repetition, this article presents only those details which regard the horse, and that which is prescribed in the *schools of the trooper and platoon* is conformed to for the commands and execution of all the movements, observing to follow the progression of these *schools* from point to point, but always with a view to the instruction of the horse.

FIRST LESSON.

The horses saddled, and with snaffle-bridles, are placed in one rank 3 paces from each other.

The lesson in mounting is given to each horse separately, the instructor holding him by the reins of the snaffle; the trooper caresses the horse on coming up to him, puts his foot carefully in the stirrup, raises himself without abruptness, seats himself in the saddle, and caresses the horse again; he pauses longer on the stirrup in proportion as the horse becomes more calm, and he mounts and dismounts successively on the right and left side, to render the horse more submissive.

To teach the horse the effect of the reins, they should be opened without abruptness, but freely, so as to leave no doubt of what is required of him.

To teach him the effect of the legs, the trooper has two switches, one in each hand; they must be of a pliant wood, sufficiently long to reach the horse behind the girths, just where the legs close. The legs are closed gradually, and if the horse does not obey, the switches are used, the force of the blow being increased progressively, until he learns to move off at the sole pressure of the legs. The switches are afterward used only when he hesitates.

To make the horse turn, open freely the rein on the side toward which he is to turn, and close the leg on the same side; if he does not obey the pressure of the leg, use the switch on that side; when the movement is nearly finished, diminish the effect of the rein and leg, sustaining him with the opposite rein and leg.

At the commencement, the horse is made to describe large arcs, and he is brought by degrees to turn upon the arcs described in the first lesson.

When all that is above prescribed is perfectly understood, the instruction commences.

The instruction is not given at a halt, as is required in the first lesson of the school of the trooper, but the march in column is performed on the track, as in the second part of that lesson; the instructor places a trained horse at the head, and the men preserve an interval of 3 paces, that they may conduct their horses more easily.

The troopers should, at first, preserve great suppleness in their position, and pliancy in their movements, that they may not discourage the horses, already annoyed by a weight to which they are not accustomed. The horses should not yet be required to march very straight; it is sufficient that they are made acquainted with the reins and legs by bringing them back to the line when they are too far from it, and by using the means prescribed for the passage of corners.

This first instruction is given at a walk, to render it easier to the horse.

It is especially in the execution of the right wheel, left

wheel, right-about wheel, and left-about wheel, that the troopers should use the reins and their legs with precision, in order that the horses may become well acquainted with them.

To make the horse back, the instructor, having dismounted, places himself in front of the horse, seizes one rein with each hand, and bears upon the snaffle.

If the horse refuses to back, the instructor, having taken both reins in one hand, with the other touches him gently on the fore-legs with a switch, caresses him when he obeys, and stops him after two or three steps. He is not required to back straight.

During the first days, the instruction should be short, and interrupted by frequent repose.

During the moments of repose, the lesson in mounting is repeated; and when the horse no longer stirs, the trooper mounts and dismounts without his being held by the instructor. If the horse is still unquiet, the instructor holds him again until he becomes calm, seeking to give him confidence, and being very careful not to ill-use him, which would only render him more restive.

After a few days' instruction, the horse is taught to hold himself straight, and more precision is exacted in the passage of the corners, as well as in all the movements and changes of direction, but always at a walk.

The trooper begins to lessen the movement of the reins a little, and to make less use of the switches, that the horse may become more and more accustomed to obey the *aids* alone.

When the horse has learned to hold himself straight, and when he obeys the hands and legs tolerably, the instructor causes him to take a moderate trot; but he is not kept long at this pace.

At a trot, the same precision is not at first required in the position and movements of the horse as at a walk; it is acquired by degrees.

The horses are practised in backing when mounted; the troopers should act with great gentleness, contenting themselves at the commencement with making the horse take two or three steps to the rear, without requiring him to back straight.

Whenever a horse has obeyed, the hand should be held lightly, and he should be caressed.

SECOND LESSON.

The horses, saddled, and bridled with a snaffle, are placed in one rank 3 paces from each other.

When the horses obey the aids sufficiently, the switches are no longer used, but they are then made acquainted with the spur; it is only used when the horse does not obey the legs. In this case, the trooper, having conformed to what is prescribed in No. 315, applies both spurs vigorously, at the moment when the horse commits the fault; at the same time the bridle-hand is slackened, unless the horse should have left the track, when he will be replaced on it. The spurs should never be applied unseasonably, in a spiritless manner, or one after the other, for fear the horse may acquire a habit of kicking.

The horses are now required to move perfectly straight on a straight line, and to bend themselves a little in turning to the right or left. They are afterward made to trot alternately to the right and to the left hand, great attention being paid to give them a free and regular gait.

When the horses have acquired suppleness and courage, the trot becomes more frequent, and lasts longer; and all the movements and changes of direction which have been executed at a walk are repeated at this gait.

The oblique march from a halt is not executed.

When the horses perform well on a straight line, they are placed in the ring, and made to take a few turns in each direction, first at a walk, and then at a trot. When the horses are in the ring, they should have the position described in No. 327.

The horses are made to execute the right wheel, left wheel, right-about wheel, and left-about wheel, and they are thus confirmed in their knowledge of the reins and legs.

At the end of the lessons, the horses, being more calm and obedient, are made to pass successively from the head to the foot of the column, which is done with great care, and those which leave the track in spite of all precautions are brought back to it with great gentleness.

This lesson is repeated, the horses being taken indiscriminately from the centre of the column.

The trot is not yet commenced from a halt, nor are the horses halted when moving at that pace.

When the horses trot well, the pace is increased, but only for one or two turns at the most.

They then take one or two turns at a gallop, merely to give them a first knowledge of this gait, to try their strength, and to increase their suppleness, without requiring them to start correctly.

Young horses are apt to run away in starting at a gallop; the troopers should endeavor to calm them, and should especially avoid exciting them too much.

BASIS OF INSTRUCTION. 157

Finally, they are taught to take a few side steps, as it is prescribed in No. 342.

This exercise, being difficult for the horse, requires great mildness and patience on the part of the instructor; a few movements of the shoulders to the right and left, and one or two side steps, are sufficient for the first time.

When a horse refuses to obey, the instructor shows him the whip, and, if that is not sufficient, he touches him lightly with it behind the girths; the horse is caressed after he has obeyed.

The lesson in backing is repeated, but with more strictness, and if the horse throws himself out of the line, he is cautiously replaced on it.

During the moments of repose, the troopers being in column, or in one rank at 3 paces from each other, the instructor causes them to mount and dismount alternately on the right and on the left side.

THIRD LESSON.

For this lesson the horses are bridled with the curb-bridle.

The instruction at a halt, which is prescribed in No. 354, is not given.

The horses marching on the track, the first thing is to accustom them to the weight of the bit; to effect this, the trooper guides his horse with the snaffle only, which he holds by the middle in his right hand, taking care to hold the reins of the curb-bridle so loose that the bit will not act.

When the horse no longer shows any uneasiness, he is taught the effect of the bit.

Whenever there is a corner to pass, the horse is *gathered* by making use of the snaffle; the horse having obeyed, and having begun to turn to the right or left, the snaffle is slackened, and the movement is completed with the bridle-hand; if the horse still shows hesitation, the bridle is slackened, and the snaffle is again used.

The snaffle, used in this manner in passing the corners, and in all changes of direction, teaches the horse by degrees the effect of the bit, and the use of it is insensibly diminished until he can be guided with the left hand alone.

The effect of the bit being much more powerful than that of the snaffle, the movements of the left hand should therefore be more progressive.

In all difficult movements, such as *to go out of the column, to passage*, &c., if the instructor finds some of the horses undecided, he will make the troopers use the snaffle.

FOURTH LESSON.

The horses being perfectly gentle to mount, and knowing how to back properly, the troopers mount and dismount in two ranks, as in Nos. 268, 292, and 293.

The instruction is the same as in the preceding lessons, but the troopers are armed. The carbine is in the boot, and the sabre in the scabbard; in proportion as the horses become accustomed to it, the carbines are slung, and the sabres drawn.

The manual of arms is then executed, first at a halt, afterward when marching at a walk and at a trot, as in the 4th lesson of the *school of the trooper*, the greatest gentleness being always used, to accustom the horse to it by degrees.

Manner of accustoming the Horses to leap the Ditch and the Bar.

At the end of the lesson, and before the horses return to the stable, they are practised in leaping the ditch and the bar.

This instruction demands many precautions and great care. The ditch is leaped before the bar, which is more difficult.

At the commencement, the ditch should be narrow and not deep, and the bar should be quite low.

The horses are always led at first, care being taken to put at their head a horse already used to this exercise.

To prevent the horse from stopping short, as it often happens, he is made to pass by the side of the ditch, and over the bar, which has been let down, in order that he may see beforehand the obstacles which he is to leap.

After these precautions have been taken, the trooper holds the end of the bridle-reins in the right hand, and runs to the ditch or bar, which he leaps the first; the instructor follows the horse, shows him the whip, and cracks it at the same time, to make him follow; the trooper caresses him after he has leaped.

If the horse refuses, the instructor forces him with the whip, using great patience, but never suffering him to return to the stable until he has leaped.

The horses should leap only once, or at most twice, a day; were it repeated too often, they would at last become discouraged.

The horse should not be made to leap mounted, until he has leaped without hesitation when led. For this purpose, each trooper, on arriving at the ditch or bar, follows what is laid down in No. 415 and the following paragraphs.

When a horse refuses to obey, it is necessary to take room and try again to make him leap, placing him, when necessary, a few paces behind another horse which leaps freely; the instructor follows, to compel him with the whip, and if, in spite of all precautions, he still refuses to leap, the trooper dismounts, leads his horse, and does not mount again until he leaps without hesitation.

Assembly of the Young Horses in a Platoon.

To accustom the young horses to the pressure of the ranks, and to the movements which they must execute together, the progression of the four articles of the *school of the platoon* is followed, conforming to what follows.

The successive alignments at a halt are not practised at first with the young horses, because they are not generally sufficiently calm.

In the formations, the troopers should keep their horses straight, and align themselves as they arrive on the line; but once in the rank and halted, they should no longer seek to put them straight, or to close, as the young horses are impatient when too long gathered, and almost always resist.

In beginning to march, by twos, by fours, and by platoon, the troopers should preserve sufficient space, taking care not to close; they should relax the thighs and legs, require little from their horses, and calm those which are excited by stopping and slackening the bridle.

When the horses are calm and march quietly, the troopers approach boot to boot, without, however, pressing each other; and it is not until then that more exactness is observed in the distances, directions, and alignments.

The horses which suffer most from pressure are placed on the flanks, and they are taken gradually toward the centre, where the pressure is more felt.

In the march in column and in line, attention is paid to the gaits, to render them equal and regular,—without changing the formation too often, until the horses are perfectly trained.

Wheeling by platoon is practised; but these movements are frequently to be interrupted by direct marches, to calm those horses to which the pressure sometimes becomes too severe. The pace of the horses near the pivot being slackened, they become impatient at being thus restrained by the hand of the rider, and they almost always resist, when they are made to wheel for a long time, and often.

They execute, at a walk only, the right wheel, left wheel,

right-about wheel, left-about wheel by fours, taking care not to repeat them too often.

They are made to gallop by twos, by fours, and by platoon, but not long at a time; no other movements are executed at this pace.

The young horses are not practised at the charge.

On the last day of their instruction they are mounted with arms and baggage; should any horse be rendered uneasy by the valise, and kick and resist, he is separated from the troop, and is accustomed by degrees to the valise by mounting him apart, and by letting him stand packed in the stable an hour or two each day.

When the horses are sufficiently trained, and some weeks before they enter the squadron, they are practised in the different formations of the *school of the platoon*, at the quick paces, the gallop being used with great moderation.

Manner of accustoming Young Horses to Firing, and Military Noises.

A few trained horses, accustomed to the firing, are mounted with the young horses; toward the end of the lesson, the troopers who mount the former separate themselves a few paces from the others and fire pistols, while the others continue to march on the track; the troopers taking care to quiet and caress those which are excited or frightened.

This method is continued during some days, the troopers approaching nearer and nearer, and finally firing inside of the square; they fire afterward when returning to the quarters, at first in rear of the column, then near the centre, and at last at the head, facing it at the distance of a few paces.

There will be an interval between the shots at first, and they will be fired more frequently in proportion as the horses become more calm, taking care not to burn them with the grains of powder.

When the young horses are somewhat accustomed to the noise of arms, the troopers who ride them, having loaded their pistols between the lessons, fire one after another at a signal from the instructor.

This lesson should be given with care, the firing being stopped when the horses become excited; after they have become more calm, the shots are repeated with shorter intervals. The carbines are afterward used.

Should there be any horses so restive as to throw the others habitually into disorder, they must be sent back to the stable;

they are then taken out separately, every morning and evening, to accustom them to the noise of arms. For this purpose they are led to the riding-ground, where pistols are fired while they are caressed, and a few oats are given them. The shots are first fired from a distance, and approach gradually. After the horses become accustomed to them, they are joined to the others, to receive the same lessons when mounted.

When the horses are no longer frightened at the successive carbine or pistol shots, they are formed at the end of the riding-ground; they are marched gently toward some dismounted men placed at the other end, who fire together several times in succession; when the horses are within fifty paces, the firing ceases, and they are marched on until they come up to the men, where they are halted and caressed.

An officer is always present at this lesson, to see that it is given properly and without disorder.

The young horses are likewise accustomed to the manual of arms, the waving of standards, colors, and the flags of lances, to the noise of drums, and finally to all military noises. This is always done at the end of the lessons, the same progression being followed and the same gentle means used.

Horses that are difficult to Train.

Young horses often offer a resistance, the cause of which should be known in order to apply a remedy.

Some jump from gayety or too much spirit; they should be brought back gently to the track, without ill-using them, and should be calmed by stopping and slackening the bridle, very little use being made of the legs.

Others jump from viciousness, and to throw their rider; they must be made to feel all the degrees of the *aids* to quiet them, punishment being employed as a last resource, as it would make them worse were it too prompt or too frequent.

In regard to horses which stop and refuse to advance, this may arise from weakness, from fear, or from obstinacy.

If it be from weakness, which may be readily seen from the conformation of the horse and the manner in which he moves, the work must be proportioned to his strength.

If it be from fear, he must be taken up gently to the object which frightens him, stopping occasionally before arriving at it, slackening the bridle, encouraging him by the voice, and using all means to give him confidence. When he has at last come up to the object, he is permitted to smell it, to show him that he has nothing to fear, and he is then caressed. In no case should a timid horse be punished, as that would only increase the evil.

Finally, if it be from obstinacy, after all gentle means have been tried, the whip must be resorted to; as the spur often induces the horse to resist still more, it is for the instructor who knows him, to prescribe or forbid the use of it.

There are some horses which have a habit of rearing. The rider must throw the upper part of the body forward, without deranging his seat; he must slacken one rein and draw upon the other.

There are other horses which kick. The rider must throw the body a little to the rear, without stiffness, raise the bridle-hand to prevent the horse from putting his head between his legs, and force him to move off by closing the legs.

It is rarely that a horse kicks up straight; he almost always throws the croup to the right or left. While conforming to what has been said above, the trooper should bear harder upon the rein on the side toward which the horse kicks, in order to oppose *the shoulders to the haunches*.

When a horse intends to kick up while in motion, it may be perceived from the slackening of the pace of his fore-legs. In the same manner, his intention to rear may be known by the slackening of his hind-legs.

If the horses have resisted both gentle means and punishment, recourse is had to the longe.

Lesson of the Longe.

This lesson requires great caution, in order not to injure the horse in trying to subdue him; the lesson should last but half an hour, or three-quarters at most, and there should be frequent repose.

The cavesson serves to moderate the pace of the horse, and to bring him near the centre when he is in the ring. It likewise serves to drive him from it, by shaking the longe. It may also be used to repress his faults.

With the whip, the pace of the horse is increased, he is driven from the centre, and he is corrected.

The instructor uses the whip and the cavesson alternately, to overcome the resistance of the horse; but he is very careful not to use both at once, nor to use them improperly, the abuse of the cavesson inclining the horse to resist, and throwing him on his haunches; that of the whip, tending to discourage him and make him restive.

The longe should be held so long as not to tire the horse by forcing him to move on too small a circle.

The horse should have a watering-bridle, and the cavesson

BASIS OF INSTRUCTION.

should be arranged in such a manner as not to impede the respiration.

An instructor and an assistant are necessary to give this lesson; the assistant holds the longe and places himself at the centre. To start the horse upon the ring, the instructor leads him by the inner rein, holding the whip behind himself with the other hand; he walks with the horse as long as necessary; in proportion as the horse moves with more confidence, he separates from him, holding the longe in the right hand (when moving to the right) and the whip in the left hand, until he is at an equal distance from the horse and the person who holds the longe. He follows the movements of the horse constantly, and uses the longe, or the whip, as may be necessary, to keep him on the ring, or to maintain the pace.

If the horse stops short when the instructor leaves him, if he backs, or pulls upon the longe, and refuses to move on at the cracking of the whip, he is again led upon the ring, that he may better understand what is required of him.

On leaving him again, the instructor shows him the whip, and even touches him with it between the shoulder and the belly, if necessary; he gives the horse more liberty in proportion as he moves with confidence.

If the horse gallops instead of trotting, the instructor shakes the longe lightly by a very gentle horizontal motion of the hand.

After a few turns, the instructor diminishes the ring and tries to stop the horse by the voice, and to make him come to him; he caresses him when he has obeyed, makes him take a few steps to the rear, and leads him upon the ring to the other hand, with the same precautions.

At the end of the lesson, and when the horse has become more docile, he is mounted, not to work in the longe, but to obtain from him that which he has refused to do; if he is submissive, little should be required of him,—he should be caressed, and the cavesson should be taken off.

If, in spite of all the precautions and patience of the instructor, the horse still refuses to obey, he is again put in the longe before being sent away, and these lessons are continued until no more resistance is offered.

The longe may also be used (but with great caution) to give suppleness to those horses which are in want of it.

ARTICLE NINTH.

DEFINITIONS AND GENERAL PRINCIPLES.

A *Troop* is composed of ranks and files.

A *Rank* is composed of men abreast of each other.

A *File* is composed of two men, one behind the other.

File-leader is a man of the front rank of a troop, relatively to the one who is behind him in the rear rank.

File-closer is an officer or sergeant posted behind the rear rank.

Front is the direction perpendicular to the alignment of a troop and before it, either in column or in line.

Centre is the middle of a troop.

Wings are the two grand divisions into which any body of men is divided, when in line.

Flank is the right or left side of a column, or line.

Interval is the vacant space between two troops, or between the fractions of a troop in line. It refers more particularly to the space which the squadrons of a regiment in line should preserve between each other.

This interval is 12 paces, (12 yards,) measured from the knees of the sergeant (not counted in the rank) on the left of a squadron, to the knees of the sergeant on the right of the squadron which follows in order of battle.

On foot, it is measured from the elbows of the same sergeants.

Distance is the vacant space from one troop to another in column, or between the ranks of a troop, either in line or in column.

The distance between the open ranks, when mounted, is 6 yards, measured from the croups of the horses of the front rank to the heads of the horses of the rear rank; on foot, this distance is 6 paces.

When the ranks are closed, the distance, if mounted, is 2 feet, measured from the croups of the horses of the front rank to the heads of those of the rear rank; on foot, it is 1 foot, measured from the breast of a man in the rear rank to the back of his file-leader.

When a troop is formed in column of platoons, or divisions, the distances prescribed are measured from the men of one front rank to those of another front rank; on foot, they are measured from the elbows of the men of one front rank to the elbows of the men of another front rank.

Depth is the space included between the head and the rear of a column.

The depth of a column of platoons is equal to the front which the troop occupied in line; it is measured from the head of the horse of the officer commanding the first platoon, to the croups of the horses of the file-closers of the last platoon.

To estimate the front of a troop, and the depth of a column, it is necessary to know that a horse, when mounted, occupies in breadth one-third of his length; this breadth is a little less than a yard. To avoid fractions, and arrive at the same result by a more simple calculation, having regard also to the room which the men must always preserve in the ranks, it is supposed to be 1 yard. The length of a horse being 3 yards, the two ranks occupy 6 yards, with a distance of 2 feet between the ranks; a space which is necessary to prevent them from interfering on the march.

Taking the above dimensions for a base, the front of a squadron will consist of as many yards as there are files, plus the two sergeants on the flanks. There will be a difference, however, according to the corps, and the manner in which the regiment is mounted; commandants of corps should satisfy themselves of it, by causing the front of their squadrons to be measured.

Alignment is the placing of men, or troops, on the same line. There are two kinds: *individual alignment* and *alignment by troop*.

Individual alignment is when men are placed abreast of each other, in a parallel direction, and without one being in front or in rear of another.

Alignment by troop is when a troop places itself on the prolongation of a line already formed.

Every troop which is to form and align itself on another, halts on a line with the file-closers, parallel to the line of formation, to place itself afterward on the alignment of the troop which is already formed.

The commandant of a troop places himself, to align it, on the side indicated by the command; it is the same if the troop which he commands serves as base of alignment to another troop. But the commander of a troop which aligns itself on another moves on the opposite side to align it.

A *Platoon* is composed habitually of 12 files; it may also be increased to 16; in that case, it is divided into 2 sections.

A *Division* is composed of 2 platoons.

A *Squadron* is composed of 2 divisions, or 4 platoons.

A *Regiment in order of battle* (or *line*) is composed of its squadrons disposed on the same line, with their intervals.

It is in *natural order* when the squadrons are placed in the order of their numbers from right to left.

It is in *inverse order* when the first squadrons are on the left of the line, and the last on the right, or when the subdivisions of each squadron are inverted. This order should be used only when circumstances require it.

A *Column* is the disposition of a troop which has broken, and of which the fractions are placed one behind another.

There are three kinds of columns: *column in route, column with distance,* and *close column.*

Column in route is formed of men by twos, or by fours.

Column with distance is formed of platoons, having between them the distance necessary to form in line in every way. This column may also be formed of divisions; but the proportion of a platoon front is the most advantageous for all movements.

Close column is formed of squadrons with a distance of 12 yards from one to another; the object of this disposition is to give the least possible depth to the column.

The column has the *right in front* when its fractions are disposed according to the order of their numbers, from front to rear.

The column has the *left in front* when the last fractions, in the order of their numbers, are in front.

Fixed points, or *points of direction,* serve to point out the direction in which a troop in line, or in column, is to march; or else to mark the right and left of a line.

Intermediate points are those taken between the fixed points. They are used to preserve the desired direction during the march, or to insure the rectitude of the formation of the lines.

General guides are the two sergeants who, in the formation of a regiment, mark the points where the right and the left are to rest.

They are selected in the first and last squadrons, and are under the orders of the adjutant and sergeant-major, for the tracing of lines.

Principal guides are the sergeants who serve to mark the intermediate points in the formation in line.

The sergeants, file-closers of the 1st and 4th platoons, are the principal guides of their respective squadrons.

Particular guides are the sergeants who place themselves on the line of formation, to mark the front of their squadrons as they arrive.

The two sergeants of the flanks, who are not counted in the rank, are the particular guides of their respective squadrons.

Guide of the march in line is the sergeant file-closer of one of the wings, who, in the march in line, replaces the particular guide in the front rank, when the latter places himself on the alignment, to insure the direction of the march by serving as an intermediate point.

Guide of the column is the man on one of the flanks of the front rank of a column; he is charged with the direction of the march.

The guide is always left when the right is in front; the exceptions to this general rule are pointed out in the title of the evolutions.

In the oblique march, the guide is on the side toward which the march is made; and when the primitive direction is resumed, after having obliqued, the guide is where it was before having obliqued.

In a column composed of cavalry and infantry, the guides of the cavalry cover the second file of the subdivisions of infantry on the side of the guides. In line, the officers, who are in front of the squadrons, align themselves on the rear rank of the infantry.

Wheel is a circular movement executed by a man, or troop, returning to the point of departure.

When a troop makes a wheel, it turns upon one of its flanks; each of the men composing it describes a circle, larger in proportion to his distance from the central point.

About face, or *wheel*, is the half of a wheel.

Right, or *left face*, or *wheel*, is the fourth of a wheel.

Right half, or *left half face*, or *wheel*, is the eighth of a wheel.

Right quarter, or *left quarter face*, or *wheel*, is the sixteenth of a wheel.

Pivot is the front-rank man of the flank on which the wheel is made. There are two kinds: the *fixed pivot*, and the *movable pivot*.

The pivot is *fixed* whenever he turns upon himself; he is *movable* when he describes an arc of a circle.

The arc of a circle described by the pivot of a rank of two, of four, of eight, or of a platoon making the fourth of a wheel, is 5 yards; for a division it is 10 yards; and for a squadron it is 20 yards.

Ployment is the movement by which a regiment forms from line into close column.

Deployment is the movement by which a regiment forms from close column into line.

Formation is the regular placing of all the fractions of a troop either in line or in column.

Paces. There are three kinds: the *walk*, the *trot*, and the *gallop*.

On foot there are two kinds of step: the *common step*, and the *quick step*.

When the command does not indicate the pace, the movement is always made at a walk, if the troop is halted; if it is marching, the movement is made at the pace at which it was already marching.

On foot the movements are executed habitually at the *quick step*, without the command being given. When they are to be executed at the *common step*, the command should signify it.

The pace, when used as a measure, is 3 feet. On foot it is 2 feet 4 inches.

A horse passes over about 100 yards per minute at a walk, 240 at a trot, and 300 at a gallop.

On foot the common step is at the rate of 90 per minute; the quick step is at the rate of 120 per minute.

The *direct march* is that which is executed by a troop in line or in column, to move off perpendicularly to its alignment.

The *march by a flank* is that by which ground is gained to the right or left after having made the fourth of a wheel.

The *diagonal march* is thus called in relation to the front from which it commences by changing direction by the eighth of a wheel to the right or left, in order to arrive at a given point on the right or left.

The *oblique march* is that by which, when moving forward, ground is gained toward one of the flanks without changing the front. There are two kinds: the *individual oblique march*, and the *oblique march by troop*.

The *individual oblique march* is that which is executed by an individual movement of each man.

The *oblique march by troop* is that which is executed by the movement, at the same time, of each of the subdivisions of a troop in line.

The *circular march* is that which is executed by describing a circle or portion of a circle.

Countermarch is a movement by which the men of each rank, after having made successively the fourth of a wheel to the right or left, form themselves facing the rear, parallel to the first formation.

The *charge* is a direct, quick, and impetuous march, the object of which is to reach the enemy.

Skirmishers (or *flankers*) are men dispersed in front, in rear, or on the flanks of a troop, to cover its movements or its position.

Obstacle is any thing in the nature of the ground which obliges a troop in line to ploy a part of its front.

Defile is a passage which compels a line to ploy into column, or a column to diminish its front.

Evolutions are the regular movements by which a regiment passes from one order to another.

Evolutions of line are these same movements executed by several regiments, on one or several lines. Their application, combined with the position or movements of the enemy, is called *manœuvres*.

Commands. There are three kinds:

The command of *caution*, which is, attention. It is the signal to preserve immobility, and to give attention.

The *preparatory command*. It indicates the movement which is to be executed.

It is at this command that the horses are *gathered*.

The command of *execution*, which is, MARCH, or HALT.

The tone of command should be animated, distinct, and of a loudness proportioned to the troop which is commanded.

The command *attention* is pronounced at the top of the voice, dwelling on the last syllable.

The commands of *execution* are pronounced in a firmer tone than the *preparatory* commands. They are prolonged, because the movement which is to follow them being communicated from the man to the horse, all jerking or abruptness is thereby avoided.

In the exercise on foot, and the manual of arms, the part of the command which causes an execution should be pronounced in a firm and brief tone.

The commands of caution, and the preparatory commands, are distinguished by *italics;* those of execution, by CAPITALS.

Those preparatory commands which, from their length, are difficult to be pronounced at once, must be divided into two or three parts, with an ascending progression in the tone of command, but always in such a manner that the one of execution may be more energetic and elevated. (*The divisions are indicated by a dash* —.) The parts of commands which are placed in a parenthesis are not pronounced.

Time, in the detailed instruction, is an action of exercise which is executed at a command or part of command, and which is divided into *motions*, to demonstrate the mechanism and facilitate the execution of it.

Soundings are the trumpet signals, which make known to the troop the movements or details of service which are to be executed.

ARTICLE TENTH.

(The book of signals is at the end of the work.)
1. The general.
2. Boots and saddles.
3. To horse.
4. The assembly.
5. To arms.
6. To the standard.
7. The march. (It also answers for a quick step on foot.)
8. The charge.
9. The rally.
10. Reveille.
11. Stable call.
12. Watering call.
13. Breakfast call.
14. Assembly of the guard.
15. Orders for the orderly sergeants.
16. Assembly of the trumpeters.
17. Retreat.
18. Fatigue call.
19. Dinner call.
20. Distributions.
21. Drill call.
22. Officers' call.
23. Common step.
24. To cease firing.
25. For officers to take their place in line after the firing.
26. Sick call.
27. Tattoo.

For the Service of Skirmishers.

1. Forward.
2. Halt.
3. To the left.
4. To the right.
5. The about.
6. Rallying of skirmishers on their chief.
7. Trot.
8. Gallop.
9. To commence firing.
10. The disperse.

Note.—To change to a *walk* from a *trot*, *halt* and *forward* are sounded.

INSTRUCTIONS

FOR

OFFICERS ON OUTPOST AND PATROL DUTY.

WAR DEPARTMENT,
September 2, 1861.

THE following detailed instructions on outpost and patrol duty are published for the information of the army, and will be distributed to regiments. Although more especially designed for cavalry, they are likewise applicable to infantry.

Grand guards will be sent out by all brigades in camp,—when in the face of the enemy, for safety; when in a friendly country, for instruction.

All colonels, and others in authority, will see to it that their commands are instructed in these duties.

The attention of officers of the regular and volunteer armies is particularly called to Article XXXVI. of the Revised Army Regulations, beginning with paragraph 473, "On Troops in Campaign." The whole article is replete with the most valuable instruction, and the safety and efficiency of all commands depend very much upon knowledge of the duties therein detailed.

SIMON CAMERON,
Secretary of War.

INSTRUCTIONS

FOR

OFFICERS AND NON-COMMISSIONED OFFICERS

ON

OUTPOST AND PATROL DUTY.

ABRIDGED FROM THE WORK OF THE LATE COLONEL ARENTSCHILD, OF THE BRITISH SERVICE, BY AN OFFICER OF THE ADJUTANT-GENERAL'S DEPARTMENT.

I. ON THE DUTIES OF AN OFFICER OR NON-COMMISSIONED OFFICER ON GRAND GUARD.

SECTION 1.

Parading the Grand Guard.

THE officer commanding a grand guard,* as soon as it has been turned over to him, takes care to have the names of his men written down, with the regiment and troop to which they belong; inspects their ammunition and fire-arms, and orders them to load. He then sees that the men are provided with provisions and forage; if not, reports the fact to their regiment, that supplies may be sent after them. He must also make himself thoroughly acquainted with his orders, and learn whither and to whom he is to send his reports.

---

* The words "grand guard" have been substituted for "picket" wherever the latter occurred in the work of Colonel Arentschild.

The terms "grand guard" and "outlying picket" are, in fact, synonymous; the former is more used in the French, the latter in the British service. By both are meant the outposts, or advanced guards thrown out in the direction of an enemy, to protect the camp from surprise, and give it time to turn out in case of a sudden attack.

The term "*picket*," met with in the Regulations, has a very different signification, being applied to the standing detail for grand guard and other service of the like nature; which, though it remains in camp, is held in constant readiness to turn out at a moment's warning. In other words, it is one and the same thing with the inlying picket of the British.

Section 2.

Marching for his Destination.

On the march to where the grand guard is to be posted, the officer must carefully examine the country, and particularly observe the places where he could make a stand in case of an attack, as, for instance, behind a bridge, a ravine, between bogs, &c., in order to keep off the enemy as long as possible. It is of the utmost importance to give the corps time to turn out; and the commander of a grand guard who retires with his men at full speed, and the enemy at his heels, deserves the severest punishment; he must retire as slowly as possible, and constantly skirmish.

Section 3.

If no Grand Guard was on the Spot before.

BY DAY.

Upon arriving at the spot chosen for the grand guard, he throws out a sentry in advance, dismounts his men, and proceeds to ascertain, by observation of the hills and roads in front, the number of vedettes and small posts necessary. He then places the vedettes in such a manner that they can each see what is coming toward the guard, as well as observe one another. Two-thirds of the guard now unbridle; the whole of a grand guard should never unbridle. The officer then carefully reconnoitres the country. Every one ambitious to do his duty well will make a little sketch, in which the following are to be marked down:

1, *roads;* 2, *rivers;* 3, *bridges and fords;* 4, *morasses, cavities, hollow roads, and mountains;* 5, *woods;* 6, *towns, villages, and their distances.*

Without an exact knowledge of the country, an officer can never feel any confidence in the security of his guard, and both exposes it to be cut off, and the army to a surprise.

By this time he will have been enabled to fix upon the spot where his guard and vedettes ought to be placed at night.

BY NIGHT.

It is impossible to lay down any fixed principles on this subject; but the general rule is, to advance the grand guard at least two or three miles in front of the main body; to place it behind a bridge, ravine, wood, or bog through which the road passes, in order to be enabled to make a stand immediately on being attacked, and to place vedettes in front and on the flanks. Small patrols of two or three men sent out in front and on both flanks, at half an hour's interval, and constantly kept in motion, will give perfect security, particularly if one of the men sometimes dismounts and listens with his ear to the ground. This precaution, by which he will hear the march of troops at a great distance, is indispensable in stormy weather. On coming by night to a new spot, particularly in a mountainous or woody country, small patrols must be pushed forward immediately on all the roads, &c., to secure in the first instance the placing of vedettes, &c.

If the enemy be near, no fire is to be lighted, and the position of the grand guard should be frequently changed. One-half of the guard should, in this case, be mounted, one hundred yards in advance; the other half stand or sit, with bridles in their hands.*

SECTION 4.

Relieving another Grand Guard.

Much of what is said in sections 1 and 2 likewise applies here. As soon as the relieving officer arrives where the other guard is to be relieved, he forms on his left flank or behind it, according to the nature of the ground, draws out a non-commissioned officer and as many vedettes as he has to relieve, (the remainder dismount,) and proceeds, with the officer commanding the old guard and his own non-commissioned officer, to relieve the vedettes. The following is to be observed on such occasions:

1. All written orders and instructions must be turned over, and the verbal orders written down and signed by the officer relieved.

2. The outlines of the sketch belonging to the commander of

---

* According to La Roche Aymon, one-third of the grand guard is told off to furnish the small posts and vedettes; one-third is on the alert, mounted, or ready to mount; and the remainder are resting, or engaged in grazing and watering their horses.

According to the same author, the small posts should be established about 600 paces in advance of the main body of the guard, and the vedettes about 500 paces in advance of the small posts,—of course, always within sight. The small posts and sentries of an infantry grand guard, however, except in a very open country, should be drawn much closer. The small posts consist usually of four or five men, and serve as a support, each one, to four or five vedettes or sentries.

These are but general recommendations, of course, and, as such, are good. No absolute rule can be laid down as to these points. Even the best military writers differ among themselves, as to each and all of them. And no general rule, even if universally accepted, could be universally applied; for the nature of the country, the strength, character, and distance of the enemy, with other elements of the problem, are always changing, and hence different dispositions must necessarily be made in each particular case.

the old guard are to be copied by the relieving officer, who will complete it afterward, at his leisure.

3. The latter must be told to whom reports are to be sent; where the grand guards on the flanks are stationed; what roads lead to them; how often patrols are exchanged between them in the night. In case the roads leading to them are little known, or difficult to find, the non-commissioned officer of the old guard must show them to the one relieving him, who will be accompanied by one of his men.

4. All the information possessed by the old guard as to the enemy, his outposts, patrols, the country, &c., must be communicated to the new guard, together with any suggestions for the better posting of the vedettes, &c.

At the relief of the vedettes, the officers of both guards should attend, and listen to the delivery of instructions from the old vedette to the new one; who must then repeat them, that there may be no mistake. The principal points of these instructions should be: on what roads and from what direction the enemy may be expected; where the neighboring vedettes are stationed; and to look out for and repeat their signals. A vedette must never move from the spot on which he is placed, as the difference of a yard may prevent his observing, or being observed, at a distance.

After all the vedettes have been relieved in this manner, the night posts of the grand guard and vedettes are to be pointed out.

The old guard then marches off. Two-thirds of the horses may then be unbridled.

Section 5.

During his Tour of Grand Guard.

BY DAY.

A dismounted sentry is posted in front of the guard, where he can observe the movements of the several vedettes.

One-third of the horses must always be bridled and ready for an advance. The men must never take off their swords and belts. One-half of them may sleep in the middle of the day, the other half in the afternoon,—that they may all be perfectly alert at night.

The men must not be allowed to leave the guard, especially if there are houses or villages in the neighborhood. Such straggling leads to irregularities, and on being rapidly attacked by the enemy the horses will be lost.

When the men water their horses, they must bridle them up, and take every thing along with them.

In short, a grand guard must be at all times ready to meet an attack in half a minute's time.

PATROLS.

How often the grand guards are to patrol, where to and how far, is generally ordered by the officer commanding the outposts. If there are no orders upon these subjects, the following patrols will be sent:

The *first*, in time to arrive at the place of its destination by daybreak; it will remain there until it is broad daylight. Whoever leads the patrol should then go to the top of some rising ground, whence he can overlook the country to a considerable distance, and, having carefully done so, he will return. The *second* patrol, at ten o'clock; the *third*, at two; the *fourth*, toward evening; the *fifth*, at midnight.

This arrangement will have to be varied according to the distance of the enemy; but the morning patrol, before daylight, must go out under all circumstances.

A patrol in returning should look often to the rear. The enemy frequently succeeds, while following up a negligent patrol, in surprising the guard. In a close country, it is very advisable, after the return of a patrol, to send forward again a few men to the distance of a mile, to make sure that the enemy did not follow the patrol.

Great care must be taken not to let the men fatigue their horses.

No man must be permitted to leave his horse a moment. Any man who attempts to misuse an inhabitant of the country, or to take any thing by force, must be severely punished,

BY NIGHT.

The proper time for the grand guard to take up its night post is when it gets too dark for the day vedettes to see at any distance; they are then called in, and the position for the night is taken.

If there are any apprehensions of being betrayed to the enemy by spies, deserters, or inhabitants of the country, the guard should change its ground again, but the vedettes remain.

At night the vedettes must be relieved every hour and visited every half-hour. The relief rides along the chain of vedettes, and serves thus as a visiting patrol. If the enemy is near, the vedettes should be doubled,—which is at all times recommended, if the strength of the guard will allow of it.

In case a man desert, the fire must be put out, and the guard instantly shift its ground to some hundred yards' distance. The vedettes are to be made acquainted with this change, and urged to increased vigilance. Every desertion must be immediately reported.

Double vedettes patrol among themselves in the following manner:

Fig. 1.

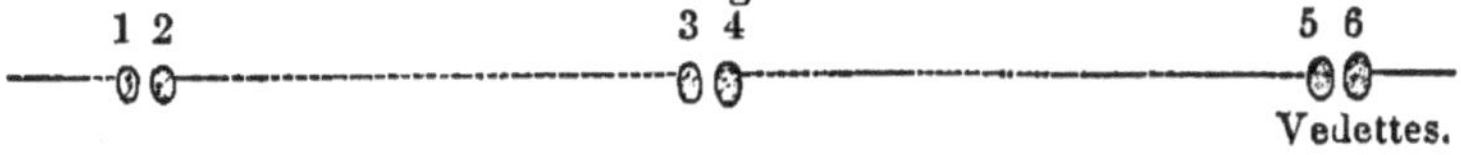

```
    1 2                    3 4                      5 6
---–Ɵ Ɵ-----------------–Ɵ Ɵ---------------------–Ɵ Ɵ---
                                                  Vedettes.
```

No. 1 patrols to his left, and on his return No. 2 proceeds to No. 3, and returns; No. 3 then patrols to No. 2, and on his return No. 4 will go to No. 5, and return; 5 and 6, and all the other vedettes, do the same. If this be done, it is almost impossible that any thing should pass unperceived. In foggy weather it must never be omitted.

When the enemy is close, the following is also to be observed: a few men are to patrol during the night beyond the chain of vedettes, in different directions, and go as close to the enemy as they can unperceived. When they have advanced near enough, one man dismounts, and listens with his ear to the ground. This is particularly recommended, as being the only means of ascertaining the secret movements of the enemy in the night;—to discover which the greatest exertions ought to be made.

Every person attempting to pass the outposts must be detained till morning. Persons suspected of carrying any papers with them are to be searched, and sent to the commanding officer, with a written statement of their case. Half an hour before daylight, the morning patrols will be sent out on the roads in front, and as soon as it is quite light, the guard and vedettes take up their position for the day.

Section 6.

Placing the Vedettes.

BY DAY.

Vedettes should be placed by day on high ground, so as to afford them an extensive view, but always near a tree or rock, so as to conceal them from the enemy, who from the position of a single vedette might guess at that of the whole line. In a mountainous country, where the ravines and narrow valleys cannot always be seen from the top of a hill, a vedette is sometimes placed at its foot.

When the vedettes are posted in such a manner as to be able to overlook their front and see each other and the ground between them, so as that nothing can pass them unperceived, they are placed as they ought to be.

In order to spare men and horses, no more vedettes than necessary are to be out.

In a thick fog, the vedettes stationed at a distance on the flanks are taken off the hills, and placed on more suitable spots. The nature of the country may require that the position fixed upon for the night should be taken up during the day; in which case the ground in front must be continually scoured in all directions by small patrols.

BY NIGHT.

By night, the vedettes are taken off the hills, and placed on the roads, behind fords, bridges, ravines, &c., by which the enemy may approach the guard; and at the bottom of hills, so as more easily to discern against the sky objects moving over the top. In clear moonshine they ought to be near a tree, or bush, to prevent their being seen by the enemy. In a close country, they should redouble their vigilance, for it may happen that he will approach them unperceived, in spite of all their care.

They must be advanced only just so far as that their firing can be distinctly heard by the guard, even in a stormy night.

SECTION 7.

Instructions for the Vedettes, and what the Officer commanding the Grand Guard has to do on their making Signals.

BY DAY.

1. When a vedette discovers any thing suspicious in the direction of the enemy, as, for instance, a rising dust or the glittering of arms, he should move his horse round in a circle, at a walk; on which the officer should instantly proceed to the vedette, accompanied by a corporal and four men, and if he cannot distinctly discover by his spy-glass the cause of the dust, &c., he should send off the men that accompanied him, as a patrol, or go himself; for if he sees troops he should be able to report how strong they are, whether consisting of cavalry, infantry, or artillery, and, particularly, in which direction they are marching. This report must be despatched in writing, without delay.

The commander of a grand guard should never omit to report occurrences of this kind, although they may have no connection with the security of his own guard. Patrols and grand guards must always report the movements of any body of troops, no matter how small in number.

2. If the vedettes positively observe troops marching toward them, but at a great distance, they ride the circle in a trot. The officer's duty is as in 1.

3. If the enemy's troops approach to within a mile, the vedettes circle in a gallop. The officer then advances with his whole guard, immediately. His duty is prescribed in the paragraph on the attack of a grand guard.

If the enemy is so close at hand that the vedettes are obliged to gallop to their guard for their own security, they should first discharge at him both their carbines and pistols.

Should a deserter approach, the vedette is to make a signal to the sentry at the guard, and a party will be immediately sent to bring him in.

BY NIGHT.

1. As soon as the vedettes hear a suspicious noise, even though at a great distance, such as the rattling of carriages or artillery, the barking of dogs in the villages in front, or if they observe any fire, one of the vedettes must instantly report it to the officer of the grand guard, in order that the circumstance may be inquired into by a patrol.

2. Any person approaching the vedette at night must be challenged in a loud tone and made to halt. Should the person refuse to halt, being twice challenged in a loud tone, the vedette is to fire, retiring, if in danger of being overpowered, by the road pointed out to him, &c. Vedettes will not allow a mounted man, nor more than one man at a time, to approach them, nor him nearer than three yards. And they will keep their cocked pistol directed all the while against him. The officer of the grand guard will then be signalled for, and must be instantly there, and examine carefully whence came the person or persons, who sent them, and for what. For when the enemy desires to surprise a grand guard, he does so frequently under the semblance of a friendly patrol; and therefore the officer should particularly inquire to what regiment they belong, the name of their brigadier, commanding officer and captains, where their regiment is encamped, &c. If able readily and correctly to answer these questions, they may be allowed to pass.

Section 8.

On the Arrival of a Flag of Truce.

No person coming from the enemy with a flag of truce must be allowed to advance farther than the chain of vedettes.

When a vedette makes the signal, the officer of the grand guard meets the flag of truce with four men, and halts the bearer of it, if possible, in a bottom, or makes him face in the direction from which he came. For it often happens that the enemy's only intention is to make observations, or see how the grand guard is placed, in order to surprise it during the night. If the bearer of the flag only bring letters, they are to be receipted for and he is sent back. If he insist upon being allowed to proceed, permission must be first obtained; he is then blindfolded, a non-commissioned officer leads his horse, and he is thus conducted to the general's quarters. Should there be more than one person with the flag, one alone will be allowed to proceed to the rear; the remainder must stay where they are. A flag of truce ought to be treated with the utmost civility; refreshments should be offered, if at hand, but no conversation relative to the army, or its position, is to be permitted.

SECTION 9.
Deserters coming from the Enemy.

BY DAY.

As they may be seen at a distance, but cannot be known as deserters, a proportionate number of the guard must already have advanced to the line of vedettes to meet them. Deserters generally make themselves known by flourishing their caps, and calling out, "Deserter!" but this is not to be depended upon; their further behavior must be carefully watched. They are then disarmed and taken to the general's quarters, one, two, or three at a time.

Whenever any private property is taken from a deserter, the act must be severely punished.

BY NIGHT.

Great caution must then be observed, especially if they are in force. The vedettes must order them to halt at some distance, and by no means allow them to come too near. The guard advances; the deserters are ordered to approach, one by one, and are immediately disarmed. They are then taken to the rear. Deserters must be examined respecting the movements, &c. of the enemy.

Section 10.

When the Grand Guard is attacked.

BY DAY.

The officer immediately sends word to the rear, and communicates the fact to the grand guards on his flanks. He then advances with his guard, but warily, so as not to be cut off, and begins to skirmish with the enemy. It will seldom be practicable to advance farther than the chain of vedettes. If obliged to retire, he must do it as slowly as possible, endeavoring to gain all the time he can, for the corps in his rear to turn out. If he has previously fixed upon places where to make a stand, (as enjoined to do in section 2,) now is the time to make use of them. The following (see fig. 2) is the best way of defending such places, (generally, a bridge, ravine, or ford:) we will suppose in this case a bridge.

On arriving within three or four hundred yards of it, the officer takes the gallop, and, passing over it with the main body of his men, posts himself in A, as close as possible to and with his right flank on it, leaving the passage clear. As soon as his skirmishers see that this has been done, they likewise gallop over the bridge, and face about again in B. The enemy is thus compelled to halt, and time is gained,—the grand object, on which may sometimes depend the honor and welfare of the whole corps.

Grand Guards on the Flanks.

When the grand guards on the flanks are not attacked at the same time, they can be sometimes of service in acting upon the enemy's flanks, though not if the nature of the ground would endanger their being cut off.

As a general rule, the grand guards that are not attacked retire in a line with those engaged, and, while doing so, omit no favorable opportunity which offers of assisting the latter.

BY NIGHT.

It is mentioned in section 7 that the vedettes, on discharging their fire-arms, must gallop back *by a certain road.* This is a point of the utmost importance, and which must be well impressed on the night vedettes,—that, in the event of being suddenly attacked, they are not to retire in the direction of the grand guard, but a hundred and fifty yards to the right or left of it, and by a circuitous route, firing all the while and doing all they can to mislead the enemy and to draw him after them. The grand guard, by this means, gains time to mount, and to

Fig. 2.

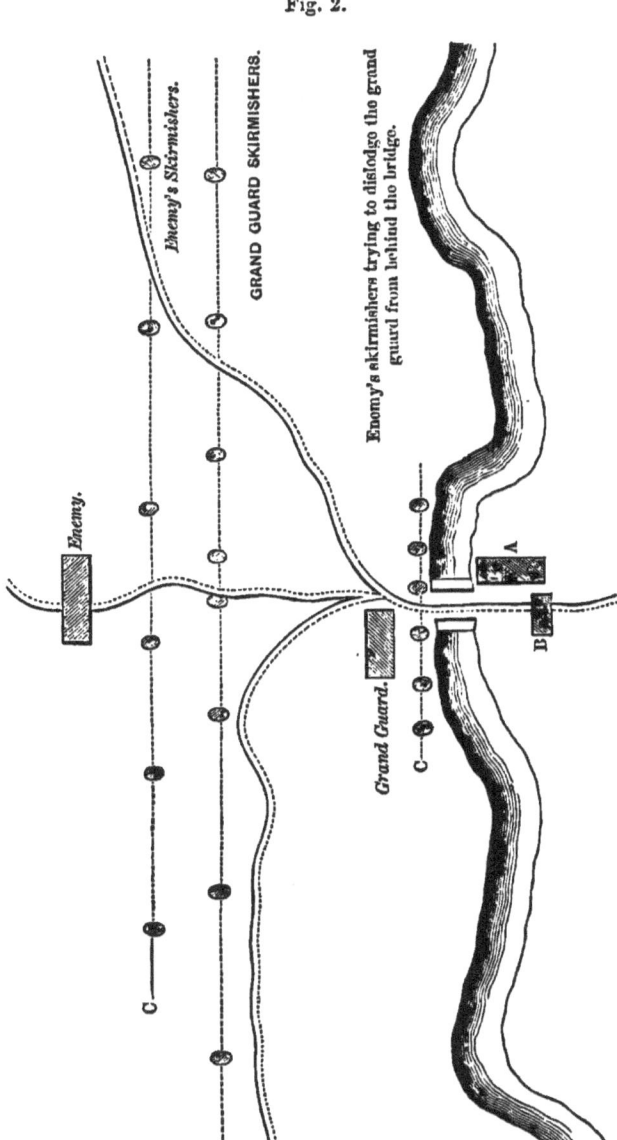

fall with a great noise on the flank or rear of the enemy, who will be thus led to suspect that he has fallen into an ambush, be thereby puzzled, and perhaps lose some prisoners. After making such an attack, it will usually be best for the grand guard to fall back again by the road fixed upon for a retreat. The men must therefore be shown, during the day, both the road which the vedettes are to take when attacked at night, and whereabout they are to rejoin the grand guard. The retreat is otherwise conducted in nearly the same way as by day, with only this difference, that there cannot be skirmishers in front, but only two or three men at the head. It is necessary to fire as much as possible, and wherever a stand can be made an obstinate defence should be attempted. It is almost unnecessary to remark that the attack, as soon as made, should be reported.

REPORTS.

All officers in command of grand guards, patrols, &c. must make written reports of any thing which occurs. There are few occasions when it is necessary to send a verbal report, and it should, as far as possible, be avoided, as it is very difficult to find non-commissioned officers and soldiers who will deliver one correctly. A commander of a post or patrol must be very cautious not to create unnecessary alarms; he must report as fully and as correctly as possible. If he reports the movements of the enemy, he must recollect that considerable confusion may arise from saying "to the right," or to "the left;" he must say to *our* right, or to *our* left, or to "the *enemy's* right," or to "the *enemy's* left." If a non-commissioned officer cannot send a written report, he must explain the message thoroughly to an intelligent private, and should the latter deliver it incorrectly, he must expect to be punished.

NON-COMMISSIONED OFFICERS.

A great deal of responsibility rests with a non-commissioned officer on outpost duty; he has frequently the command of patrols, small posts, &c.; it is therefore necessary for him to obtain a thorough knowledge of his duty. He is to recollect that the safety and honor of his regiment may frequently depend upon the manner in which he executes his duty. Unless, therefore, he can enforce the strictest discipline, and make the men under him conform scrupulously to their orders, he is not fit for his situation.

II. ADVANCE GUARD OF A COLUMN IN MARCH.
BY DAY.

Should the same consist of one officer, two non-commissioned officers, and twenty-four men, the officer commanding will tell them off as in fig. 3.

Fig. 3.

This gives an extension of 1,500 yards,—which is sufficient for twenty-four men. The larger the column, the stronger and more extended will be the advance guard. The principle on which an advance guard, rear guard, or flank guard is thrown out, is to give time to the column to make the necessary preparations for an attack or a retreat in case of the enemy's being discovered. The quantity of ground to be taken up will be regulated by this consideration and by the strength of the guard. The several divisions of each and all of these different guards must always keep their support in sight, and be careful to preserve the same distances. When the column halts, the advance guard does the same, but the three men at the head should instantly occupy the neighboring heights, if any there be within four or five hundred yards' distance.

If the advance guard comes to a wood, supposed to be 2,000 yards broad, the sergeant reinforces the three men at the head with six more, who extend themselves on a line with, and just so far to the right and left of the first three, as to be able to see each other and what lies concealed between them, and with the two men left him he follows in rear of the three men in advance. Should the wood be larger, the officer must send two men to the right, and as many to the left, around it, who are carefully to examine whether they can see any traces of troops leading into the wood, and if so will immediately report the fact. The column halts until this is ascertained.

Never less than three men should be at the head of the advance guard. Their duty is as follows: If there is a height in front, the centre man of the three trots on until he can look over it and beyond; if one is seen to the right or left of the road, one of the other two men must do the same. Near an enemy this precaution must never be omitted, not even if the hill be 2,000 yards distant. Men that go up a hill to reconnoitre in this manner (they may belong to an advance guard or a patrol) must proceed with more than ordinary caution, remembering that it is of as much importance not to be seen by as to see the enemy. For this reason, when nearly on top, they should take off their caps and creep up only just far enough to be enabled to look over.

On approaching a village, one of the three goes round it to the right, another to the left, and the third straight through. The non-commissioned officer of the advance guard quickens his gait, reinforces this last man with three others; of whom one is sent to the right, and the other to the left, through the by-streets, while the third, keeping the leading man always in sight, follows him through the middle of the village. Should these men, in patrolling the village, find no inhabitants, they are to look into the windows, ride into the yards, and examine carefully, if perhaps the enemy has not concealed himself. Those going round the village examine the roads and paths, to see if there are any traces of troops leading into it. The sergeant, with the rest of his men, follows slowly. When he has passed through, he collects his men, sends on three in advance again, and reports to his officer—who meantime has halted behind the village—that it has been patrolled, &c.

BY NIGHT.

The advance guard is told off as by day, but the distances between the several divisions must not be so great. The officer's division is only a hundred yards from the column, the sergeant's a hundred from the officer's, and the three men in advance, fifty ahead of the sergeant's party. The communication between them is further kept up by a chain of single men, who ride just so far apart as to be able, each, to see the man before and behind him.

If the advance guard, at night, should unexpectedly fall in with the enemy, it has no choice but instantly to attack him. The non-commissioned officer at once disperses his men to the right and left, and fires as much as possible; the officer advances rapidly with his division, and charges. In no other way can the column gain time for preparation. It is therefore an unpardonable fault in an advance guard to get frightened and fall back upon the column. Every thing would then be confusion; it would have been much better to have no advance guard.

Should the advance guard, after a gallant struggle with a superior force, be compelled to retire, its retreat must be made on either side of the column, but never *on* the column, for fear of throwing the latter into confusion.

On all these subjects the men should be well instructed beforehand. Every commanding officer of a detached party must consider it as one of his first duties to give his men clear and circumstantial instructions how to act in every case. Unless he do so, they will frequently act in a manner contrary to his ideas, even with the best intentions.

III. REAR GUARD

Is told off in separate divisions in the same way as an advance guard, only in reverse order, (fig. 4.)

The object of a rear guard is to prevent the enemy's approaching the column unperceived. Two men at the extreme rear are sufficient, but they must be picked men. They should often halt on the heights they are passing, carefully screening themselves from observation while doing so, to see if, perchance, the enemy is not following. When a mountain is at hand, the officer will do well to ride to the top of it, and search, thence, the country with his spy-glass.

If the enemy should follow closely with only a few men, it may be well either to try and drive him off, or, by leading him into an ambuscade, to take some prisoners from him. But should the rear be attacked it must instantly be supported by the sergeant's troop, and this be supported by the officer's troop. Both of these must immediately advance, and do their utmost to prevent the enemy from coming too near the column. The commanding officer of the column will either support them, or give them directions to retire slowly. If the enemy should follow with a more considerable force, say one squadron, *without* attacking, the rear guard will follow the column in the manner about to be described. Halting until the column has got a thousand yards ahead of him, the officer trots on to the ordinary distance of five hundred yards, halts, and fronts; as soon as the sergeant sees the officer fronted, he trots on likewise to five hundred yards' distance from the officer, halts, and fronts; the two men in the rear do the same. In this way the enemy is kept off, while at the same time an engagement is avoided and the horses are saved. Whenever the column halts, the different parties of the rear guard face to the enemy.

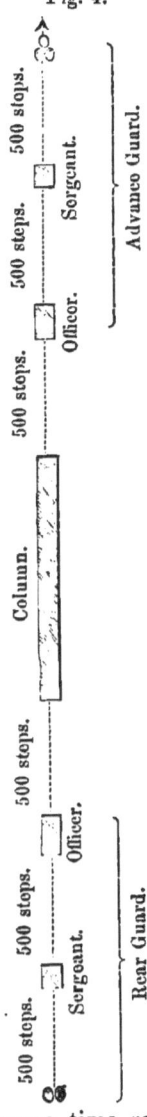

Fig. 4.

At night, the rear guard observes the rules laid down for an advance guard; that is to say, the intervals between the several troops are to be shortened, with single men interspersed through them in sufficient proximity to each other to keep up a connected communication with each other and the column.

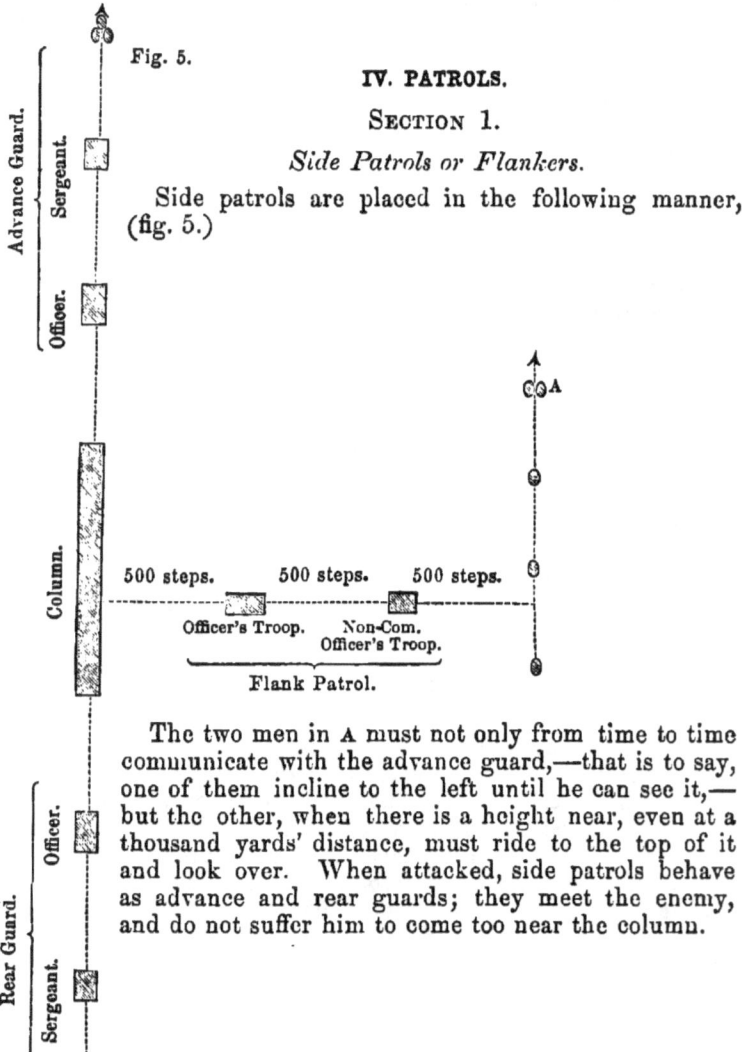

IV. PATROLS.

SECTION 1.

Side Patrols or Flankers.

Side patrols are placed in the following manner, (fig. 5.)

The two men in A must not only from time to time communicate with the advance guard,—that is to say, one of them incline to the left until he can see it,—but the other, when there is a height near, even at a thousand yards' distance, must ride to the top of it and look over. When attacked, side patrols behave as advance and rear guards; they meet the enemy, and do not suffer him to come too near the column.

When a side patrol meets with a wood in the direction of its march, the disposition is altered. (Fig. 6.)

The officer detaches the sergeant's troop to the right, the corporal and four men to the left, and himself remains with his men in the centre. The sergeant sends two men to the skirts of the wood; these must look at the tracks, and one of them occasionally ride to the top of a height, if any be near; the remainder divide themselves to the left of these two men, at such a distance that they can keep one another in sight. The corporal divides his men in the same manner, between the right flank of the column and the officer's troop. If the officer perceive that these two lines are not extensive enough to cover the ground toward his troop, he detaches a sufficient number of men to the right and left to form a perfect line, which line must be careful never to get at the head of the column. The non-commissioned officers endeavor to keep their men in the same line with the officer's division. All this should be done quietly, without hurry or fuss, and will be so done wherever the men have been previously instructed in their duty. To see men unnecessarily galloping and fatiguing their horses on such occasions, from mere want of instructions, and without doing any more good than if at a walk, really excites one's pity.

Section 2.

Patrolling a Wood.

This is done in the manner just described (section 1) for a side patrol, with the difference that two men are also sent round to the left skirt of the wood.

Section 3.

Patrols of Discovery

Consist generally of a considerable force, so as to be enabled to defend themselves against small parties or patrols of the enemy, and are sent for the purpose of ascertaining whether a certain place is in the enemy's possession, whether he is on the move against us, or whether a certain district is occupied by him. Such a patrol usually has three men for an advance and two for its rear guard; and, if necessary, sends one man to its right, and another to its left, along the heights.

As, frequently, not only the safety of the patrol, but the very object for which it is sent, depends upon its not being seen by the enemy, it is of the utmost importance to impress well upon the men in front that they are not to be satisfied with merely

Fig. 6.

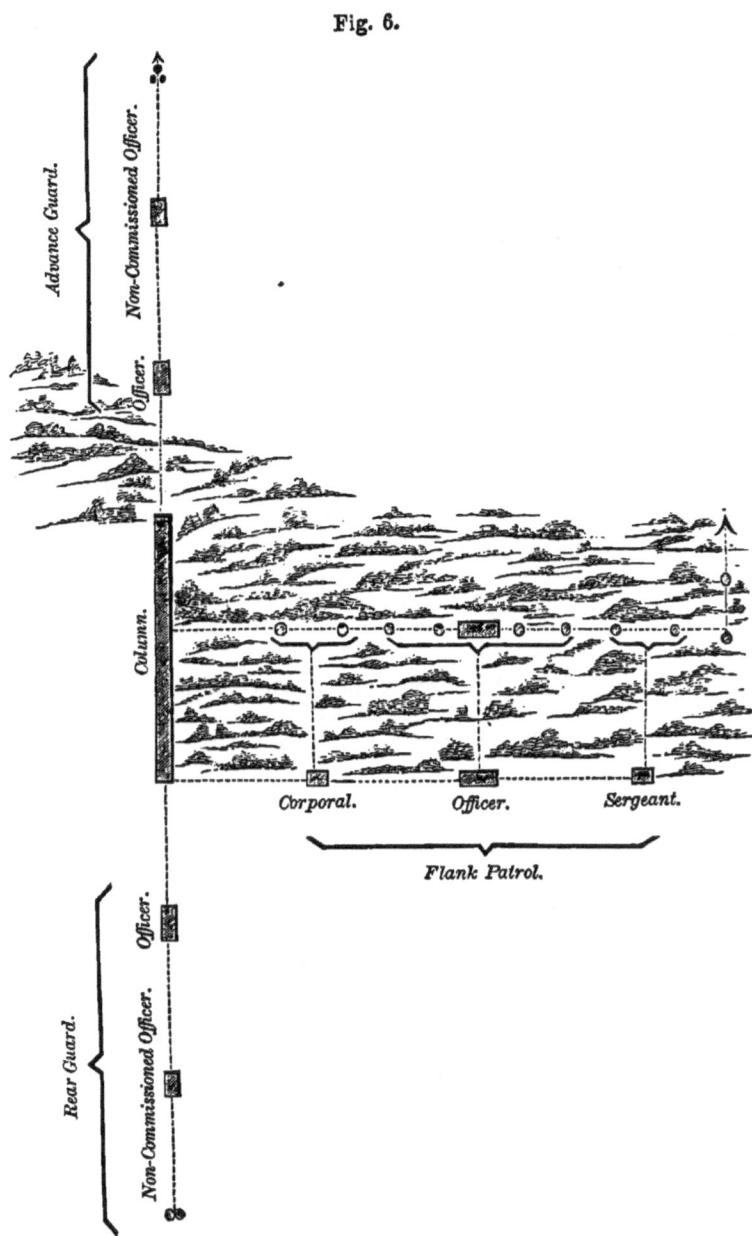

looking out before them, but to examine closely the tracks along the cross-roads, ascend the hills with caution, &c.

If this be done, the patrol will sometimes have a chance of making prisoners. A patrol, which sees the enemy advancing toward it with not too strong a force, must conceal itself, and, at the proper moment, attack him vigorously; whereby he will be thrown into confusion, fly, and perhaps lose some prisoners. When the enemy is too strong, the patrol avoids him, and, if circumstances permit, continues its march, and endeavors to carry out the object for which it was sent.

A patrol must never enter a village or wood which has not been examined; but this is to be so managed as not to delay the patrol. For it must be borne in mind that the officer who sent it out has calculated the time of its return; should it not come back at that time, he may get apprehensive, and send another one out to look for it; whereby men and horses will be unnecessarily fatigued.

In passing at night a village which the enemy may have occupied, the patrol is to halt about five or six hundred yards from it. When no vedettes of the enemy are visible, a few men are sent to the right and left, who approach stealthily, to ascertain if the entrances to the village are occupied by troops, and to try and pick up an inhabitant, whom they may bring back with them. If nothing can be learned in this way, the patrol moves on, observing the precautions mentioned in a former section.

When a patrol is ordered to ascertain by night whether a village is occupied, and how, three of the best-mounted men are picked out for the lead; eight others follow at a distance of twenty-four yards, and the remainder of the patrol at a hundred yards. The enemy's vedettes are then approached without noise, and as soon as one challenges, the three men in advance bear down on him at full speed, to take him prisoner. Should they not succeed, they with the other eight must make a dash at the guard, to bring off a prisoner, with whom they retire. The alarm will be given in the village, to a certainty, and the sounding of trumpets or beating of drums will enable the patrol to judge by what kind of troops it is occupied. If a patrol go so far as to be obliged to feed, it must never stop to do so in a village, but always in an open country under some trees, and vedettes are to be placed during the time. The horses must be watered and fed by detachments,—never all at the same time,—so as to guard against surprise.

Provisions and forage, if it be necessary to get them out of villages, must be brought out by the inhabitants.

On such occasions, as on all others, the inhabitants are to be treated with kindness; any attempt to rob or ill treat them must be promptly and most severely punished.

But the object had in view by the patrol, and the direction of its route, must be carefully concealed from them. Guides that are sent home must be deceived, if possible, by the patrols marching in a false direction until they are out of sight. If information about the road be wanted, the inquiry must embrace several roads, that the true one may not be suspected.

Section 4.

Secret Patrols.

These only consist of a few men, say six or eight, and are generally sent out on the flanks, sometimes in rear of the enemy's army. They have frequently to go far, and be long gone, to make the necessary observations; and of all the duties of light cavalry, therefore, this is the most difficult to perform.

Many of the rules laid down for other patrols are likewise applicable here.

A patrol of this kind marches without advance or rear guard. Only one man must be detached to look over the country from the hill-tops. The high-roads must be avoided as much as possible, and the patrol march by by-roads, deep valleys, &c. A guide on horseback will be of great service to such a patrol; but he is to be paid for it, and well treated. The patrol to feed must go off the road into a thicket or wood, and a look-out be set from a tree. If any thing hostile approach, the patrol must escape unperceived, and seek out another place of concealment, until it may continue its march without danger. A fire can rarely be lighted,—never without being very careful to hide it; but it is better to do without one. An inhabitant who meets with the patrol at night must remain with it until the march is resumed. Should a secret patrol be discovered by the enemy in spite of all these precautions, it must fly. But, as soon as the enemy gives up the pursuit, it must make a renewed attempt to get, by roundabout ways, to where it is to execute its commission.

A well-informed and clever officer is required for this kind of duty,—one who speaks the language of the country, and has a knowledge of the customs, habits, hopes, and fears of the inhabitants.

It is to be remarked, in conclusion, that if the leader of a patrol, when returned, cannot answer the following questions about the roads he has passed over:

As to whether they are rocky, sandy, or boggy?

How many streams were passed; their distance from one another; their breadth, depth, and strength of current?

The character of their banks; whether steep, miry, &c.?

Whether fordable at every season for cavalry, infantry, or artillery, &c.?

How many bridges span them; whether of wood or stone, massive or slight?

How many villages on the road; their names; and the distances from one to the other?

Whether the road run much through woods, or at some distance from them; the woods, of what size and kind, &c.?

he has lost sight of one of the chief points of his duty.

CONCLUSION.

The foregoing is but a sketch of the duties performed by light cavalry. The young and inexperienced soldier may look upon it as an introduction to his duties,—nothing more. Knowing this much, he will have still much to learn; but less than this he could hardly know and still remain an officer.

SKIRMISH DRILL

FOR

MOUNTED TROOPS.

SKIRMISH DRILL

FOR

MOUNTED TROOPS.

ARTICLE I.

§ 1.—Composition of a company acting singly, and posts of officers, non-commissioned officers, &c., &c.

A COMPANY consists of one captain, one first lieutenant, one second lieutenant, one brevet second lieutenant, four sergeants, four corporals, one farrier, one blacksmith, two buglers, and sixty-four privates minimum, seventy-four maximum.

A company is divided into two platoons, which are numbered, from the right, FIRST platoon and SECOND platoon.

Each platoon contains two sections. The first and second sections make up the first platoon; the third and fourth sections make up the second platoon.

The sections are called from the right in the order in which they stand,—first, second, third, and fourth section.

Each section is made up of "sets of four," which are called in the order in which they stand in their respective sections, from the right, "first set," "second set," "third set," &c.

Posts of officers and non-commissioned officers of a company in line of battle, viz.:

No. 1. Captain, ten yards in front of centre of company. } Measured from face to face.
No. 2. 1st lieutenant, five yards in front of centre of 1st platoon.
No. 3. 2d lieutenant, five yards in front of centre of 2d platoon.

No. 4. Brevet 2d lieutenant, five yards in rear of centre of company, (not replaced when absent.)

No. 5. 1st sergeant, on right of 1st section, not counted in the rank.

No. 6. 2d sergeant, on right of 2d section, not counted in the rank.

No. 7. 3d sergeant, on right of 3d section, not counted in the rank.

No. 8. 4th sergeant, on right of 4th section, not counted in the rank.

No. 9. 1st corporal, on left of 1st section, not counted in the rank.

No. 10. 2d corporal, on left of 2d section, not counted in the rank.

No. 11. 3d corporal, on left of 3d section, not counted in the rank.

No. 12. 4th corporal, on left of 4th section, not counted in the rank.

Farrier and blacksmith in the rank; bugler near and behind the captain, or on right of 1st sergeant, and one yard from him.

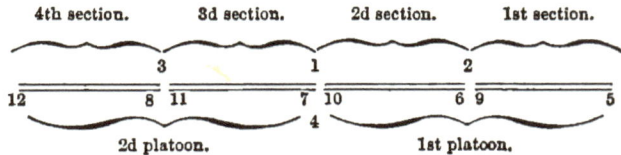

In line of battle there will be an interval of one yard between the corporal on the left of each section and the sergeant on the right of next section. In column of platoons the same interval will be observed.

In column of platoons the captain will be habitually on the side of the guide, and about ten yards outside the centre of the column. The other officers, non-commissioned officers, &c., will occupy the positions above indicated.

In column of sections the captain will be ten yards outside the flank of the column on the side of the guide.

The first lieutenant will be five yards outside the flank of the column on the side of the guide, and opposite the centre of the interval between the 1st and 2d sections.

The second lieutenant will be five yards outside the flank of the column on the side of the guide, and opposite the centre of the interval between the 3d and 4th sections.

The sergeants will be one yard in front of the centre of their respective sections, and will command them. The corporals will be in the rank of their respective sections.

The buglers will accompany the captain, or will be on the right of the leading sergeant of the column.

In column of fours, twos, or file, the captain will be ten yards outside of the centre of the flank of the column, on the side of the guide.

The first lieutenant will be five yards outside of the centre of the flank of his platoon, on the side of the guide.

The second lieutenant will be five yards outside of the centre of the flank of his platoon, on the side of the guide.

The sergeants (except the sergeant of the leading section) will be abreast of the leading four, two, or file, of their respective sections, and on the side opposite the guide.

The sergeant of the leading section will be in front of its leading four.

In all columns the brevet second lieutenant, when there is one serving with the company, will be five yards outside of the centre of the flank of the column, and on the side opposite the guide.

The corporal will, in all columns of fours, twos, and file, be on the side opposite the guide, abreast of the last set, two, or file. In columns of companies, platoons, or sections, he remains in the rank.

The company, having been thus formed, will be drilled by the means and directions laid down in U. S. Cavalry Tactics for the squadron.

The section will be drilled by the means and directions laid down in U. S. Cavalry Tactics for the platoon.

The only changes necessary in order to make the one answer for the other, are those which result from the diminished depth of the rank, and the use of the words "company" and "section" instead of "squadron" and "platoon :"—(*e.g.*)

In forming to left into line from column of fours, the command must be changed to, "By fours, left wheel."

To mount.

§ 2.—The command being dismounted in line of battle, the men standing to horse, to mount, the commands of the chief are:

1. *Prepare to mount.*
2. MOUNT.

At the first command, the sergeant and numbers two and four of each section move five yards to the front, stepping off with the left foot and regulating by the right. The corporal and numbers one and three stand fast until the others have cleared them; all then prepare to mount according to the principles laid down in

U. S Cavalry Tactics, except that they take the end of the reins in the right hand, draw them through the left, which holds them above the middle of the neck of the horse between the thumb and hand, with the palm down, until the horse just feels the bit; then with the right hand adjust the stirrup to the left foot, and with the left hand take up a lock of the mane so that its end comes out by the thumb; then take the surplus part of the reins in the right hand, between the thumb and hand, with the palm up, and seize the right side of the pommel with the right hand.

At the second command, all mount together, and the corporals and numbers one and three immediately move forward, and place themselves boot to boot with the sergeants and numbers two and four.

The chief corrects the alignment, if it be necessary, commanding "Right dress." The assistant places himself at this command on the right of the line, looking along it, and correcting the files who are out of place.

The chief remains in front, in order to superintend the alignment. The assistant commands "Steady," when the files are all correctly aligned; and then the chief commands "Front."

To dismount.

§ 3.—The command being mounted in line of battle: to dismount it, the commands are:

1. *Prepare to dismount.*
2. Dismount.

At the first command, the sergeant and numbers two and four in each section move to the front five yards; the corporals and numbers one and three stand fast. All then prepare to dismount in other respects as laid down in U. S. Cavalry Tactics, except that they take the reins in the left hand with a lock of the mane, and carry the right hand to the right side of the pommel.

At the second command, all dismount, leaving the reins over the pommel; the sergeants and numbers two and four stand to horse, while the corporals and numbers one and three lead forward and form rank with them.

To link.

To link after dismounting, the man stands to horse, faces about to the rear, takes the link which hangs from the halter-ring of the horse of his left file in his right hand, seizes his own horse by the bit near the mouth, and draws the horse of his left file toward his own until he can hook the snap into the curb-ring; in hooking, the nails of his right hand are down.

When he dismounts, he leaves his reins over the pommel of the saddle.

To facilitate the linking, the horse-holder should bear his horse's head well toward number three.

§ 4.—Form and course of inspection for the single-rank formation: The company being formed in line, in one rank, mounted, the officers and non-commissioned officers in their places, (see section 1,) to inspect it—the commands are:

1. *For inspection—Prepare to dismount.*
2. DISMOUNT.

At the *first command*, the first and second lieutenants move forward ten yards. The brevet second lieutenant places himself upon the line with them, in front of the left file of the company; they all then return sabre and prepare to dismount.

The non-commissioned officers move forward ten yards, and prepare to dismount.

Numbers two and four move forward five yards, and prepare to dismount.

Numbers one and three prepare to dismount in their places.

At the *second command*, all dismount and stand to horse. They then shift the pistol-holster toward the front of the body sufficiently to enable the inspecting officer readily to withdraw the pistol. The men then unsling rifles, order arms, and spring rammers without noise, with the right arm passed through the rein; they then allow the rifle to fall across the body obliquely into the hollow of the left arm, which holds it, with the forearm extended down, the barrel between the thumb and closed fingers. In this position they await the inspection.

As soon as the inspecting officer perceives that the second command has been executed, he returns his sabre, dismounts, gives his horse to a trumpeter to hold, and commences his inspection on the right of the line of officers. He passes along the front of the line, around its left, and along its rear; he then passes to the front of the line of non-commissioned officers, which he inspects in the same manner. He draws and inspects the pistol of each man as he comes to him, and, after inspecting, returns it to the holster. He then passes to the right of the front line of men, draws and inspects the pistol of the man on the right of that line, returns it to the holster, takes the rifle from the position in which it rests, and, after inspecting, returns it to that position; and so on throughout the line. Each man slings his rifle and readjusts his pistol, as soon as the inspector has passed one file beyond him. After having completed his inspection of the men, horses, arms, equipments, &c., from the front, the officer passes around the left and along the rear of the line, examining, as he goes, the condition of men, horses, arms, and equipments. He then inspects the rear line of men in the same manner.

After which he mounts, and commands:

   1. *Prepare to mount.*
   2. MOUNT.
   3. FORM RANK.
   4. RIGHT DRESS.
   5. FRONT.

At the first command, all prepare to mount in their places. At the second command, all mount, and the rear line of men move forward to their places, boot to boot with the front line of men. All then move forward together to the line of non-commissioned officers, on which they are aligned by the fourth and fifth commands.

The sabres are then inspected, as directed in the U. S. Cavalry Tactics, by the command:

   1. INSPECTION SABRE.

If the company be in tents or other quarters, the valises or saddle-bags and clothing are inspected in the quarters.

If in the field, the men will unstrap and display them on the ground at their feet, as they stand to horse, before they unsling rifles.

The trumpeters will be near and in rear of the inspecting officer when he gives the first command. They will dismount with the rest. One of them holds the horse of the other who goes to take that of the inspector.

ARTICLE II.

SKIRMISH DRILL FOR MOUNTED TROOPS.

§ 5. Preliminary remarks.

For this drill the men should be dressed so as to secure the greatest freedom of action, as in the blouse or sack, and in the forage-cap with the chin-strap down. The revolver will be worn in a belt-holster upon the right side of the man. The gun will be slung across his back, with the butt near his right hip. In addition to the usual equipment of a cavalry soldier, each man will be provided with a "link," for the purpose of securing his horse whenever he dismounts. It will be buckled in the halter-ring of the headstall, and when not wanted for immediate use will be hooked up by the snap in the same ring.

At the signal "boot and saddle," the horses will be saddled and bridled.

At the signal "to horse," the command will be formed according to the instructions already given in section 2.

Should the command be less than a complete company, the officer in charge of it will make such changes in its organization as are necessary in consequence of the absence of members.

Every command, be it a full company or a scouting-party less than a company, will be divided into four equal sections if possible.

A section must contain at least eight men.

Some portion of every command will be held in reserve, unless it is so small as to manifestly render it unwise to divide it. Any section may form the reserve; and its commander will be assigned by selection, and not according to rank.

A "set of four" means the four men who tell off together.

A "chief of four" is the right file of the set, or "number one" of the set, and will be habitually the guide of his set; when in column of fours, he will command the set to which he belongs.

He will be responsible that the men of his set *never* separate from each other, and for the interval, distance, and alignment.

The senior officer on drill is termed the "chief;" his next in rank is termed the "assistant."

Before skirmishing, two or three men will be detailed to accompany and protect the chief.

Preparatory to skirmishing, a section will take *open order*.

The interval between men in open order, measured from "boot to boot," is twenty-seven inches.

In a column of fours, open order, the distance between the sets of four, from croup to head, is four yards.

In a column of twos, open order, the distance from croup to head is eighteen inches.

In a column "by file," open order, the distance from croup to head is eighteen inches.

These distances and interval are deduced from the length and breadth of the horse, and from the agreement which must exist between the depth of a column and the length of the line into which it will wheel.

The interval of twenty-seven inches will be found in practice ample to enable the men to mount and dismount in their places in line or in column, without the necessity of the alternate files moving out to the front for that purpose.

In an enemy's country, or when in danger of sudden attack or ambuscade, the leading section of the company or scouting-party should march in open order, so as to be able to get at once into action.

To take open order.

§ 6. Being in line, right in front, the commands of the chief are:

1. *1st section,* (*or* 2d *or* 3d, *as the case may be,*) *open order*—GALLOP.
2. MARCH.

At the first command, all gather their horses; at the second command, all take the gallop, except the centre file of the section, which trots out directly to the front. Those on the right of the centre oblique to the right, each man continuing to oblique until he has an interval of twenty-seven inches between him and the next file on his left; those on the left of the centre continue to oblique to the left, until each man has twenty-seven inches interval between him and the next file on his right. They all then align themselves on the centre, take up its gait, and continue to move to the front until the next command of the chief.

To return to close order.

Being in line, right in front, in open order, the commands of the chief are:

1. *Close order*—TROT.
2. MARCH.

At the first command, all gather their horses; at the second command, the centre file moves to the front at the walk, the others close in toward him at the trot; each in succession taking up the walk, and aligning on the centre as he gains his position in the line.

§ 7. The section being in line, right in front, open order, breaks into columns of fours by the commands:

1. *By fours*—TROT, (*or* GALLOP.)
2. MARCH.

At the first command, the first set of four gathers its horses, and takes the trot together at the second. After the first set has cleared the front of the line, or marched three yards, the second set moves out at the trot, (or gallop,) marches straight to the front until clear of the line, and then obliques to the right until in position in column exactly behind the first set, and at four yards' distance from it, when it marches to the front to take its place. in column. The third set follows the second, and so on throughout the section, according to the foregoing directions.

Care must be taken to avoid losing distance in this movement. The sets of four must move out promptly in turn, and oblique together. The chief commands "Guide right" when the first set is out.

A column of "twos" and "file" may be formed on the same principles and by the same means, except that the distance in these cases is only eighteen inches from head to croup.

In all formations of this drill, the same principles will be observed in regard to increasing the gait as are now established in the U. S. Cavalry Tactics.

When in column of fours, twos, or file, the various methods of forming into line (front, right, or left) can be executed by the commands and means laid down in the U. S. Cavalry Tactics for the platoon.

Observe that, as there is no rear rank, lines can be formed at once on either flank by wheeling by fours to the right or left. When the right of the column is in front, and the wheel is made by fours to the right, the sets will be in line by inversion. The men of each set will not be inverted.

When the men are not well instructed in the drill, the deployments from close order into open order, and from open order into skirmishing order, should be made at the walk or trot. Habitually they should be executed at the gallop, and, in action, with the greatest possible celerity compatible with steadiness.

In deploying, the officers and non-commissioned officers will fall to the rear of the line, in order to superintend the movement.

Every movement not fully described in the following pages will be understood to be executed, as is now ordered, in the system already in use.

§ 8.—To form column of twos, open order, from column by file, marching at the walk, right in front, the commands are:

1. *Form twos, open order*—TROT.
2. MARCH.

At the second command, numbers two and four oblique to the left at the trot, and move to the front when in rear of their places in column of twos, until in line with their respective ones and threes. The leading set of twos then being at the walk, all the others close up at the trot to their places, with distance of eighteen inches, and interval from boot to boot of twenty-seven inches.

§ 9.—To form column of fours, open order, from column by file, when marching at the walk, right in front, the commands are:

 1. *Form fours, open order*—TROT.
 2. MARCH.

At the first command, number one of each set continues to march at the walk to the front; twos, threes, and fours of every set oblique to the left at the trot, each moving to the front when in rear of the place he will occupy in his set of four; when they have gained their places in line with numbers one, the leading set being at the walk, the others take up the trot, which they keep until each has arrived at the distance of four yards from the one preceding it; each in turn then takes up the walk. The chief commands "Guide right" when the first set is formed.

§ 10.—To form column of fours, open order, from column of twos, open order, when marching at the walk, with right in front, the commands are:

 1. *Form fours*—TROT.
 2. MARCH.

At the second command, threes and fours oblique to the left at the trot, until opposite their places in the sets of four, when they move to the front, taking up the walk when in line with ones and twos. The chief commands "Guide right" when the movement is completed. Ones and twos preserve the walk and direction during the movement, and after the other files have moved out must take care not to diminish the distance left by them. If the column is trotting when the movement is ordered, it will be executed at the gallop.

§ 11.—To break from column of fours into column of twos, open or close order, marching at the walk, with right in front, the commands are:

 1. *By twos.*
 2. MARCH

At the second command, numbers three and four halt until numbers one and two have cleared them, when they oblique to the right, promptly, into their places in column of twos. The chief commands "Guide right" as soon as the movement is completed.

§ 12.—To break a column of twos, in open or in close order, into column by file, when marching at the walk, right in front, the commands are:

    1. *By file*—TROT.
    2. MARCH.

At the second command, number one of the leading set takes the trot. As soon as he has cleared number two of the first set, number two obliques to the right at the trot, and enters the column behind number one. Number three then moves in his place in column at the trot, followed by number four; who, by obliquing at the trot, takes his place in rear of number three; and so on throughout the column, each even-numbered file obliquing at the trot as soon as the odd-numbered file on his right has cleared him. The files must move very promptly and exactly in their proper time, so as not to lose distance, in this movement.

Being in column of twos, wheels to the left may be executed when the right is in front, or to the right with the left in front; but not the reverse of these, for then the twos would be inverted in their respective fours, and confusion would result on account of the change in position of the horse-holder.

§ 13.—To deploy forward as skirmishers, from a line, right in front, halted, or marching at any gait, the commands are:

    1. *On (such) set—Deploy as skirmishers*—GALLOP.
    2. MARCH.

At the second command, all take the gallop except the designated set, which trots out to the front. Those on the right and left of it oblique at the gallop to the right and left, each set taking up the trot when on line with the directing set, and at fifteen yards from the nearest file of the next set on the side of direction.

In this movement the chiefs of four will be held responsible for the direction and interval and alignment of the men of their respective sets, and will see that the sets are at proper intervals from each other. The chief will halt the line when it has reached the point where it is to act.

The following movements will enable cavalry, when on a march, to get into action with the least possible delay, in case of an attack when passing a defile or of any other ambuscade.

It is understood that always, when dismounted to fight, the horse-holders remain mounted, unless otherwise ordered.

In all the manœuvres of this article the commands numbered "1" are cautionary.

ARTICLE III.

§ 14. To dismount to fight when in column of fours, open order, right in front, halted, or marching at any gait, to meet an enemy on the left of front, the commands are:

1. DISMOUNT TO FIGHT.
2. ACTION FRONT AND LEFT.
3. COMMENCE FIRING.

At the first command, all halt, spring to the ground, link horses, unsling rifles, and step one yard to the front. At the second command, the first set moves forward four yards, and at the third command commences firing. The other sets move at the double-quick obliquely to the left, and take their places on the line with the first set. Each set, as soon as it arrives upon the line, commences firing.

In case it be desired to form the line toward the right of the head of the column, the commands are: 1. DISMOUNT TO FIGHT. 2. ACTION FRONT AND RIGHT. 3. COMMENCE FIRING. All the sets except the first will then gain their places in the line by obliquing to the right. The sets will be in line by inversion. The men in each set will be in direct order.

§ 15. Being in column of fours, open order, right in front, marching at any gait, or halted, to meet an attack on left of rear, the commands are:

1. DISMOUNT TO FIGHT.
2. ACTION REAR AND LEFT.
3. COMMENCE FIRING.

At the first command, all halt, spring to the ground, link horses, unsling rifles, and step one yard to the front. At the second command, the men of the rear set face to the right, and, led by their chief, file to the right around the rear set of horses to a line five yards in rear of their croups.

At the second command, all the other sets face to the left, and move at the double-quick. Each man as he clears the column moves obliquely to the left and rear to his place on the line with the rear set.

If it be desired to get at once into action, the chief commands "Commence firing" as soon as the set first on the line is established. This set then commences the fire; and each of the others takes it up in succession as it arrives upon the line; and in all of the following movements the same rule will be observed.

§ 16. Being in column of fours, open order, right in front, marching at any gait, or halted, to meet an attack from the right of the column, the commands are:

   1. DISMOUNT TO FIGHT.
   2. ACTION RIGHT.

At the first command, all halt, spring to the ground, link horses, unsling rifles, and step one yard to the front. At the second command, all move briskly upon a line five yards outside the right flank of the column, where they take their places, in line of battle, faced to the right. The sets will be in order by inversion; but the men in each set will be in direct order, the chief being on the right. From this position they may be deployed forward as skirmishers, if it be desired.

§ 17. When in column of fours, open order, right in front, halted or marching, to meet an attack from the left, the commands are:

   1. DISMOUNT TO FIGHT.
   2. ACTION LEFT.

At the first command, all halt, spring to the ground, link horses, unsling rifles, and step one yard to the front. At the second command, all move briskly to the left, and place themselves on a line five yards outside the left flank of the column, facing to the left of it, and in their proper places in line of battle. From this position they may be deployed forward as skirmishers, if desired.

§ 18. Being in column of twos, with right in front, marching at any gait, or halted, to meet an enemy on left of front, the commands are:

   1. *By twos, left wheel*—MARCH.
   2. DISMOUNT TO FIGHT.
   3. ACTION FRONT AND LEFT.

At the first command, the twos wheel to the left and halt. At the second command, all dismount, link horses, unsling rifles, and step one yard to the front. At the third command, the leading set moves to a line five yards to the right of the right flank, as now formed, and facing in that direction. The others move obliquely to their right and front, at the double-quick, and take their places on line with the first.

If it be desired to form the line toward the right of the head of the column, the commands are:

1. *By twos, left wheel*—MARCH.
2. DISMOUNT TO FIGHT.
3. ACTION FRONT AND RIGHT.

Each of the sets in rear of the leading set will then gain its place in the line by passing through the interval on the right of its set of horses, and moving obliquely to the right and front, to its place in line with the leading set. The sets will be in line by inversion.

§ 19. Being in column of twos, right in front, marching at any gait, or halted, to meet an enemy in rear, the commands are:

1. BY TWOS, LEFT WHEEL.
2. DISMOUNT TO FIGHT.
3. ACTION REAR AND LEFT.

At the first command, all wheel by twos into line to the left, and halt. At the second command, all dismount, link horses, unsling rifles, step one yard to the front, and await the next command. At the third command, the rear set faces to the left, and moves at the double-quick to its place on a line five yards to the left of the left flank, as now formed, and facing in that direction. The other sets face obliquely to the left, and move off at the double-quick to their places in the line with the rear set.

If it be desired to form the line to the right instead of the left, the first two commands are the same as in the other case; the third command is: "ACTION REAR AND RIGHT;" at which the rear set takes its place on the line as before, and the others pass through the intervals to the left of their sets of horses, respectively, and take their places in succession on the left of the set first established. The sets will then be in line by inversion.

§ 20. Being in column of twos, marching at any gait, or halted, with right in front, to dismount to fight, in order to meet an enemy on the right flank, the commands are:

1. *By twos, left wheel*—MARCH.
2. DISMOUNT TO FIGHT—ACTION RIGHT.

At the first command, the twos wheel into line to the left and halt. At the second command, all dismount and link. In linking the men remain faced to the front, and take the link in the left hand and the bit in the right. After linking they face about, unsling rifles, and take their places in a line five yards outside the croups of the horses. The cautionary words "ACTION RIGHT" should be uttered immediately after "DISMOUNT TO FIGHT."

The method of linking is changed in this instance to avoid the inconvenience which might result from the men having to stoop under the links, after linking, in order to pass to their position in rear of the horses.

§ 21. Being in column of twos, right in front, marching at any gait, or halted, to dismount to fight, to meet an enemy on the left, the commands are:

1. *By twos, left wheel*—MARCH.
2. DISMOUNT TO FIGHT.

At the first command, wheel by twos into line to the left and halt; and at the second command, all dismount, link horses, unsling rifles, step five yards to the front, and stand fast.

In case it should be desired in any of the preceding manœuvres to form the line in an oblique direction, the commands would be the same; but the set first in the line would be placed in the desired direction, and the others would conform to it. The chief will judge from the circumstances which of the manœuvres to adopt,—whether the flank, the front, or the rear.

In all the cases of this article the command "Commence firing" will be the signal for the set first on the line to open fire. The other sets, if not on the line when it is given, will commence firing as soon as practicable after they arrive on the line.

ARTICLE IV.

§ 22. To deploy as skirmishers, when dismounted, the command is:

1. *On (such) set*—*Deploy*—FORWARD.

At this command, the section springs forward at the double-quick. The sets on the right of the directing set move obliquely toward the right until opposite their places in line of battle, when they move to the front, aligning by the left.

The sets on the left of the directing set move obliquely toward the left until opposite their places in line of battle, when they move to the front, aligning by the right. All move forward until halted by the chief.

When in proper position in line of battle, thus deployed, there will be fifteen yards between sets and three feet between files in each set.

The firing will commence at the command of the chief.

If it be desired to deploy on the line already occupied, the command will be "ON (*such*) SET—DEPLOY."

The directing set stands fast; the sets to the right and left of it face to the right and left, respectively, and move at the double-quick to take their intervals; then face to the front, and align themselves on the directing set.

§ 23. To deploy as skirmishers, mounted, from a column of fours, right in front, the commands are:

1. *On (such) set—Deploy*—GALLOP.
2. MARCH.

At the second command, the directing set trots out to the front; those in front of it oblique to the right at the gallop; those in rear to the left at the gallop; and all take the trot when they have gained their intervals of fifteen yards, aligning themselves by the directing set. The chief will halt the line when it has arrived where it is to act.

To assemble the skirmishers into line or column again, the chief will place himself at, or otherwise indicate, the point at which the directing set is to rest, and have the rally sounded. At this signal the sets will close in at the gallop upon the indicated point and take their places in line of battle.

When the line is formed, it will be broken into column, in order to advance or retire as may be necessary

§ 24. Having been thus deployed into line for skirmishing, to commence action, the commands are:

1. DISMOUNT TO FIGHT.
2. FORWARD.
3. HALT.
4. COMMENCE FIRING.

At the first command, all, save the horse-holders, dismount, link horses, unsling rifles, step one pace to the front, and await the next order. At the second command, the line moves forward at the double-quick until halted. At the fourth command, the right file of each set delivers his fire, and he is followed in succession by the other two.

The chief of four will take care that there is always one gun loaded in his set; this will never be neglected, whether in advancing or retreating. The files of each set must depend upon each other for support and assistance; they must never separate; every kind of cover must be seized and occupied by the skirmishers; each chief of four must be alert to perceive such advantages for his set, taking care, however, that in attempting to secure them he does not separate too far from the other sets of the line to receive or give support when necessary.

The horses will be habitually kept at about one hundred yards in rear of their riders, though they should be nearer when they can find shelter from fire which will admit of it. Fifty yards will be far enough when the enemy does not use fire-arms.

They will be under charge of a non-commissioned officer, and, when it is desired to remount rapidly, should be advanced to meet their riders. The reserve will be kept mounted, and where it can best protect the horses of the dismounted men and get into action best.

The deployed line will be manœuvred by the commands, signals, and means provided in the U. S. Cavalry Tactics.

If it be desired to fight mounted, the chief will command the charge. The men will then draw sabre or pistol, and charge.

§ 25. The section being in column of fours, open order, right in front, and at the walk, to take close order, the commands are:

1. *Close order*—TROT.
2. MARCH.

At this command, number one of the leading set marches to the front at the walk, the other men of his set closing upon him at the trot until each has gained his place in the set of four in close order. The set then walks. The other sets close at the trot in the same manner, each walking when it has closed to eighteen inches from that in its front.

§ 26. The section being in column of twos, right in front, open order, to take close order, the commands are:

1. *Close order.*
2. MARCH.

At this command, numbers two and four incline to the right, slightly quickening the gait, and place themselves boot to boot with numbers one and three.

§ 27. To form column of fours, in close order, when marching in column of file at the walk, with right in front, the commands are:

    1. FORM FOURS.
    2. *Trot*—MARCH.

At the second command, number one of the leading set continues to march to the front at the walk. All the others oblique to the left at the trot; each man marching to the front when in rear of his place in his set of fours in close order, and aligning by number one of his set. All of the sets (except the leading set) continue the trot until they have closed up to within eighteen inches of each other, and then take the walk.

ARTICLE V.

§ 28. To sling rifles, from carry arms, the command is:

    1. SLING RIFLES.

At this command, raise the piece with the right hand a little higher than the hip, inclining the barrel over the right shoulder, and in rear of the head; at the same time, with the left hand near the right shoulder, move the sling out from the barrel, thrust the head, right shoulder, and right arm through the opening, let the piece fall into its position, steadying it with the right hand, and drop the hands by the side.

To unsling rifles, the command is:

    1. UNSLING RIFLES.

At this command, pass the right hand through the opening between the sling and piece near the right hip, bear the piece toward the front with the right arm, seize it with the right hand as in carry arms, and raise it a little above the right hip; at the same time, with the left hand, free the sling from the head and lower the piece to the position of carry arms.

§ 29. All of the movements described herein are supposed to be executed when the right is in front. It will be understood that they can all be executed when the left is in front upon the same principles by inverse means.

The men should always, after dismounting, leave their reins over the pommel of the saddle.

When more than two full companies are serving together, and their front in single rank would be unduly extended, all lines should be formed of companies in column of platoons at wheeling distance.

As far as possible, the composition of the different sets will remain unchanged; and every thing should be done which will promote the mutual dependence of the men of each set on each other.

They should act together as much as possible on all kinds of duty, as well in the fatigue duties of the camp or garrison as when on drill or in action.

All details should be made as much as practicable of sets of four rather than of individuals from different sets; and the chief of four should be always in command of his set, and invested with the authority of a non-commissioned officer over it. He must see that his men stand by each other in action, and, whether in the charge, in pursuit, or in retreat, that they never separate. After the men and horses are familiar with the drill, all of its movements should be executed at the gallop.

The men should be made to saddle up with the greatest possible despatch whenever the "boot and saddle" sounds.

Always before using their *guns* the men must dismount.

In order to avoid fretting the horses, the men should be at least five yards from them before they commence firing.

When the men are in action on foot, they should be manœuvred with due reference to the safety of their horses.

While the horses should be so far in rear of the men as to be out of the range of the enemy's fire, they should not be so far that their riders cannot reach them before the enemy, if an attempt should be made to capture or stampede them. Generally, in open ground, one hundred yards will be about the maximum distance. They should be nearer, if they can be safe from fire.

One of the non-commissioned officers of each section should be left in charge of its horses when the men dismount to fight; and he will be held responsible for their security and proper management. The other will dismount with his section, linking his horse to that of the nearest number one.

In this drill, inversions of platoons, of sections, and of sets of four should be frequently practised, but the individual men of the sets should never, either when mounted or on foot, be inverted in their sets.

When the company is about to be formed, two or three men will be detailed to accompany the chief during the drill or skirmish.

Whenever the men are dismounted, at the command "mount" they will run to their horses without unnecessary noise, unlink, and mount.

When the "rally" is sounded, the skirmishers will close upon the indicated point at the gallop, and by the quickest means.

When charging in line with pistols or sabres, the officers must ride in the rank; the captain on the right of the first platoon, the first lieutenant on the left of it, the second lieutenant on the right of the second platoon, and the brevet second lieutenant on its left. In case of the absence of any one of them, his place must not be supplied by the next in rank, except on the flank of the company.

All the commands should be habitually given with the trumpet; and on drill the trumpeters should always accompany the chief. It is very important that in this drill the men should learn perfectly what the signals mean.

THE END.

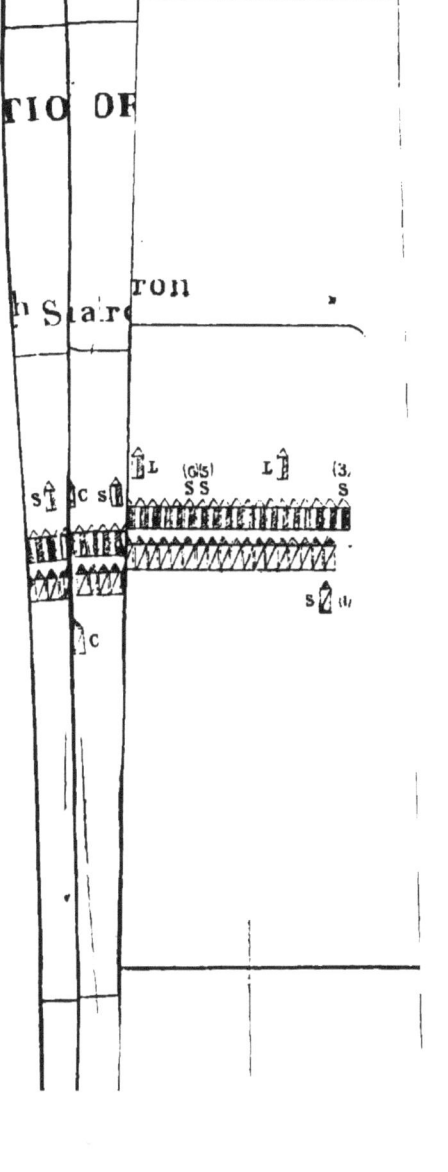

the sets should never, either when mounted or on foot, be inverted in their sets.

When the company is about to be formed, two or three men will be detailed to accompany the chief during the drill or skirmish.

Whenever the men are dismounted, at the command "mount" they will run to their horses without unnecessary noise, unlink, and mount.

When the "rally" is sounded, the skirmishers will close upon the indicated point at the gallop, and by the quickest means.

When charging in line with pistols or sabres, the officers must ride in the rank; the captain on the right of the first platoon, the first lieutenant on the left of it, the second lieutenant on the right of the second platoon, and the brevet second lieutenant on its left. In case of the absence of any one of them, his place must not be supplied by the next in rank, except on the flank of the company.

All the commands should be habitually given with the trumpet; and on drill the trumpeters should always accompany the chief. It is very important that in this drill the men should learn perfectly what the signals mean.

THE END.

FORMATION OF A REGIMENT OF FIVE SQUADRONS IN ORDER OF BATTLE

INST

Pl. 2

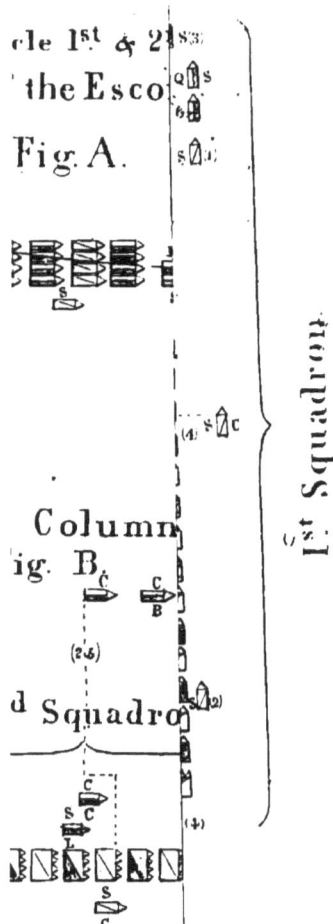

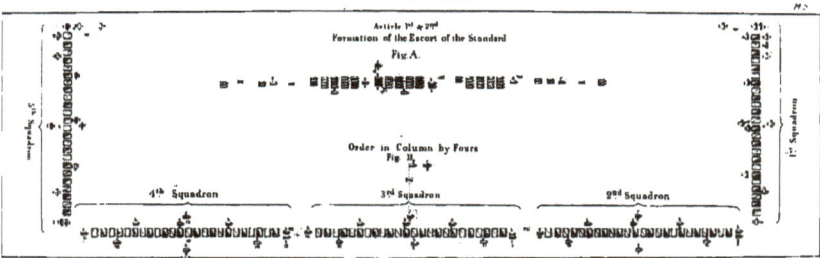

Article 1st & 2nd
Formation of the Escort of the Standard
Fig. A.

Order in Column by Fours
Fig. B.

Pl. 3.

Fig. A.

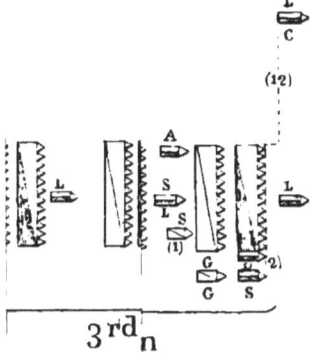

3rd n

BASIS OF INSTRUCTION

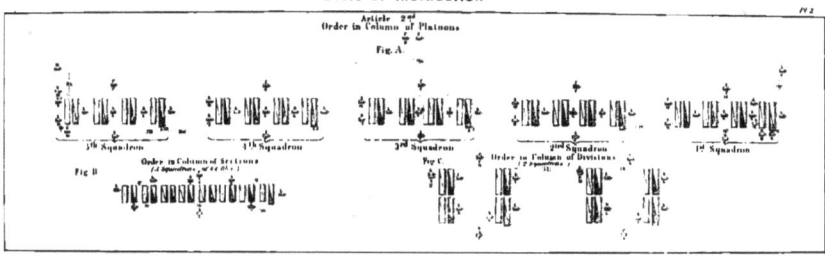

BASIS OF INSTRUCTION.

Article 2nd.
Order in close Column.

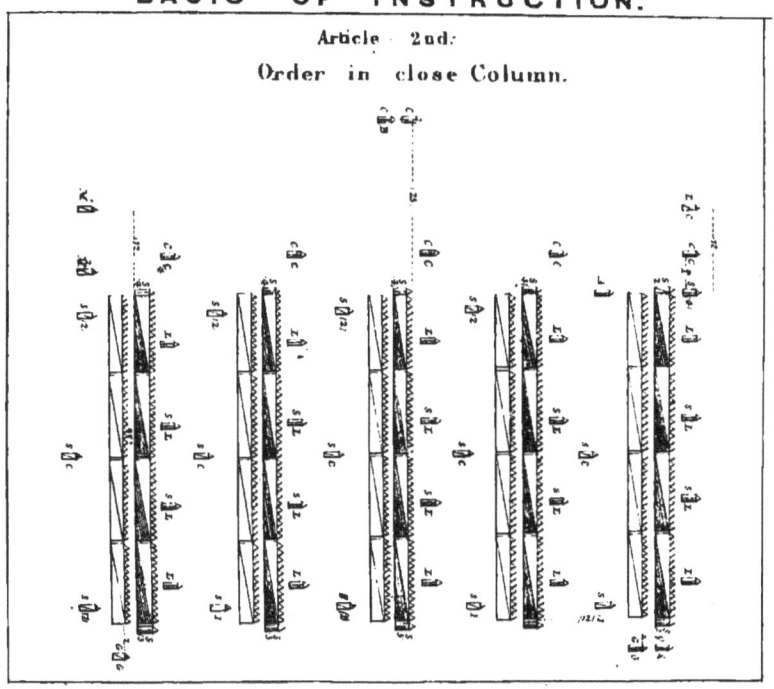

OF IN

Artic
of th

g E.

3

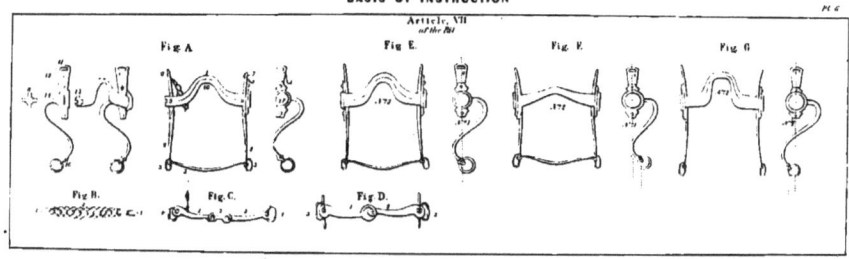

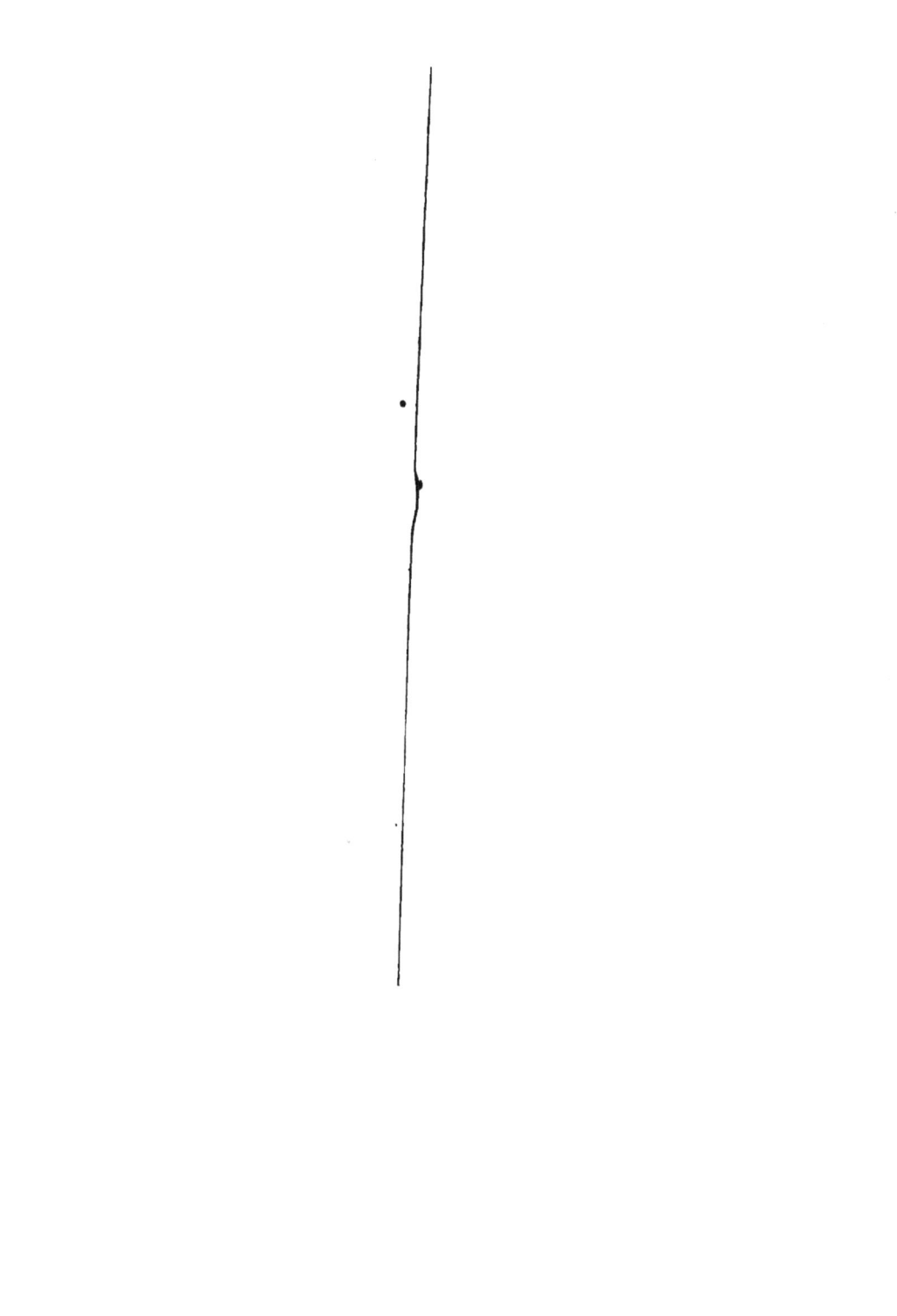

BUGLE SIGNALS.

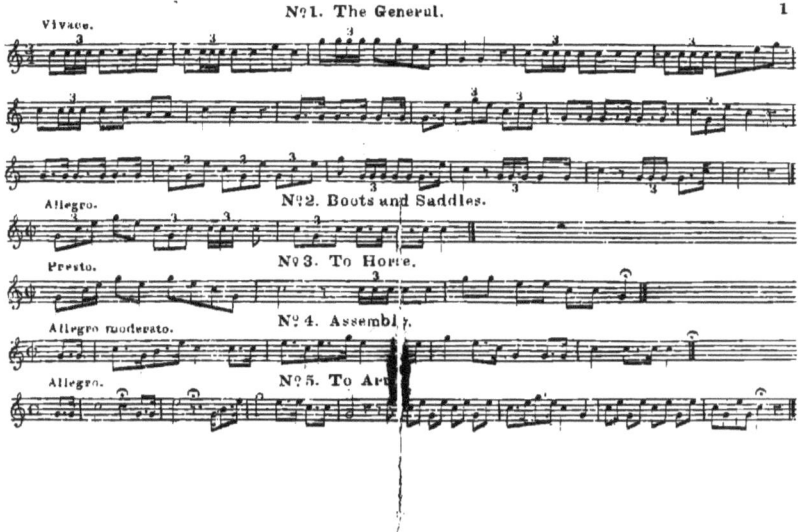

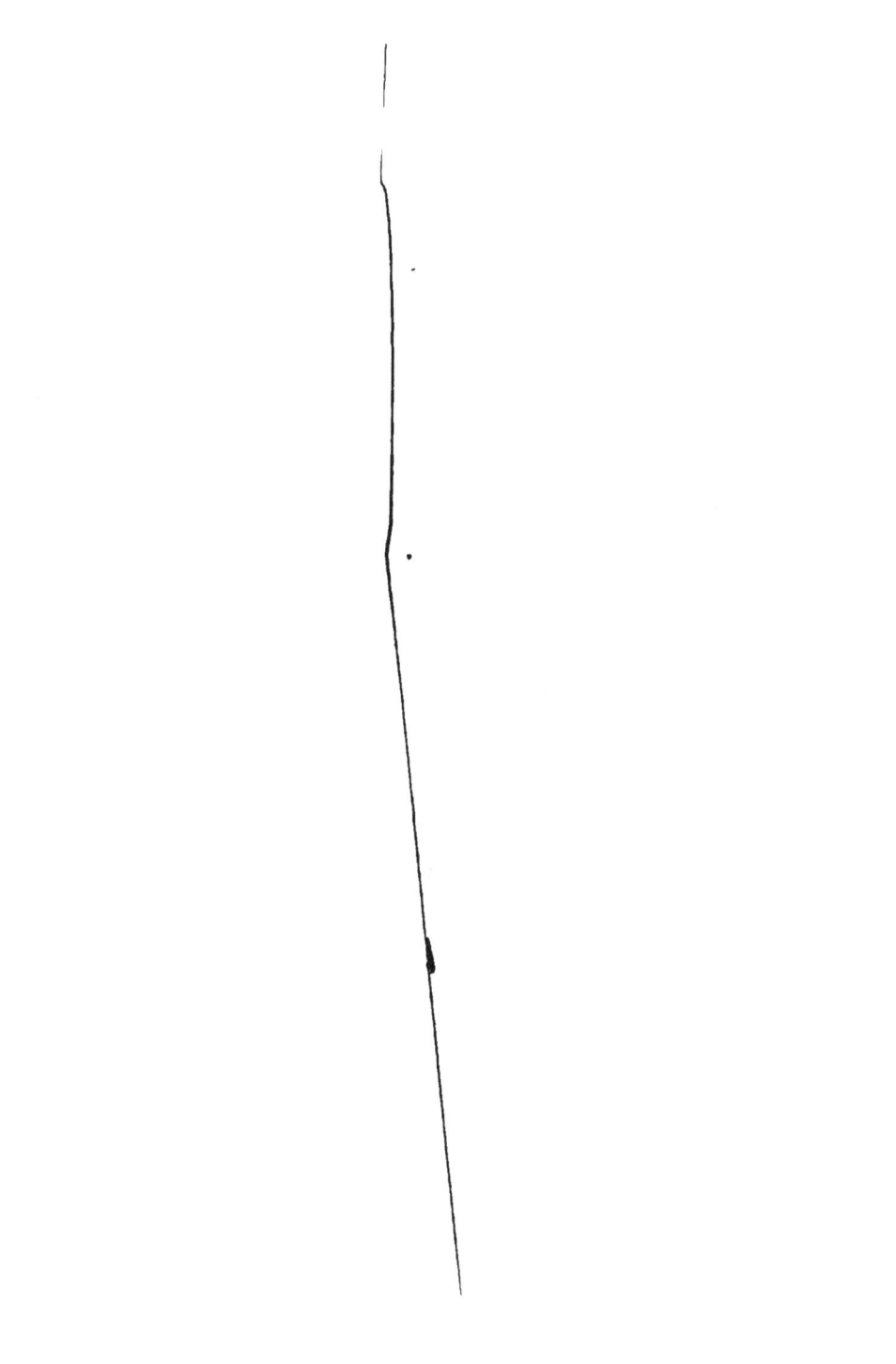

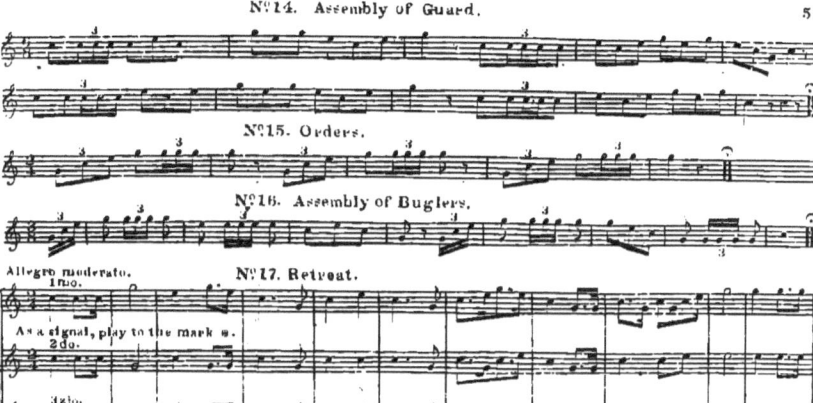

Nº 24. Cease firing.

Nº 25. Officers take place.

Nº 26. Sick Call.

Nº 27. Tattoo.

FOR THE SERVICE OF SKIRMISHERS.

Nº 1. Forward.

QUICK MARCH.

10

MILITARY BOOKS

PUBLISHED BY

J. B. LIPPINCOTT & CO.
PHILADELPHIA.

Major-General McClellan's Works.

The Armies of Europe; comprising descriptions in detail of the Military Systems of England, France, Russia, Prussia, Austria, and Sardinia. Adapting their advantages to all arms of the United States Service. Embodying the Report of Observations in Europe during the Crimean War, as Military Commissioner from the United States Government in 1855-56. By GEO. B. MCCLELLAN, Major-General U.S. Army. Originally published under the direction of the War Department, by order of Congress. 1 vol. 8vo. Illustrated with a fine steel Portrait and several hundred Engravings. $3.50.

This most interesting volume, prepared with great labor by General MCCLELLAN, from copious notes taken during his tour of observation in Europe, under orders from the War Department, opens to the reader much of his own military history and culture. Here will be found his matured views on subjects of immediate and absorbing interest, and the noble and bold suggestions contained herein he is now in position to realize, and is, in fact, every day applying in practice. The book is a striking prophecy, of which his present position and his assured fame are the bright fulfilment.

Regulations and Instructions for the Field Service of the U.S. Cavalry in Time of War. By GEO. B. MCCLELLAN, Major-General U.S. Army. To which is added, the Basis of Instruction for the U.S. Cavalry, from the authorized Tactics,—including the formation of regiments and squadrons, the duties and posts of officers, lessons in the training and use of the horse,—illustrated by numerous diagrams, with the signals and calls now in use; also, instructions for officers and non-commissioned officers on outpost and patrol duty. With a drill for the use of cavalry as skirmishers, mounted and dismounted. 1 vol. 12mo. Fully illustrated. $2.

European Cavalry, including details of the organization of the Cavalry Service among the principal nations of Europe; comprising England, France, Russia, Prussia, Austria, and Sardinia. By GEO. B. MCCLELLAN, Major-General U.S. Army. 1 vol. 12mo. Fully illustrated. $1.25.

Manual of Bayonet Exercises. Prepared for the Use of the Army of the United States. By GEO. B. MCCLELLAN, Major-General U.S. Army. Printed by order of the War Department. 1 vol. 12mo. Fully illustrated. $1.25.

Hon. C. M. CONRAD, Secretary of War.

Head-Quarters of the Army, Washington, D.C., Dec. 81, 1851.

SIR :—Herewith I have the honor to submit a system of Bayonet Exercises, translated from the French by Captain GEO. B. MCCLELLAN, Corps Engineers, U.S. Army.

I strongly recommend its being printed for distribution to the army, and that it be made, by regulation, a part of the "System of Instruction."

The enclosed extracts from reports of the Inspector-General, &c., show the value.

I have the honor to be, sir, with high respect, your most obedient servant,

WINFIELD SCOTT,

R. JONES, *Adjutant-General.*

Approved. C. M. CONRAD, *Secretary of War.* Jan. 2, 1852.

Revised Regulations for the Army of the United States. 1861. By authority of the President of the United States and the Secretary of War. With a full Index. 1 vol. 8vo. 559 pp. $2.00. JUST PUBLISHED.

War Department, Washington, August 10, 1861.

WHEREAS, it has been found expedient to revise the Regulations for the Army, and the same having been approved by the President of the United States, he commands that they be published for the information and government of the military service, and that, from and after the date hereof, they shall be strictly observed as the sole and standing authority upon the matter therein contained.

Nothing contrary to the tenor of these Regulations will be enjoined in any part of the forces of the United States by any commander whatsoever.

SIMON CAMERON,

Secretary of War.

Important changes and additions have been made to this REVISED edition of the Army Regulations, and it should at once be in the hands of all who have the previous editions.

United States Infantry Tactics. For the Instruction, Exercise, and Manœuvres of the U.S. Infantry, including Infantry of the Line, Light Infantry, and Riflemen. Prepared under the direction of the War Department, and authorized and adopted by SIMON CAMERON, Secretary of War. Containing the School of the Soldier, the School of the Company, Instructions for Skirmishers, the General Calls, the Calls for Skirmishers, the School of the Battalion, the Articles of War, and a Dictionary of Military Terms. 1 vol. complete, illustrated with numerous Engravings. $1.25.

War Department, Washington, May 1, 1861.

This System of United States Infantry Tactics for Light Infantry and Riflemen, prepared under the direction of the War Department, having been approved by the President, is adopted for the instruction of the troops when acting as Light Infantry or Riflemen, and, under the act of May 12, 1820, for the observance of the militia when so employed.

SIMON CAMERON, *Secretary of War.*

The above system of Infantry Tactics, based upon the latest improvements in French military experience, and adapted to the peculiar wants of our service, has been prepared by order of the United States Government, and is now, after the most satisfactory evidence of its efficiency, authorized and adopted by the Secretary of War for the Instruction of the troops.

Infantry is divided into Heavy Infantry,—also called Infantry of the Line, and Light Infantry. The difference between Heavy and Light Infantry is twofold: 1st. In their weapons and equipment; the former being armed with the musket, and the latter with the rifle when it may be had. 2d. In the order of battle; Heavy Infantry being in compact order, while Light Infantry is dispersed or deployed as skirmishers, the men being separated and more independent in delivering their fire as sharp-shooters.

In the School of the Company and of the Battalion, *the instruction for Heavy and Light Infantry is the same*, every regiment of Infantry having one company of Light Infantry as a part of its organization, and all these companies being drilled as Infantry of the Line.

The system now presented gives a complete course of instruction for both kinds of Infantry, in the Schools of the Company and Battalion, and has, besides, a special drill for Light Infantry when employed as skirmishers.

The advantages claimed by this system of tactics over former ones are numerous and decided; greater celerity in movements, forming in line from column without halting, changing direction from front to rear while marching, doubling the files when marching by a flank, the omission of unnecessary commands, or parts of commands, more varied formation of squares against cavalry, and many others.

It is believed that, with the same *matériel*, this system will render a company or regiment much more effective than any other.

With a view to insure uniformity in a system of instruction the merits of which are acknowledged by the highest authority, it is now presented to the volunteers and militia called into service, as the authorized drill for the U. S. Infantry, and that by which they will be instructed and disciplined.

WASHINGTON, D.C., May 1, 1861.

4   J. B. LIPPINCOTT & CO.'S MILITARY PUBLICATIONS.

The Ordnance Manual, for the use of the Officers of the Army and others. Prepared under the direction of the War Department. Third edition. 1 vol. demi-8vo. Fully illustrated. $2.50.

CONTENTS.—CHAP. I. Ordnance. II. Shot and Shell. III. Artillery Carriages. IV. Machines, etc., for Siege and Garrison Service. V. Artillery Implements and Equipments. VI. Artillery Harness and Cavalry Equipments. VII. Paints, Lackers, etc. VIII. Small Arms, Swords, and Accoutrements. IX. Gunpowder, Lightning-Rods. X. Ammunition of all kinds, Fireworks. XI. Equipment of Batteries for Field, Siege, and Garrison Service. XII. Mechanical Manœuvres. XIII. Artillery Practice, Ranges, Penetration, etc. XIV. Materials, Strength of Materials. XV. Miscellaneous Information, Tables of Weights and Measures, Physical Data, Mathematical Formulæ, Ballistics, Tables, etc.

This most valuable work to persons engaged in the military service and in the preparation of any of the various military supplies, (the construction of which is given in minute detail,) will also prove useful to mechanics generally for the valuable tables and miscellaneous information which it contains.

Hardee's Rifle and Light Infantry Tactics, for the Exercise and Manœuvres of Troops when acting as Light Infantry or Riflemen. Prepared under the direction of the War Department. By Brevet Lieutenant-Colonel W. J. HARDEE, U.S.A. 2 vols. complete. VOL. I. Schools of the Soldier and Company; Instruction for Skirmishers. VOL. II. School of the Battalion. $1.50.

Henderson on the Examination of Recruits. Hints on the Medical Examination of Recruits for the Army, and on the discharge of Soldiers from service on Surgeon's Certificate. Adapted to the service of the United States. By THOMAS HENDERSON, M.D., Asst. Surgeon U.S. Army. A new edition, revised by RICHARD H. COOLIDGE, M.D., Asst. Surgeon U.S. Army. 1 vol. 12mo. $1.00.

A Manual of Military Surgery; or, Hints on the Emergencies of Field, Camp, and Hospital Practice. By S. D. GROSS, M.D., Professor of Surgery in the Jefferson Medical College of Philadelphia. 1 vol. 18mo. 50 cents.

Cavalry Tactics. Published by order of the War Department. FIRST PART.—School of the Trooper, of the Platoon and of the Squadron Dismounted. SECOND PART.—Of the Platoon and of the Squadron Mounted. THIRD PART.—Evolutions of a Regiment. 3 vols. 18mo. $3.75.

War Department, Washington, Feb. 10, 1841.

The system of Cavalry Tactics adapted to the organization of Dragoon regiments, having been approved by the President of the United States, is now published for the government of the said service.

Accordingly, instruction in the same will be given after the method pointed out therein; and all additions to, or departures from, the exercises and manœuvres laid down in this system are positively forbidden. J. R. POINSETT, *Secretary of War.*

Instruction in Field Artillery. Prepared by a Board of Artillery Officers. 1 vol. demi-8vo. $2.50.

Baltimore, Md., Jan. 15, 1859.

COL. S. COOPER, Adjt. Gen. U.S.A.

SIR:—The Light Artillery Board assembled by Special Orders No. 134, of 1856, and Special Orders No. 116, of 1858, has the honor to submit a revised system of Light Artillery Tactics and Regulations recommended for that arm.

WM. H. FRENCH, Bt. Major, Captain First Artillery.
WILLIAM F. BARRY, Captain Second Artillery.
HENRY J. HUNT, Bt. Major, Captain Second Artillery.

War Department, March 6, 1860.

The system of instruction for Field Artillery, prepared by a Board of Light Artillery Officers, pursuant to orders from this Department, having been approved by the President, is herewith published for the information and government of the army.

All exercises, manœuvres, and forms of parade not embraced in this system are prohibited in the Light Artillery, and those herein prescribed will be strictly observed.

BY ORDER OF THE SECRETARY OF WAR.

The Handy-Book for the United States Soldier, ON COMING INTO SERVICE. Containing a Complete System of Instruction in the School of the Soldier; embracing the Manual for the Rifle and Musket, with a preliminary explanation of the Formation of a Battalion on Parade, the Position of the Officers, &c. &c. Also, Instructions for Street-Firing. Being a First Book or Introduction to the authorized United States Infantry Tactics. Complete in 1 vol. 128 pages, illustrated. 25 cents.

To the recruit just mustered into service, the system of tactics seems extensive and difficult.

The design of this little Handy-Book is to divide the instruction, and, by presenting a complete system for the drill of the individual soldier, to prepare him for the use and study of the authorized United States Infantry Tactics, in the school of the company and the battalion.

6   J. B. LIPPINCOTT & CO.'S MILITARY PUBLICATIONS.

MILITARY BOOKS IN COURSE OF PREPARATION.

New U.S. Cavalry Tactics. By Colonel PHILIP ST. G. COOKE, U.S. Army. Approved by a Board of Cavalry Officers. (*Immediately*.)

Jomini's Art of War. [*Précis de l'art de la guerre.*] Summary of the Art of War; or, A new Analytical Compend of the Principal Combinations of Strategy, Grand Tactics, and Military Policy. By BARON DE JOMINI, General in Chief, Aide-de-Camp General to the Emperor of Russia. A new and accurate translation, from the last Paris edition, (just published,) by Lieut. WM. P. CRAIGHILL, of the Military Academy, West Point, First Lieut. of Engineers, U.S. Army.

A Comprehensive Encyclopædia of Military Science, Art, and History; containing a Complete Explanation of all Military Terms, with their Pronunciation, and Descriptions of the Principal Battles in the World's History. Fully illustrated.

Marmont's Spirit of Military Institutions, from the latest Paris edition. Translated, with notes, by HENRY COPPÉE, Professor in the University of Pennsylvania, and late a Captain in the Army of the United States.

This book contains, in a small compass, the principles of the art of war, as learned and practiced by this great marshal during the Napoleonic wars. It treats of strategy, tactics and grand tactics,—of the organization and formation of armies—the principles of fortification—of military justice, wars offensive and defensive, marches and encampments, reconnoissances, battles,—and various important topics, including the tactics of the three arms as applied in actual movements before the enemy,—with the peculiar characteristics and duties of general officers.

Register of the Officers and Graduates of the U.S. Military Academy, at West Point, N.Y., from March 16, 1802, to the present time. Compiled from the official records of the War Department, and other reliable sources, by GEO. W. CULLUM, Lieut. Col. and A.D.C. to Lieut. Gen. WINFIELD SCOTT.

The Artillerist's Manual and U.S. Soldier's Compendium. By JOSEPH ROBERTS, Capt. 4th Artillery U.S. Army.

The Army of the United States:
its constitution and organization; with a complete description of every corps in the service, and accurately-colored illustrations of the uniforms and equipments of officers and soldiers of every grade.

This captivating book contains the most valuable information on the topic of present absorbing interest. It is not designed merely to please the eye with its fine colored engravings of our officers and troops of every grade, but, prepared by an experienced military hand, it contains important instruction as to the formation and history of the various arms,—infantry, artillery, and cavalry; of the scientific corps,—engineers, topographical engineers, ordnance; of the various staff departments; with details of the uniforms and equipments of every corps and grade. As a book for a splendid gift,—for the centre-table of a lady's drawing-room,—it can have no superior.

The Field Manual of Evolutions of the Line,
arranged in a tabular form, for the use of officers of the U.S. Infantry; being a sequel to the authorized U.S. Infantry Tactics. Translated, with adaptation to the U.S. Service, from the latest French authorities.

A most valuable and timely book: every officer should have it in his pocket in the manœuvres of brigades and divisions. It contains a condensed and tabular statement of the commands of the instructor and of the battalion commanders, with short but sufficient explanations accompanying each.

Many of our officers find *the evolutions of the line* a most complicated study. They are here rendered easy both of knowledge and reference.

Mississippi Delta Report.
Report upon the Physics and Hydraulics of the Mississippi River, upon the protection of the alluvial region against overflow, and upon the deepening of the mouths. Based upon surveys and investigations, made under the act of Congress directing the Topographical and Hydrographical Survey of the Mississippi River, with such investigations as might lead to determine the most practicable plan for securing it against inundation, and the best mode of deepening the channels at the mouths of the river. Prepared by Capt. A. A. HUMPHREYS and Lieut. H. L. ABBOT, Corps of Top. Engineers, U.S. Army. Submitted to the Bureau of Top. Engineers, War Department, 1861. 1 vol. quarto. Illustrated with maps and charts.

Guthrie's Surgery of War. Commentaries on the Surgery of the War in Portugal, Spain, France, and the Netherlands, from the battle of Roliça, in 1808, to that of Waterloo, in 1815, with additions relating to those in the Crimea in 1854-55; showing the improvements made during and since that period in the great art and science of Surgery on all the subjects to which they relate. By G. J. GUTHRIE, F.R.S. 1 vol. 12mo.

Macleod's Surgery of the War in the Crimea. Notes on the Surgery of the War in the Crimea, with Remarks on the Treatment of Gunshot Wounds. By GEORGE H. B. MACLEOD, M.D., F.R.C.S., Surgeon to the General Hospital in Camp before Sevastopol, &c. 1 vol. 12mo.

Florence Nightingale's Notes on Hospitals. Notes on Hospitals: being Papers read before the National Association for the Promotion of Social Science, at Liverpool, in October, 1858, with evidence given to the Royal Commissioners on the state of the Army in 1857. By FLORENCE NIGHTINGALE.

Longmore's Gunshot Wounds. A Treatise on Gunshot Wounds. By THOMAS LONGMORE, Surgeon.

A LIBERAL DISCOUNT made to parties ordering by the quantity; or single copies will be forwarded by mail (postpaid) on receipt of the price, in gold or postage stamps, by the Publishers.

Constantly on hand, and for sale at wholesale or retail, a large stock of AMERICAN and FOREIGN MILITARY BOOKS, SCHOOL and COLLEGE TEXT-BOOKS, standard LAW, THEOLOGICAL, and MEDICAL works, and Miscellaneous Books of every department of Literature.

J. B. LIPPINCOTT & CO.
Philadelphia.

www.ingramcontent.com/pod-product-compliance
Lightning Source LLC
Chambersburg PA
CBHW032043230426
43672CB00009B/1454